Oracle Press™

Effective MySQL

Backup and Recovery

D0630991

About the Author

Ronald Bradford has worked in the relational database field for over 20 years. With his professional background and a decade of working knowledge in database architecture, performance tuning, and management of large enterprise systems using Ingres and Oracle, Ronald has for the past 13 years worked primarily with MySQL, the world's most popular open source database. He has worked both at Oracle Corporation (1996–1999) as an Oracle Consultant and MySQL, Inc. (2006–2008) as a senior MySQL Consultant. His contributions to the MySQL community include being recognized as the all-time top individual MySQL blog contributor at Planet MySQL (2010), and international recognitions include being named an Oracle ACE Director (2010) and MySQL Community Member of the Year (2009).

Ronald combines his extensive consulting expertise with a passion to share the knowledge and benefits of using MySQL. Starting in 2006, his many public speaking engagements have included over 60 presentations in 20 countries in 2010–2011.

About the Technical Editors

Hans Forbrich has been working with computers since the early 1970s, in particular with entity-relationship and relational databases starting in 1979 using an engine on IBM mainframes called GERM (General Entity Relationship Model). Since that time, Hans has been a DBA, an operations architect for a number of organizations, and an Oracle University instructor but always heavily involved in high availability and recoverability.

As a fellow ACE Director, Hans is pleased and honored to have been a technical reviewer for this book. Backup and recovery is an important and often overlooked area of MySQL, and Ronald's expertise and experience in this area shines through.

Chris Schneider has been a MySQL community member, user, and evangelist for the past ten years. Throughout his career he has designed, implemented, and maintained small to large scale MySQL installations while training and mentoring teams of DBAs. This has included building architecture from the ground up and improving on those that are currently in place while emphasizing scalability, performance, and ease of use. Since 2009, Chris has been an expert speaker at many U.S. conferences including the MySQL Conference and Expo, ODTUG KScope, and Oracle Open World.

Lenz Grimmer first encountered MySQL in 1995, when he had his first job as a systems administrator in a small Internet startup company, which already used what was later called the "LAMP stack" to provide web hosting services for customers. He then worked as a distribution developer at SUSE Linux from 1998–2002, before he joined MySQL AB as a Release Engineer in charge of producing the official MySQL builds for all platforms. After having been with the MySQL team for nine years, he recently returned to Linux, as a member of the Oracle Linux product management team at Oracle. Lenz is the maintainer of the mylvmbackup script and has given numerous talks on the topics of MySQL backup and recovery. In his spare time, Lenz enjoys spending time with his family or tinkering with remote controlled quadrocopters, powered by the Arduino platform.

Oracle Press™

Effective MySQL

Backup and Recovery

Ronald Bradford

New York   Chicago   San Francisco
Lisbon   London   Madrid   Mexico City
Milan   New Delhi   San Juan
Seoul   Singapore   Sydney   Toronto

The **McGraw·Hill** Companies

Cataloging-in-Publication Data is on file with the Library of Congress

McGraw-Hill books are available at special quantity discounts to use as premiums and sales promotions, or for use in corporate training programs. To contact a representative, please e-mail us at bulksales@mcgraw-hill.com.

Effective MySQL: Backup and Recovery

1 2 3 4 5 6 7 8 9 0   DOC DOC   1 0 9 8 7 6 5 4 3 2

ISBN   978-0-07-178857-1

MHID   0-07-178857-3

Sponsoring Editor	**Technical Editors**	**Production Supervisor**
Paul Carlstroem	Hans Forbrich	Jean Bodeaux
Editorial Supervisor	Chris Schneider	**Composition**
Patty Mon	Lenz Grimmer	Cenveo Publisher Services
Project Manager	**Copy Editor**	**Illustration**
Sapna Rastogi,	Lisa McCoy	Cenveo Publisher Services
Cenveo Publisher Services	**Proofreader**	**Art Director, Cover**
Acquisitions Coordinator	Paul Tyler	Jeff Weeks
Ryan Willard	**Indexer**	**Cover Designer**
	Karin Arrigoni	Pattie Lee

For MySQL culture, past, present, and future.
To many in the MySQL and growing Oracle community:
you are more than colleagues;
you are, and always will remain, great friends.

CONTENTS

ACKNOWLEDGMENTS

Thanks to the readers who have already enjoyed the first book of the Effective MySQL series for providing valuable feedback, both good and bad. A positive comment tells me I am meeting your needs; a negative one means I need to continue to do better. Both are important to ensure continued improvements in this series. It is also a great feeling to receive an e-mail asking when the next book will be available.

As I write my acknowledgments for this book, I realize the timeline of my own changing immediate family. In my first book from 2010 I acknowledged my fiancé, Cindy, and in my second book my now wife Cindy. For this third book my family has again increased with Chance, our two-year-old dachshund rescue. In such a short time he has become integral to our daily routine and in finding a balance between work, life, and writing. Significant time, effort, and support from family is needed to create a book; however, I write this material for the benefit of all who have a desire to learn, appreciate, and master using MySQL effectively.

Without the technical abilities of the team at McGraw-Hill this publication would not be possible. Many thanks to Ryan Willard, my coordinating editor; Paul Carlstroem, my sponsoring editor; and the production team, who all remained very patient during some significant unforeseen delays.

My technical editors, Hans, Chris, and Lenz, and the extended review team have been invaluable for this book.

The many years of database wisdom and extensive training expertise of Hans Forbrich brings the necessary Oracle expertise to the team and ensures this material meets the needs of an experienced Oracle DBA for understanding and learning to master backup and recovery for MySQL.

I am indebted to Chris Schneider, who in addition to being a technical editor of this book and co-author for the next book in this Effective MySQL series, was able to assist greatly in supplementing content in the later chapters and perform additional reviews as I was overcoming illness. His expertise as an operational MySQL DBA working with the demanding needs of systems requiring real life disaster recovery needs in his daily role ensures the syntax, examples, and options described in this book mirror the needs of many MySQL production systems.

Lenz Grimmer, long time MySQL community advocate, good friend, and sponsor of the open source MySQL backup tool mylvmbackup, has added another well rounded perspective and technical validation with his many years of database and system administration knowledge.

While the words written in this text are mine, this does not become a published book without the help, input, clarification, and discussion of these trusted and respected senior technical advisors.

Several others have also contributed to making this a great reference. Thanks to the MySQL Enterprise Backup (MEB) team at Oracle including Sagar Jauhari, Lars Thalmann, and Sanjay Manwani in their review of all things MEB. Also to Ken Ashcraft from Google and Vipu Sabhaya from HP for their feedback on the respective offerings of MySQL in the cloud. Mark Leith contributed an actual code patch to mysqldump in one day as the result of a blog post providing an example hack for a workaround. Great work, Mark. That is the MySQL community spirit and open source in action. Further thanks to Patrick Galbraith who provided early input around MySQL replication. Finally, several individuals and companies named or anonymous helped to provide many colorful disaster scenarios detailed in Chapter 7.

INTRODUCTION

Disaster is inevitable. Total failure is avoidable.

While many organizations plan, practice, and invest for scalability, few plan and practice for business resilience as the result of a disaster or a "Choas Monkey*". One of the most critical tasks of an operational database administrator (DBA) is to perform, test, document, and verify adequate backup and recovery procedures to ensure business continuity. While this may be considered a much loathed and less prioritized task, this is the single most comforting element in a well functioning and stable production environment. Backups are not just used for recovery. Other uses of backups that can be incorporated into daily operations to assist in the verification process can include additional scalability and higher availability infrastructure, testing, and benchmarking.

Understanding what limitations and quirks exist with the various approaches to MySQL backups is important in being confident that the crucial business information is backed up. The methods you have used to recover your information must meet your business needs to obtain a mean time to recovery (MTTR) and the recovery point objective (RPO).

MySQL provides no one single unbreakable solution as yet. The use of MySQL storage engines, MySQL replication, configuration settings for durability, hardware configuration, database uptime, and locking requirements are all factors in choosing an applicable approach matching your business requirements. This book will cover these approaches detailing the relative strengths and weaknesses and leading the reader to identify and implement an appropriate backup and recovery strategy.

The final chapter of this book also discusses advancements in MySQL availability in the cloud and the benefits and risks for an optimal backup and recovery strategy.

---

*The "Choas Monkey" and the "Simian Army" created by Netflix highlight that proactively creating disasters esures the best approach for being prepared. More at http://techblog.netflix.com/2011/07/netflix-simian-army.html

Conventions

All code examples are provided in a proportional font. For example:

```
mysql> SHOW SCHEMAS;
+--------------------+
| Database           |
+--------------------+
| information_schema |
| blog               |
| mysql              |
+--------------------+
3 rows in set (0.00 sec)
```

Any SQL syntax within text or code examples will be in uppercase. For example, the FLUSH TABLES WITH READ LOCK statement will hold a global read lock. These statements are not provided in a different font. If a specific syntax or value from a code example is described in general text, this is provided in a proportional font, for example, the --log-bin configuration option.

For any Unix/Linux command, this is prefixed with a $ to indicate a shell prompt. For example:

```
$ which mysql
```

Any MySQL SQL statement that can be executed is prefixed with mysql> to indicate execution with the mysql command line client that is included with a full MySQL distribution. For example:

```
mysql> SELECT VERSION();
```

All SQL statements listed with this prefix can generally be performed in any alternative MySQL client GUI tool; however, some additional syntax may not be applicable—for example: \G for vertical display is a mysql command line client specific directive.

About MySQL

The MySQL database server is an open source product released under the GPL V2 license. More information about the GPL license can be found at http://www.mysql.com/about/legal/licensing/index.html. The copyright owner of MySQL at the time of this publication is Oracle Corporation. Oracle Corporation provides continued product development and also provides commercial licenses for OEM providers and comprehensive subscription services for websites and enterprises.

More information about MySQL can be found at the official MySQL website at http://mysql.com and the MySQL developer zone at http://dev.mysql .com.

The current generally available (GA) version of MySQL is version 5.5. This book is written to support MySQL versions 5.0 and better with specific version differences noted when applicable. The current development version of MySQL 5.6 is also referenced to indicate expected new functionality in an upcoming release; however, these features may operate differently or not be provided in any final future MySQL product.

Code Examples

All examples detailed in this book are available for download from the Effective MySQL site at http://effectivemysql.com/book/backup-recovery/. Code, scripts, and sample data are also available at GitHub.

A separate text document of all URLs used is also included on the website to enable quick access to these references.

References

The MySQL Reference Manual on the MySQL developer zone is an invaluable resource. This can be found at http://dev.mysql.com/doc/refman/5.5/en/index.html.

Access to manuals for older MySQL versions can also be found at http://dev.mysql.com/doc.

The Planet MySQL website at http://planet.mysql.com provides an aggregation of thousands of MySQL bloggers detailing great insight on all things MySQL.

Additional open source products referenced in this book including XtraBackup and Percona Toolkit from Percona, mylvmbackup, and mydumper have various sources of additional online information. These are detailed at the appropriate time.

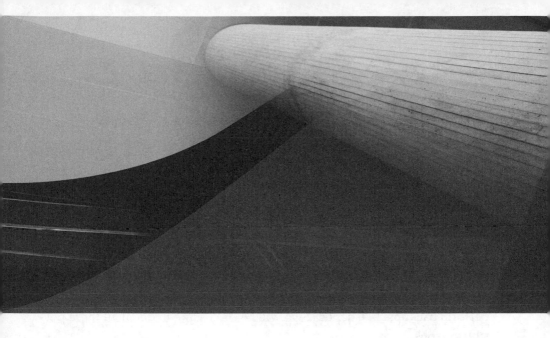

1

The Five Minute DBA

You have just inherited a production MySQL system and there is no confirmation that an existing MySQL backup strategy is in operation. What is the least you need to do? Before undertaking any backup strategy there are some necessary prerequisites about your database size and storage engine usage that have a direct effect on your system availability during any backup approach.

In this chapter we will discuss the approach necessary to identify a minimum functionality backup, including:

- Determine your database size
- Determine your storage engine usage
- Locking and downtime implications

Approaching a MySQL Backup

There is more than one strategy to back up a MySQL environment. These strategies also depend on the number of servers in the MySQL topology. There are a number of various open source and commercial tools available to perform backups. In Chapter 2 we will be discussing in detail all these possible options.

At this time you have an environment with a single server and you want to create a consistent backup. You have at your disposal for all MySQL environments two immediate options. The first option is to stop your MySQL instance and take a full filesystem cold backup. This would result in your system being unavailable for an undetermined time, and you would need to ensure you make a copy of all the right information including MySQL data, transaction and binary logs if applicable, and the current MySQL configuration.

Your second option is to use a client tool included with the standard MySQL installation. The `mysqldump` command can produce a consistent MySQL backup without stopping the MySQL instance. However, before running `mysqldump`, several important decisions are required to make an informed decision of the best options to use. These are:

- What is the size of the database to backup?
- What locking strategy is necessary to produce a consistent backup?
- How long will the backup take?

Determining Your Database Size

An important consideration for performing a MySQL backup is the size of your backup when backing up to local disk. This is required to ensure you have available diskspace to store your backup file.

The following SQL statement provides the total size in MB of your current data and indexes:

```
mysql> SELECT  ROUND(SUM(data_length+index_length)/1024/1024)
    ->         AS total_mb,
    ->         ROUND(SUM(data_length)/1024/1024) AS data_mb,
    ->         ROUND(SUM(index_length)/1024/1024) AS index_mb
    -> FROM    INFORMATION_SCHEMA.tables;
+----------+---------+----------+
| total_mb | data_mb | index_mb |
+----------+---------+----------+
|      927 |     847 |       80 |
+----------+---------+----------+
```

Your `mysqldump` backup will be approximately the same size as your data with an appropriate safety margin of 10 to 15 percent. There is no precise calculation; however, your backup produces a text based output of your data. For example, a 4 byte integer in the database may be 10 character bytes long in a `mysqldump` backup file. It is possible to compress your backup concurrently or to transfer to a different network device. These options and their limitations are discussed in Chapters 2 and 8.

From this SQL statement the database data size is 847MB. For later reference, the size of the backup file as described in the section running `mysqldump` reports a size of 818MB using the common default options. The example database in Chapter 8 with a data size of 4.5GB produces a backup file of 2.9GB.

Choosing a Locking Strategy

The locking strategy chosen will determine if your application can perform database write operations during the execution of a backup. By default, `mysqldump` performs a table level lock to ensure a consistent version of all data using the LOCK TABLES command. This occurs with the `--lock-tables` command line option, which is not enabled by default. This option is part of the `--opt` option that is enabled by default. You can elect to not lock tables; however, this may not ensure a consistent backup. When using the MyISAM storage engine, `--lock-tables` is necessary to ensure a consistent backup.

Alternatively, `mysqldump` provides the `--single-transaction` option that creates a consistent version snapshot of all tables in a single transaction. This option is only applicable when using a storage engine that supports multiversioning. InnoDB is the only storage engine included in a default

MySQL installation that is applicable. When specified, this option automatically turns off --lock-tables.

The following SQL statement will confirm the storage engines in use for your MySQL instance:

```
mysql> SELECT  table_schema, engine, COUNT(*) AS tables
    -> FROM    information_schema.tables
    -> WHERE   table_schema NOT IN
    ->             ('INFORMATION_SCHEMA','PERFORMANCE_SCHEMA')
    -> GROUP BY table_schema, engine
    -> ORDER BY 3 DESC;
+--------------------+--------+--------+
| table_schema       | engine | tables |
+--------------------+--------+--------+
| shopping_cart      | MyISAM |    109 |
| cust_db            | InnoDB |     48 |
| mysql              | MyISAM |     21 |
| analytics          | InnoDB |     20 |
| phpmyadmin         | MyISAM |      8 |
| newsletter         | MyISAM |      8 |
| cust_db            | MyISAM |      3 |
| mysql              | CSV    |      2 |
+--------------------+--------+--------+
```

In this example, the MySQL instance has several different schemas that support various functions including a shopping cart, newsletter, and administration tool. An all InnoDB application may look like:

```
+--------------------+--------+--------+
| table_schema       | engine | tables |
+--------------------+--------+--------+
| prod_db            | InnoDB |    122 |
| mysql              | MyISAM |     21 |
| mysql              | CSV    |      2 |
+--------------------+--------+--------+
```

As you see in the example the mysql meta-schema uses MyISAM. There is no ability to change this. If your database is all InnoDB you will have two options regarding the MyISAM mysql tables that we will discuss later in this chapter.

Execution Time

The most important requirement is to determine how long your backup will take. There is no calculation that can give an accurate answer. The size of your database, the amount of system RAM, the storage engine(s) in use, the MySQL configuration, the hard drive speed, and the current workload all contribute in the calculation. What is important when performing a backup is that you collect this type of information for future reference. The execution time is important, as this is an effective maintenance window for your database. During a database backup there may be a limitation of application functionality, a performance overhead during the backup, and your backup may limit other operations including batch processing or software maintenance.

Combining Information

The following is a recommended SQL statement that combines all information for an audit of your database size:

```
$ cat storage_engines.sql
SELECT  table_schema, engine,
        ROUND(SUM(data_length+index_length)/1024/1024) AS total_mb,
        ROUND(SUM(data_length)/1024/1024) AS data_mb,
        ROUND(SUM(index_length)/1024/1024) AS index_mb,
        COUNT(*) AS tables
FROM  information_schema.tables
GROUP BY table_schema, engine
ORDER BY 3 DESC;

mysql> source storage_engines.sql
+--------------------+--------+----------+---------+----------+--------+
| table_schema       | engine | total_mb | data_mb | index_mb | tables |
+--------------------+--------+----------+---------+----------+--------+
| analytics          | InnoDB |    10903 |   10525 |      378 |     20 |
| cust_db            | InnoDB |     1155 |     962 |      194 |     48 |
| newsletter         | InnoDB |      514 |     278 |      237 |      7 |
| shopping_cart      | MyISAM |       27 |      19 |        8 |    109 |
| cust_db            | MyISAM |        9 |       3 |        7 |      3 |
| mysql              | MyISAM |        1 |       0 |        0 |     21 |
| information_schema | MyISAM |        0 |       0 |        0 |      8 |
| information_schema | MEMORY |        0 |       0 |        0 |     20 |
| mysql              | CSV    |        0 |       0 |        0 |      2 |
+--------------------+--------+----------+---------+----------+--------+
```

Performing a MySQL Backup

Now that you have gathered prerequisite information, you have the details necessary to make an informed decision.

The choice of how to perform a backup, when to perform, and how you monitor and verify is a more complex process that is discussed in more detail starting with Chapter 2.

One additional consideration during a backup process is to disable any cron or batch processes during the backup to minimize additional workload. This can minimize database contention and shorten the window of time needed.

Running mysqldump

In the simplest form, you can perform a backup using `mysqldump` with the following syntax:

```
$ time mysqldump -uroot -p --all-databases > backup.sql
$ echo $?
$ ls -lh backup.sql
```

- The first command runs the `mysqldump` for all databases producing an ASCII dump in the `backup.sql` file.

- The second command confirms the exit status of the first command. A non-zero result is an indication of a problem during the backup process. If any errors occur, these are generally shown in the screen output.

- The third command shows the size of your backup file for later reference.

For example:

```
$ time mysqldump -uroot -p --all-databases > backup.sql
real     0m35.493s
user     0m9.808s
sys      0m3.021s
$ echo $?
0
$ ls -lh backup.sql
-rw-rw-r-- 1 uid gid 818M Aug 10 21:37 backup.sql
```

This is a successful backup file totaling 818MB that took 35 seconds to execute. The original size of the database data as shown previously for this MySQL instance was 847MB.

> **TIP**   *Prefixing the* `mysqldump` *command with the* `time` *command will provide valuable information on the actual time taken. Recording your backup time and size is an important administration step all DBAs should do. This time is useful for scheduling other system requirements, for an additional verification step if a successful backup has a significantly different time, and is helpful in benchmarking using different arguments, MySQL configuration settings, or changes in physical hardware.*

An example of an error condition may look like:

```
$ time mysqldump -uroot -p --all-databases > backup.sql
mysqldump: Got error: 1142: SELECT,LOCK TABL command denied to user
'root'@'localhost' for table 'cond_instances' when using LOCK TABLES
real    0m7.692s
user    0m1.780s
sys     0m0.313s
$ echo $?
2
$ ls -lh backup.sql
-rw-rw-r-- 1 uid gid 94M Aug 10 21:28 backup.sql
```

A backup file as per this example may in isolation appear to be completely valid. That is, this file contains valid and complete SQL statements and can be successfully used to restore data in one or more schemas; however, it is incomplete as a full backup of all data. The execution time, error status, and size are all important information for verification of a successful backup.

Creating a backup is only the first step in a suitable strategy. It is important this backup file can be used successfully in recovery. This is discussed in Chapter 5.

Securing Your Backup

The final step in a minimal backup approach is to ensure the security of your data. The backup is currently on the same system as your data. A loss of this system would include the data and your backup. The minimum you should undertake is to copy your backup to a secondary location. For example:

```
$ time gzip backup.sql
$ time scp backup.sql.gz   another-server:backup-dir
```

Benefits with mysqldump

The mysqldump command provides a SQL based backup file. This can be ideal for creating a backup that can be executed on different versions of MySQL, and on different operating systems. You can, for example, view this file directly and see SQL statements. For example:

```
$ more backup.sql

--
-- Current Database: `mysql`
--
CREATE DATABASE /*!32312 IF NOT EXISTS*/ `mysql`
```

```
    /*!40100 DEFAULT CHARACTER SET latin1 */;
USE `mysql`;
--
-- Table structure for table `help_topic`
--
DROP TABLE IF EXISTS `help_topic`;
/*!40101 SET @saved_cs_client     = @@character_set_client */;
/*!40101 SET character_set_client = utf8 */;
CREATE TABLE `help_topic` (
  `help_topic_id` int(10) unsigned NOT NULL,
  `name` char(64) NOT NULL,
  `help_category_id` smallint(5) unsigned NOT NULL,
  `description` text NOT NULL,
  `example` text NOT NULL,
  `url` char(128) NOT NULL,
  PRIMARY KEY (`help_topic_id`),
  UNIQUE KEY `name` (`name`)
) ENGINE=MyISAM DEFAULT CHARSET=utf8 COMMENT='help topics';
/*!40101 SET character_set_client = @saved_cs_client */;
--
-- Dumping data for table `help_topic`
--
LOCK TABLES `help_topic` WRITE;/*!40000 ALTER TABLE `help_topic` DISABLE KEYS */;
INSERT INTO `help_topic` VALUES (0,'MIN',16,'Syntax:\nMIN([DISTINCT] expr)\n\n
Returns the minimum value of expr. MIN() may take a string argument; in\nsuch
cases, it returns the minimum string value.See\nhttp://dev.mysql.com/doc/refman/
5.1/en/mysql-indexes.html. The DISTINCT\nkeyword can be used to find the minimum
of ...
```

More Information

For more information about the various options with `mysqldump`, you can obtain a list of valid options with the following syntax:

```
$ mysqldump --help
```

You can find detailed information in the MySQL Reference Manual at http://dev.mysql.com/doc/refman/5.5/en/mysqldump.html.

Other Options

If your database uses all InnoDB tables, the default locking strategy is restrictive. You have to consider the impact of the `mysql` schema on MyISAM tables. Under normal circumstances you can generally ignore the consistency requirement providing you do not perform operations that change the meta-data. This includes adding or changing users and privileges, as well as creating or dropping database schemas. Alternatively you may elect to perform two separate backups. The first backup excludes the `mysql` schema using the `--single-transaction` option. The second backup only includes the `mysql` schema and uses the default locking approach. This will be discussed more in Chapter 2.

Conclusion

An appropriate MySQL backup strategy is an essential component for any running production system. For a simple installation, the implementation of a backup strategy can occur in minutes as demonstrated in this chapter. However, a backup strategy is only as good as the process to perform a successful, timely, and complete recovery using the backup strategy. Chapter 5 will provide a detailed explanation for a successful recovery.

There are a number of important considerations when using the output of `mysqldump` for recovery that may affect how you execute your backup command. Chapter 2 will discuss these points.

This chapter also introduced a number of common terms including consistent, valid, complete, and point in time. We will define these terms in greater detail in Chapter 2.

The SQL statements and web links listed in this chapter can be downloaded from http://effectivemysql.com/book/backup-recovery/.

2

Understanding Backup Options

MySQL supports various different options for the backup of your database data. Each of these options has its relative strengths and weaknesses that need to be considered to determine what is most applicable for your production environment. The choice of operating system, hardware, and software configuration can affect the availability of options. There are also open source and commercial considerations for your choice of product.

In this chapter we will discuss:

- Different backup strategy needs and approaches
- Various popular MySQL backup options
- Hardware considerations

Terminology

Chapter 1 introduced a number of important terms that are essential to fully understand the principles for backup and recovery with MySQL.

Term	Description
static backup	This is a backup of data at a given point in time. Generally a MySQL backup would be performed daily, for example 2:00 A.M.
consistent backup	This is a backup of data where all information pertaining to the backup is consistent. For example, a filesystem backup on a running production system would produce an inconsistent backup when copying files sequentially. This could lead to a mismatch of information between individual files.
static recovery	A recovery process involves two important initial steps; the first is the static recovery and the second is the verification of a valid static backup.
point in time recovery (PITR)	Following a successful static recovery, it is generally necessary to perform a PITR recovery of current transactions. These are all the data operations that have occurred since the static backup, i.e., since 2:00 A.M.
maintenance window	A backup is generally performed when the system is under less utilization, or in pre-determined times known as a maintenance window. This is when administration tasks including backups, software upgrades, and other maintenance can be performed with limited or restricted application access.

Choosing a Backup Strategy

Several factors affect the choice of the type of backup you should implement for your MySQL environment. This chapter covers the bases of what backup strategies exist and what limitations you need to consider for each strategy. For a clear description of the following backup options, these are demonstrated for a single server environment. This highlights the relative strengths and weaknesses for evaluation. The design of your MySQL topology can also affect an appropriate backup and recovery strategy. The use of MySQL replication in the context of backup and recovery can be a great benefit to overcoming some of the limitations listed in this chapter. In Chapter 4 we will discuss the considerations for combining replication with the various strategies.

Before choosing a backup approach, various MySQL architecture and schema design decisions may have an impact.

Database Availability

If access to your database is not required for a period of time—for example, you are not running a 24/7 operation—there may be a common time when your database may not be required to be available. This is called a maintenance window, and it provides an opportunity for backup strategies that may not be possible if such a window is not available.

Storage Engines

As highlighted in Chapter 1, the choice of storage engine for your underlying tables can have an effect on your strategy, particularly in relation to locking and data availability with the primary included storage engines and additional storage engines supported via a plugin architecture. The InnoDB, MyISAM, ARCHIVE, MERGE, MEMORY, and BLACKHOLE engines included with the official MySQL binaries have different locking requirements and needs for consistency, which also drive different backup strategies.

In the following section we will be discussing InnoDB specific options that provide the best approach for a true hot backup.

Locking Strategies

For any backup strategy that operates with a running MySQL instance there is an important consideration of an applicable locking strategy to ensure a *consistent* backup. An applicable locking strategy is necessary because MySQL supports different concurrency and DML locking approaches. In MySQL not all engines support multi-versioning concurrency control (MVCC). MySQL provides two SQL commands that directly control table level locking. These are the LOCK TABLES and FLUSH TABLES commands. Many backup options detailed in this chapter handle applicable locking.

This information is provided to define what options are used and available for custom management.

LOCK TABLES

The LOCK TABLES command can provide a READ or WRITE lock for one or more specified tables. The LOCAL option enables concurrent inserts to continue when applicable for MyISAM tables only. Concurrent inserts for a MyISAM table are possible when there are no holes (from deletes) in the table, or when the `concurrent_insert` configuration variable is set appropriately.

This command is used when the `--lock-tables` option is enabled with `mysqldump`. See the later section on SQL dump for a detailed explanation of when this option is auto-enabled.

The UNLOCK TABLES command is used to release all current locks for a session. In addition to the UNLOCK TABLES command, a session termination, a START TRANSACTION, or a LOCK TABLES on the same table name also produce an implied UNLOCK TABLES.

CAUTION   *Any backup that takes longer to execute then* `wait_timeout` *or* `interactive_timeout` *can result in the session being closed. This will cause an implied UNLOCK TABLES.*

For more information see http://dev.mysql.com/doc/refman/5.5/en/lock-tables.html.

FLUSH TABLES

The FLUSH TABLES command, when used with the optional keywords WITH READ LOCK, will enable a consistent view of data when the command completes successfully. This occurs by taking a globally held read lock, then closing all currently open tables. This can take time to complete as this requires all running SQL statements to complete. This is not the same type of lock as a LOCK TABLES command on a list of all tables. This lock is released by issuing an UNLOCK TABLES command, or any operation that implicitly runs an UNLOCK TABLES command. This last point is very important as shown in the following example.

In session 1:

```
mysql> DROP TABLE IF EXISTS t1;
Query OK, 0 rows affected, 1 warning (0.00 sec)
mysql> CREATE TABLE t1(i int);
Query OK, 0 rows affected (0.03 sec)
mysql> INSERT INTO t1 VALUES (1);
Query OK, 1 row affected (0.01 sec)
mysql> FLUSH TABLES WITH READ LOCK;
Query OK, 0 rows affected (0.02 sec)
```

In session 2:

```
mysql> SET SESSION lock_wait_timeout=10;
Query OK, 0 rows affected (0.00 sec)
mysql> INSERT INTO t1 VALUES (2);
ERROR 1205 (HY000): Lock wait timeout exceeded;
try restarting transaction
```

The command in session 2 does not complete as expected. We can confirm this by looking at the current threads in the processlist before the timeout occurs.

In session 1:

```
mysql> SHOW PROCESSLIST\G
*************************** 1. row ***************************
      Id: 1391205
    User: root
    Host: localhost
      db: book
 Command: Query
    Time: 0
   State:
    Info: SHOW PROCESSLIST
*************************** 2. row ***************************
      Id: 1391211
    User: root
    Host: localhost
      db: book
 Command: Query
    Time: 5
   State: Waiting for global read lock
    Info: INSERT INTO t1 VALUES (2);
mysql> EXIT;
```

As soon as session 1 is closed, an implied UNLOCK TABLES is performed. This releases the global read lock, and the pending statement in session 2 completes immediately if the SQL statement has not timed out as per this example.

CAUTION   *A common flaw with backup strategies that use FLUSH TABLES WITH READ LOCK is the need to use two independent threads for the executing backup process. Running a FLUSH TABLES WITH READ LOCK command, then exiting from the current connection will automatically perform an UNLOCK TABLES. After the successful return of FLUSH TABLES WITH READ LOCK, any backup option must occur in a different concurrent thread. Only when the applicable backup option is complete should an UNLOCK TABLES be executed.*

NOTE   *The risk of using a FLUSH TABLES WITH READ LOCK command for a highly concurrent system is this may take some time (i.e., seconds to minutes) to complete. This is due to any other long running statements executing. It is important that this command is monitored and terminated if necessary. While this statement is popular with snapshot options, this risk must be carefully considered for the true impact for an online application.*

For more information see http://dev.mysql.com/doc/refman/5.5/en/flush.html.

A recent article on the popular MySQL Performance Blog provided a detailed description of how the combination of FLUSH TABLES WITH READ LOCK, MySQL 5.5, and InnoDB can produce an unexpected wait in order to complete locking all tables. The combination of versions, storage engines, and SQL commands can vary the expected outcome. As always, testing is a sound business practice. For more information see http://www.mysqlperformanceblog.com/2012/03/23/how-flush-tables-with-read-lock-works-with-innodb-tables/.

MySQL Topology

The decision of a backup strategy for a single server installation can be very different then for a MySQL topology that includes MySQL replication. While it may not be possible to stop or limit access to a primary MySQL instance, this approach may be possible with a MySQL replicated slave.

A full copy of your MySQL instance using MySQL replication is actually the easiest backup strategy to implement. This approach, when correctly configured, can also serve as a primary recovery option with minimal impact on production operation. Chapter 4 discusses the impacts of using MySQL replication with your backup and recovery strategy.

Static Backup Options

MySQL provides no single backup option. The following are the various popular and most common approaches to performing a static backup of a MySQL instance. This is a necessary prerequisite for a database recovery that includes a static recovery and then a possible point in time recovery (if configured).

The following options are possible for a backup of a given MySQL instance:

- Filesystem cold backup
- SQL dump
- Table extract
- Filesystem warm snapshot
- InnoDB hot backup

Filesystem Backup

When you stop the MySQL instance with a clean and proper shutdown, it is possible to perform a filesystem backup. This is a physical copy of files on the filesystem. To ensure you successfully back up all important MySQL data, the following MySQL configuration variables define various file locations that should be carefully reviewed and when applicable included in the list of files to back up. These variable values should be obtained while the server is running. Not all variables may be defined in the `my.cnf` file. MySQL will use pre-configured defaults for all variables not defined.

- `datadir`   The MySQL data directory
- `innodb_data_home_dir`   The InnoDB Data directory
- `innodb_data_file_path`   The individual InnoDB data files, which may contain specific different directories
- `log-bin`   The binary log directory
- `log-bin-index`   The binary log index file
- `relay-log`   The relay log directory
- `relay-log-index`   The relay log index file

In addition, it is critical you also back up the MySQL configuration file as these settings are particularly necessary to successfully run MySQL. In particular the `innodb_data_file_path` and `innodb_log_file_size` include underlying file sizes that when not configured in identical size will result in your MySQL instance failing to start. Refer to Chapter 6 for more information regarding MySQL configuration variables.

Restricting application SQL access to the MySQL server to perform a file copy of a running MySQL instance is highly recommended. A file copy is a sequential process, and there is no guarantee all files will be consistent for the full copy. This is especially applicable when using InnoDB, as additional background threads operate to flush and persist underlying data from the InnoDB Buffer pool even after all MySQL access is restricted.

Disadvantages
There are several key disadvantages to this approach.

- The MySQL instance is not available during the backup.
- The recovery process requires a similarly configured system with the same operating system and directory structures.
- The MySQL instance memory buffers will be re-initialized when MySQL is restarted. This can take some time for the system to provide optimal performance for running SQL statements.

Advantages
- Simple process.
- This enables a backup to be performed with any filesystem backup tool.

SQL Dump

MySQL provides a SQL based backup option with the included client command `mysqldump`. This command was first introduced in Chapter 1. Using `mysqldump` is a practical way that requires no additional software; however, this solution is not without a number of limitations. A common use of `mysqldump` would be:

```
$ mysqldump -u[user] -p --routines --master-data --complete-insert \
   --all-databases > backup.sql
```

This command creates a backup that includes all tables, views, and stored routines for all database schemas and the master binary log position.

The one additional option that is most commonly used is `--single-transaction`; however, this is only applicable for an InnoDB only environment, or transactional storage engine that supports MVCC.

A number of the options shown are described in further detail.

--opt

This option is enabled by default and is equivalent to `--add-drop-table`, `--add-locks`, `--create-options`, `--quick`, `--extended-insert`, `--lock-tables`, `--set-charset`, and `--disable-keys`.

--lock-tables

This option is actually implied by the `--opt` option, which is enabled by default. The underlying implementation of the LOCK TABLES command uses the syntax:

```
USE [schema]
LOCK TABLES [tablename] READ LOCAL, [tablename] READ LOCAL, etc
UNLOCK TABLES
USE [schema]
...
```

The `mysqldump` with `--lock-tables` only locks the tables of one schema at one time—not all tables for all schemas. If application logic writes to two different schemas and you use a storage engine that does not support transactions, it is possible to have inconsistent data during a backup.

--lock-all-tables

This option will perform a FLUSH TABLES WITH READ LOCK command in order to produce a consistent view of data in all schemas.

--routines

Using `mysqldump` to back up all databases does not back up all of your schema meta-information. MySQL routines are not included by default. This can be a significant shortcoming if your recovery process does not fully test the validity of your backup. If your database includes stored procedures or functions the `--routines` option is necessary.

--master-data

This option is essential for any point in time recovery, which is the general requirement for all disaster recovery situations. When enabled, the output will produce a SQL command like:

```
CHANGE MASTER TO MASTER_LOG_FILE='log-bin.000122', MASTER_LOG_POS=211885601;
```

You can also specify --master-data=2, which will embed this SQL statement as a comment only so this is not physically executed during the restoration of data with the mysqldump output. The importance of this option and the prerequisite configuration is discussed in the following section on point in time requirements.

--all-databases

As the name implies, all database schemas are referenced for the mysqldump command. You can also specify individual database schemas and tables on the command line. To specify specific databases use the --database option; for specific tables use --tables, and to define schemas with an exclusion list of tables use --ignore-table.

--complete-insert

The --complete-insert option provides a practical syntax for a higher level of compatibility as shown:

```
$ mysqldump -u[user] -p --skip-quote-names --databases book --tables colors
...
INSERT INTO colors VALUES
('RED','Apples,Sun,Blood,...'),
('ORANGE','Oranges,Sand,...')
...

$ mysqldump -u[user] -p --skip-quote-names --complete-insert \
  --databases book --tables colors
...
INSERT INTO colors (name, items) VALUES ('RED','Apples,Sun,Blood,...'),('ORANGE'
,'Oranges,Sand,...'),
...
```

This is important if you separate your schema and data using mysqldump to trap errors when loading data.

By default MySQL will combine a number of rows for individual INSERT statements. This is due to the --extended-insert option that is enabled by default. If you want to generate a backup with individual INSERT statements use the `--skip-extended-insert` option. This will affect the recovery time of your backup.

--skip-quote-names

By default MySQL will automatically add a back tick (`) around every object name. This is used to support using reserved words and spaces in object names, two practices that are strongly not recommended. `mysqldump` does not quote only those objects that need this syntax, but all objects including table names, column names, index names, etc.

This is a cumbersome syntax that can be removed with `--skip-quote-names`, and providing you avoid the two conditions mentioned the backup file will be correctly restored.

--single-transaction

When using a storage engine that supports MVCC it is possible to get a consistent view of data using the `--single-transaction` option. This works, for example, with the InnoDB storage engine. It does not work with the MyISAM storage engine. This option does have an overhead, as this is one long running transaction.

--hex-blob

When your database contains binary data, the `--hex-blob` option will provide maximum compatibility especially when using your backup for restoration on different MySQL systems.

MySQL Replication Specific Options

Chapter 4 will discuss a number of important `mysqldump` options to consider when working with a MySQL slave including `--master-data`, `--apply-slave-statements`, and `--dump-slave`.

Additional Options

The following syntax provides a full list of possible options with `mysqldump`:

```
$ mysqldump --help
```

Benefits

As mentioned in Chapter 1, one of the benefits of mysqldump is the ASCII nature of the data. You can look at the backup file with a text editor and you can use simple tools to manipulate the data—for example, to perform a global string substitution to change the storage engine. mysqldump can also support the extraction of individual schemas and tables, providing a level of flexibility not possible with other options discussed in this chapter. While mysqldump may not be the tool of choice for your full backup and recovery strategy, understanding this command for partial data situations is important.

This command uses the MySQL client/server protocol so the mysqldump command does not have to be performed on the same host. This can help reduce the I/O writing requirement and disk capacity necessary; however, this can increase the time the command executes and network utilization. When used on a Linux or Unix operating system additional piping and redirection can enable additional features including encryption and compression.

One advantage of the SQL backup is that it enables a cross operating system compatible solution. A backup using mysqldump on Linux can be restored on a Windows platform. In addition, mysqldump also provides a --compatible option to support SQL statements that can be used with previous MySQL versions.

Because mysqldump output is an ASCII representation of data, it is possible that the size of the backup is larger than the database. For example, a 4 byte integer can be 10 characters long in ASCII.

Recovery Considerations

A backup process is only as good as a successful recovery. A mysqldump file is only a static backup. Regardless of your backup approach, this is one common component required for a true recovery solution that is to support a point in time recovery. This important recovery step has two additional requirements when producing a SQL dump. The first requirement is the master binary logs, which are enabled with --log-bin. The second is the binary log position at the time of the backup; this is obtained by the --master-data options. Chapter 6 discusses these options in detail.

Recommended Practices for Database Objects

It is recommended that you separate your table objects and table data. This has multiple benefits including ease of comparison for schema objects, ability to re-create your schema only—for example, with a test environment—and provides an easier way to split your data file for possible parallel loading. Regardless of your ultimate backup process, I would always recommend you run the following two commands to back up your schema definition and objects:

```
$ mysqldump -u[user] -p --no-data --all-databases > schema.sql
$ mysqldump -u[user] -p --no-data --all-databases \
  --no-create-info --routines > routines.sql
```

A simple approach to schema comparison is to perform a difference between files that are created with each backup. This approach is only approximate, as the order of objects is not guaranteed, and the syntax may and does change between MySQL versions. You can use this technique, however, as a quick check and confirmation of no schema changes, which is an important verification and audit.

TIP   A mysqldump *of database objects can provide an easy means of confirming that no objects have changed between scheduled backups. This can provide a level of auditability for system architecture.*

Using Compression

Using mysqldump you can leverage the operating system to support compression. The simplest approach is to pipe the output directly into a suitable compression algorithm. For example:

```
$ mysqldump [options] | gzip > backup.sql.gz
```

While this will ensure a much smaller backup file, compression adds time to the backup process, which could affect other considerations including locking and recovery time. See Chapter 8 for a more detailed discussion on using compression to optimize the backup process.

Leveraging Network Devices

You can also use mysqldump across the network, either with a pull or push process, for example, to pull the data from the database server to another server.

```
#  db-server is the database
#  bak-server is the remote server
bak-server $ mysqldump [options] -C -hdb-server > backup.sql
```

The -C option enables compression in the communication when supported between the mysqldump client command and the database server. This does not compress the result, only the communication.

The push of mysqldump output can be performed several ways including with the nc (netcat) command. For example:

```
bak-server $ nc -l 9000 > backup.sql
db-server  $ mysqldump [options] | nc db-server 9000
```

Chapter 8 provides more information regarding different options and considerations for streaming a backup.

Disadvantages

mysqldump is ideal for smaller databases. Depending on your hardware, including available RAM and hard drive speed, an appropriate database size is between 5GB and 20GB. While it is possible to use mysqldump to back up a 200GB database, this single thread approach takes time to execute. It is also impractical to restore in a timely manner due to the single threaded nature of the restoration of a mysqldump output. Ideally, leveraging techniques of separating static and online data into multiple files can provide an immediate parallelism. The mydumper utility aims to improve these features by offering parallelism capabilities. This open source utility is discussed in Chapter 8.

Table Extract

An additional form of ASCII backup is to produce a per table data file, also called a data snapshot. This option is not practical for a full system backup; however, it is ideal for time series, write once, and archival data, especially if the data has been manually partitioned. Using a hybrid approach for a backup strategy can reduce both the time and size required for your backup. This method, when used with static data, i.e., eliminating a consistency problem, and combined with mysqldump of other data, can provide a much smaller backup both in execution time and filesize. This can also translate to reduced recovery times. Generally this approach is not practical as a complete solution because it is difficult to reconcile with point in time recovery.

You can use the mysqldump command with the --tab option or SELECT INTO OUTFILE SQL syntax to achieve a per table data file. By default, these commands produce a tab separated column format, with a newline terminator for rows. If you wanted to produce a comma separated variable (CSV) dump of data, you could use the following syntax:

```
$ cd /tmp
$ mysqldump -u [user] -p --no-create-info --tab=.
  --fields-terminated-by=,
  --fields-optionally-enclosed-by=\" book colors

$ ls -l colors.txt
-rw-rw-rw- 1 uid gid 308 Sep  1 00:40 colors.txt

$ cat /tmp/colors.txt
"RED","Apples,Sun,Blood,..."
"ORANGE","Oranges,Sand,..."
"YELLOW","..."
"GREEN","Kermit,Grass,Leaves,Plants,Emeralds,Frogs,Seaweed,Spinach,
Money,Jade,Go Traffic Light"
"BLUE","Sky,Water,Blueberries,Earth"
"INDIGIO","..."
"VIOLET","..."
"WHITE","..."
"BLACK","Night,Coal,Blackboard,Licorice,Piano Keys,..."
```

or

```
mysql> SELECT * FROM colors
    -> INTO OUTFILE '/tmp/colors.csv'
    -> FIELDS TERMINATED BY ',' OPTIONALLY ENCLOSED BY '"';
Query OK, 9 rows affected (0.00 sec)

$ ls -l /tmp/colors.csv
-rw-rw-rw- 1 uid gid 308 Sep  1 00:42 /tmp/colors.csv
$ diff /tmp/colors.txt /tmp/colors.csv
# NOTE: No difference from mysqldump generated file
```

One advantage of the `mysqldump` command is a greater flexibility of the underlying file permissions necessary to write the output file. Using the SELECT INTO OUTFILE syntax requires the `mysqld` process owner (generally `mysql`) to have appropriate write permissions where the outfile is defined. This also produces an additional problem when compressing or moving the file, as a normal operating system user generally cannot perform this on the file created by the `mysql` user.

Filesystem Snapshot

A more practical solution for a larger MySQL instance is to perform a filesystem snapshot. This is not actually a MySQL specific strategy, but rather a disk based operating system command using Logical Volume Manager (LVM) for direct attached drives, or applicable snapshot technology for Storage Area Network (SAN) or Network Attached Storage (NAS) providers. This may also be a feature of certain file systems, e.g., the Btrfs file system on Linux and ZFS on Solaris.

Your disk must be correctly configured with LVM prior to using any of these commands. The EffectiveMySQL website provides a detailed article on installing and configuring LVM at http://effectiveMySQL.com/article/configuring-a-new-hard-drive-for-lvm/ and on installing MySQL to utilize this LVM volume at http://effectiveMySQL.com/article/using-mysql-with-lvm.

Assuming you have a MySQL instance running on an LVM volume you can use the following command to take a filesystem snapshot:

```
$ sudo su -
$ sync ; lvcreate -L1G -s -n dbsnapshot /dev/db/p0
```

This command uses the logical volume group (dev/db/p0) and a very small undo size for this example (-L1G). These would be modified accordingly for your environment. Calculating the necessary undo size can be difficult. If the space is not large enough, the snapshot command will report an appropriate error.

NOTE   *A snapshot volume does not need to be the same size as the underlying volume that contains your MySQL data. A snapshot only has to be large enough to store all data that is going to change over the time the snapshot exists.*

CAUTION   *Always ensure you have sufficient diskspace to perform a snapshot. The pvdisplay and lvdisplay commands show total available space and the percentage of space allocated to snapshots.*

CAUTION   *Having an active LVM snapshot comes with a performance penalty for all disk activity. While ideal for recovery purposes to have the current snapshot online, for general database performance it is best to discard the snapshot as soon as it is no longer in use. Having multiple snapshots will further degrade I/O performance.*

The verification process of taking a filesystem snapshot would include:

```
$ sudo su -
$ mkdir -p /mnt/dbsnapshot
$ mount -o ro /dev/db/dbsnapshot /mnt/dbsnapshot
```

```
$ du -sh /mnt/dbsnapshot
$ ls -al /mnt/dbsnapshot
$ diff -rq /original/volume /mnt/dbsnapshot
```

LVM snapshots operate under the filesystem; they are thus application and filesystem agnostic. Whatever application uses these files—in this case, MySQL—needs to ensure that the files on disk are in a consistent state when the snapshot is taken. This backup approach works; however, it creates an inconsistent snapshot of MySQL. Depending on the storage engines used, the recovery process may perform an automatic recovery for this inconsistent view, or it may produce errors, for example, with MyISAM tables, which can increase the total system recovery time. Historically, automatic recovery time with InnoDB could also take a long time. This has been greatly improved with newer versions of MySQL 5.1 and 5.5.

The correct approach when using a filesystem snapshot is to place the MySQL instance into a consistent state before any command. This is achieved with the FLUSH TABLES WITH READ LOCK command. As described in the earlier section on locking, this command, when used incorrectly, does not ensure a consistent view.

The recommended steps for using a filesystem snapshot are:

- Generate a consistent MySQL view with FLUSH TABLES WITH READ LOCK. It can be difficult to predict how long this will take.

- Obtain the MySQL binary log position with SHOW MASTER STATUS and/or SHOW SLAVE STATUS.

- Run the snapshot command in a different thread. It is important you do not exit from the MySQL session for the previous commands.

- Optionally run a FLUSH BINARY LOGS.

- Release locks with UNLOCK TABLES.

- Verify the filesystem snapshot.

- Make an appropriate copy of the snapshot backup on a different server or site.

- Discard the snapshot (for optimal I/O performance).

NOTE   *The most common backup needed for a disaster recovery is the most recent backup. The underlying LVM logical volume for the filesystem snapshot is actually an I/O performance overhead to maintain. The backup of the snapshot and movement to an external system is a common approach. The restoration of these compressed backup files from an external system can be the most significant time component of the recovery strategy. Chapters 3 and 5 discuss these impacts in more detail.*

For more information about the theory of LVM see http://en.wikipedia .org/wiki/Logical_Volume_Manager_(Linux).

Using mylvmbackup

The `mylvmbackup` utility now maintained by longtime MySQL community advocate Lenz Grimmer is a convenience script that wraps all of this work into a single command. You can find this utility at http://www.lenzg.net/ mylvmbackup/. For example, the use of `mylvmbackup` when correctly installed and configured is:

```
$ sudo su -
$ mylvmbackup
20110902 17:11:24 Info: Connecting to database...
20110902 17:11:24 Info: Flushing tables with read lock...
20110902 17:11:24 Info: Taking position record into
/tmp/mylvmbackup-backup-20110902_171124_mysql-RzDzAn.pos...
20110902 17:11:24 Info: Running: lvcreate -s --size=5G
--name=p0_snapshot /dev/db/p0
File descriptor 4 (socket:[120367]) leaked on lvcreate invocation.
Parent PID 7594: /usr/bin/perl
  Logical volume "p0_snapshot" created
20110902 17:11:31 Info: DONE: taking LVM snapshot
20110902 17:11:31 Info: Unlocking tables...
20110902 17:11:31 Info: Disconnecting from database...
20110902 17:11:31 Info: Mounting snapshot...
20110902 17:11:31 Info: Running: mount -o rw /dev/db/p0_snapshot/
var/tmp/mylvmbackup/mnt/backup
20110902 17:11:31 Info: DONE: mount snapshot
20110902 17:11:31 Info: Copying /tmp/mylvmbackup-backup-20110902_171124_
mysql-RzDzAn.pos to /var/tmp/mylvmbackup/mnt/backup-pos/backup-20110902_171124_
mysql.pos...
20110902 17:11:31 Info: Copying /mysql/etc/my.cnf to
/var/tmp/mylvmbackup/mnt/backup-pos/backup-
20110902_171124_mysql_my.cnf...
20110902 17:11:31 Info: Taking actual backup...
20110902 17:11:31 Info: Creating tar archive
/var/tmp/mylvmbackup/backup/backup-
20110902_171124_mysql.tar.gz
20110902 17:11:31 Info: Running: cd '/var/tmp/mylvmbackup/mnt' ;
```

```
'tar' cvf - backup/  backup-pos/backup-20110902_171124_mysql.pos
 backup-pos/backup-20110902_171124_mysql_my.cnf| gzip --stdout
--verbose --best -> /var/tmp/mylvmbackup/backup/backup-
20110902_171124_mysql.tar.gz.INCOMPLETE-BlfzQH
...
backup-pos/backup-20110902_171124_mysql.pos
backup-pos/backup-20110902_171124_mysql_my.cnf
20110902 17:14:59 Info: DONE: create tar archive
20110902 17:14:59 Info: Cleaning up...
20110902 17:14:59 Info: Running: umount /var/tmp/mylvmbackup/mnt/backup
20110902 17:15:00 Info: DONE: Unmounting /var/tmp/mylvmbackup/mnt/backup
20110902 17:15:00 Info: LVM Usage stats:
20110902 17:15:00 Info:    LV   VG   Attr   LSize Origin Snap%  Move Log
Copy% Convert
20110902 17:15:00 Info:    p0_snapshot db   swi-a- 5.00g p0        0.01
20110902 17:15:00 Info: Running: lvremove -f /dev/db/p0_snapshot
  Logical volume "p0_snapshot" successfully removed
20110902 17:15:00 Info: DONE: Removing snapshot


$ ls -lh /var/tmp/mylvmbackup/backup/
total 153M
-rw-r--r-- 1 uid gid 153M 2011-09-02 17:14 backup-20110902_171124_mysql.tar.gz
```

This command supports many additional features including backing up to a remote server using rsync. The Effective MySQL article at http://effective-MySQL.com/article/creating-mysql-backups-using-lvm/ provides additional information on how to correctly install and configure `mylvmbackup` and also lists several valuable external references.

TIP   A snapshot is a great way to perform software updates. There is no need to back up and remove the snapshot for this operation. If the update fails you can roll back to the snapshot just taken.

Designing Appropriate LVM Volumes

There are several considerations for optimizing the use of LVM and MySQL. Ensure you have a dedicated logical volume for your MySQL instance. This should include the data and InnoDB transactional logs. This is critical for a successful recovery. A snapshot is an atomic operation for all files at the same time per logical volume. Having data and InnoDB transaction logs on separate volumes would not ensure a consistent snapshot, as this would be performed separately per volume. While the MySQL binary logs are good to keep with your MySQL backup, for a highly loaded system, it may be beneficial to separate this from your MySQL data volume. MySQL log files, or other monitoring or instrumentation, can also cause overhead; the goal should be to minimize your disk footprint to ensure the most optimal recovery time.

Limiting other operations that affect your data during the execution of a filesystem snapshot can also improve the performance. For example, disabling or limiting batch processes and reporting can reduce additional system load.

Other Considerations

Using filesystem snapshots can be a disk I/O intensive operation. If your system is already heavily loaded, the addition of an active snapshot is an overhead that could add up to 20 percent extra load. In addition, the compressing and/or copying of the snapshot, while necessary for a backup strategy, may add more stress to the system.

The ZFS filesystem, available with Solaris, FreeBSD, and other free Solaris derivative operating systems, provides a native snapshot command that works very efficiently with the designed copy-on-write principle. The Btrfs filesystem for Linux is another snapshot efficient option. Other filesystem types such as xfs can provide different performance benefits for disk I/O and management with snapshots.

InnoDB Hot Backup

For an InnoDB only MySQL instance there are two products that can perform a hot non-blocking backup. These are MySQL Enterprise Backup (MEB), formally known as InnoDB Hot Backup, and XtraBackup.

The process of performing a hot backup is different from both the `mysqldump` and filesystem snapshot approaches, as it integrates with features and functionality within InnoDB to produce a solution that provides a consistent version of data in a non-locking manner. These tools duplicate some of the features of the InnoDB storage engine by keeping a copy of all InnoDB transactional log engines (aka redo logs) and performing a copy of data consistent with InnoDB data page management. Both products will also perform a warm backup of a MySQL installation that has a mixture of InnoDB and other storage engines.

NOTE   In addition to supporting an InnoDB only application, these hot backup options do support MyISAM backups for the mysql meta-schema and any other tables; however, this requires table locking.

MySQL Enterprise Backup (MEB)

MEB is available as part of MySQL Enterprise Edition, a commercial offering that is provided by Oracle when purchasing a MySQL subscription. MEB provides a hot backup solution for a MySQL environment.

Downloading the Software   You can download MySQL Enterprise Backup for evaluation from the Oracle Software Delivery website at https://edelivery .oracle.com/. You must first sign up for free, accept the licensing agreement, and download the appropriate version via a web browser. Currently MySQL Enterprise Backup is available in the following distribution packages:

- RHEL/OL 4 32bit/64bit

- RHEL/OL 5 32bit/64bit

- RHEL/OL 6 32bit/64bit

- SuSE 10 32bit/64bit

- SuSE 11 32bit/64bit

- Generic Linux 32bit/64bit

- Windows 32bit/64bit

- Solaris 10 32bit/64bit

The following steps install a downloaded version of the generic Linux 64bit software:

```
$ sudo su -
$ cd /opt
$ unzip /path/to/V30004-01.zip
Archive:  V30004-01.zip
  inflating: meb-3-7-0-linux2-6-x86-64bit/README.txt
  inflating: meb-3-7-0-linux2-6-x86-64bit/manual.html
  inflating: meb-3-7-0-linux2-6-x86-64bit/mysql-html.css
  inflating: meb-3-7-0-linux2-6-x86-64bit/bin/mysqlbackup
  inflating: meb-3-7-0-linux2-6-x86-64bit/bin/ibbackup
  inflating: meb-3-7-0-linux2-6-x86-64bit/bin/innobackup
$ ln -s /opt/meb-3-7-0-linux2-6-x86-64bit/ /opt/meb
$ export PATH=/opt/meb/bin:$PATH
$ mysqlbackup --help
```

Running a Full Backup

```
$ sudo su - mysql
$ mkdir /mnt/backup/meb
$ time /opt/meb/bin/mysqlbackup --user=root --password=passwd \
  --backup-dir=/mnt/backup/meb/test1 backup-and-apply-log
MySQL Enterprise Backup version 3.7.0 [2011/12/19]
Copyright (c) 2003, 2011, Oracle and/or its affiliates. All Rights Reserved.

INFO: Starting with following command line ...
 /opt/meb/bin/mysqlbackup --user=root --password=passwd
        --backup-dir=/mnt/backup/meb/test1 backup-and-apply-log

INFO: Got some server configuration information from running server.

IMPORTANT: Please check that mysqlbackup run completes successfully.
           At the end of a successful 'backup-and-apply-log' run mysqlbackup
           prints "mysqlbackup completed OK!".


-------------------------------------------------------------------
                    Server Repository Options:
-------------------------------------------------------------------
  datadir                        = /var/lib/mysql/
  innodb_data_home_dir           =
  innodb_data_file_path          = ibdata1:10M:autoextend
  innodb_log_group_home_dir      = /var/lib/mysql/
  innodb_log_files_in_group      = 2
  innodb_log_file_size           = 5242880


-------------------------------------------------------------------
                      Backup Config Options:
-------------------------------------------------------------------
  datadir                        = /mnt/backup/meb/test1/datadir
  innodb_data_home_dir           = /mnt/backup/meb/test1/datadir
  innodb_data_file_path          = ibdata1:10M:autoextend
  innodb_log_group_home_dir      = /mnt/backup/meb/test1/datadir
  innodb_log_files_in_group      = 2
  innodb_log_file_size           = 5242880

mysqlbackup: INFO: Unique generated backup id for this is 13312305018224421
mysqlbackup: INFO: Uses posix_fadvise() for performance optimization.
mysqlbackup: INFO: System tablespace file format is Antelope.
mysqlbackup: INFO: Found checkpoint at lsn 915847942.
mysqlbackup: INFO: Starting log scan from lsn 915847680.
120308 18:15:01 mysqlbackup: INFO: Copying log...
120308 18:15:01 mysqlbackup: INFO: Log copied, lsn 915847942.
        We wait 1 second before starting copying the data files...
120308 18:15:02 mysqlbackup: INFO: Copying /var/lib/mysql/ibdata1

(Antelope file format).
mysqlbackup: Progress in MB: 200 400
 mysqlbackup: INFO: Preparing to lock tables: Connected to mysqld server.
120308 18:15:13 mysqlbackup: INFO: Starting to lock all the tables....
```

```
120308 18:15:14 mysqlbackup: INFO: All tables are locked and flushed to disk
 mysqlbackup: INFO: Opening backup source directory '/var/lib/mysql/'
120308 18:15:14 mysqlbackup: INFO: Starting to backup all files in

subdirectories of '/var/lib/mysql/'
 mysqlbackup: INFO: Backing up the database directory 'music1'
 mysqlbackup: INFO: Backing up the database directory 'music2'
 mysqlbackup: INFO: Backing up the database directory 'music3'
 mysqlbackup: INFO: Backing up the database directory 'music4'
 mysqlbackup: INFO: Backing up the database directory 'music5'
 mysqlbackup: INFO: Backing up the database directory 'mysql'
 mysqlbackup: INFO: Copying innodb data and logs during final stage ...
 mysqlbackup: INFO: A copied database page was modified at 915847942.
          (This is the highest lsn found on page)
          Scanned log up to lsn 915850010.
          Was able to parse the log up to lsn 915850010.
          Maximum page number for a log record 23494
120308 18:15:14 mysqlbackup: INFO: All tables unlocked
 mysqlbackup: INFO: All MySQL tables were locked for 0.000 seconds
120308 18:15:14 mysqlbackup: INFO: Full backup completed!
 mysqlbackup: INFO: Backup created in directory '/mnt/backup/meb/test1'
120308 18:15:14 mysqlbackup: INFO:  ibbackup_logfile's creation parameters:
          start lsn 915847680, end lsn 915850010,
          start checkpoint 915847942.
InnoDB: Starting an apply batch of log records to the database...
InnoDB: Progress in percents: 0 1 2 3 4 5 6 7 8 9 10 ... 97 98 99
Setting log file size to 0 5242880
Setting log file size to 0 5242880
120308 18:15:14 mysqlbackup: INFO: We were able to parse ibbackup_logfile up to
          lsn 915850010.
120308 18:15:14 mysqlbackup: INFO: The first data file is '/mnt/backup/meb/
test1/datadir/ibdata1'
          and the new created log files are at '/mnt/backup/meb/test1/datadir/'
 mysqlbackup: INFO: System tablespace file format is Antelope.
120308 18:15:14 mysqlbackup: INFO: Full backup prepared for recovery
successfully!


-------------------------------------------------------------
   Parameters Summary
-------------------------------------------------------------
   Start LSN                 : 915847680
   End LSN                   : 915850010
-------------------------------------------------------------


mysqlbackup completed OK!

real    0m12.614s
user    0m2.144s
sys     0m1.928s

$ du -sh /mnt/backup/meb/test1/
446M    /mnt/backup/meb/test1/
$ ls -lh /mnt/backup/meb/test1/
```

```
total 12K
-rw-rw-r-- 1 mysql mysql  188 2012-03-08 18:15 backup-my.cnf
drwx------ 8 mysql mysql 4.0K 2012-03-08 18:15 datadir
drwx------ 2 mysql mysql 4.0K 2012-03-08 18:15 meta
```

NOTE   *The* `--with-timestamp` *option will create an appropriate date/time sub-directory for each backup using MySQL Enterprise Backup.*

This example showed the `backup-and-apply-log` option. It is also possible to create a backup with two separate commands by running MEB with `backup` and then `apply-log`.

For more information see the MySQL documentation at http://dev.mysql .com/doc/mysql-enterprise-backup/3.7/en/mysqlbackup.backup.html.

Chapter 8 discusses additional options for MySQL Enterprise Backup including compression, incremental, and remote backups.

Security   To improve access permissions for a privileged user performing a backup with MEB, the following privileges are required:

```
mysql> CREATE USER dbbackup@localhost IDENTIFIED BY 'backup-password';
mysql> GRANT RELOAD, REPLICATION CLIENT, SUPER, CREATE TEMPORARY TABLES
    -> ON *.* TO dbbackup@localhost;
mysql> GRANT CREATE,INSERT,DROP ON mysql.ibbackup_binlog_marker
TO dbbackup@localhost;
mysql> GRANT CREATE,INSERT,DROP ON mysql.backup_progress TO dbbackup@localhost;
mysql> GRANT CREATE,INSERT,DROP ON mysql.backup_history TO dbbackup@localhost;
```

For more information refer to the MEB manual at http://dev.mysql.com/ doc/mysql-enterprise-backup/3.7/en/mysqlbackup.privileges.html.

Monitoring   In addition to text output of the `mysqlbackup` command, information is recorded in the `mysql` schema. For example:

```
mysql> SELECT * FROM backup_history\G
...
*************************** 3. row ***************************
             backup_id: 13312305018224421
             tool_name: /opt/meb/bin/mysqlbackup --user=root
--backup-dir=/mnt/backup/meb/test1 backup-and-apply-log
            start_time: 2012-03-08 18:15:01
              end_time: 2012-03-08 18:15:14
            binlog_pos: -1
           binlog_file: BINLOG-DISABLED
     compression_level: 0
               engines: MEMORY:MyISAM:InnoDB:CSV:
```

```
       innodb_data_file_path: ibdata1:10M:autoextend
          innodb_file_format: Antelope
                   start_lsn: 915847680
                     end_lsn: 915850010
         incremental_base_lsn: 0
                 backup_type: FULL
               backup_format: DIRECTORY
              mysql_data_dir: /var/lib/mysql/
         innodb_data_home_dir:
 innodb_log_group_home_dir: /var/lib/mysql/
 innodb_log_files_in_group: 2
        innodb_log_file_size: 5242880
          backup_destination: /mnt/backup/meb/test1
                   lock_time: 0.000
                  exit_state: SUCCESS
                  last_error: NO_ERROR
             last_error_code: 0


mysql> SELECT * FROM backup_progress WHERE backup_id=13312305018224421\G
*************************** 1. row ***************************
    backup_id: 13312305018224421
    tool_name: mysqlbackup
   error_code: 0
error_message: NO_ERROR
 current_time: 2012-03-08 18:15:01
current_state: Started mysqlbackup.
*************************** 2. row ***************************
    backup_id: 13312305018224421
    tool_name: mysqlbackup
   error_code: 0
error_message: NO_ERROR
 current_time: 2012-03-08 18:15:13
current_state: mysqlbackup locking tables and copying .frm + other engines data.
*************************** 3. row ***************************
    backup_id: 13312305018224421
    tool_name: mysqlbackup
   error_code: 0
error_message: NO_ERROR
 current_time: 2012-03-08 18:15:14
current_state: mysqlbackup unlocked the tables.
*************************** 4. row ***************************
    backup_id: 13312305018224421
    tool_name: mysqlbackup
   error_code: 0
error_message: NO_ERROR
 current_time: 2012-03-08 18:15:14
current_state: mysqlbackup applying log.
*************************** 5. row ***************************
    backup_id: 13312305018224421
    tool_name: mysqlbackup
   error_code: 0
```

```
error_message: NO_ERROR
 current_time: 2012-03-08 18:15:14
current_state: mysqlbackup returns success.
5 rows in set (0.02 sec)
```

This can be disabled with the `--no-history-logging` option.

More Information For more information on the features of MySQL Enterprise Backup visit http://www.mysql.com/products/enterprise/backup .html.

XtraBackup

XtraBackup is an open source offering by Percona that can perform an InnoDB hot backup. This tool also has additional features for the support of the XtraDB storage engine, an open source variant of InnoDB.

Downloading the Software XtraBackup is available in three different versions. This is because XtraBackup actually includes an embedded version of the MySQL server and MySQL client libraries. You can download the software from http://www.percona.com/downloads/XtraBackup/.

For example, when using the Ubuntu 64bit MySQL 5.5 version of XtraBackup, the following commands download and install the software. Refer to the previously mentioned link to obtain the most current version of XtraBackup for your applicable operating system. At the publication of this book the current version is 2.0.0.

```
$ wget http://www.percona.com/redir/downloads/XtraBackup/XtraBackup-2.0.0/
       deb/oneiric/x86_64/percona-xtrabackup_2.0.0-417.oneiric_amd64.deb
$ sudo apt-get install -y libaio1
$ sudo dpkg -i percona-xtrabackup_*.deb
$ xtrabackup -help
```

CAUTION *XtraBackup may require the installation of the library package for Asynchronous I/O (libaio1 on Ubuntu, libaio on RHEL). This is also required for MySQL versions 5.5 or greater.*

NOTE *In the prior version of XtraBackup, the package name was* xtrabackup. *It is now* percona-xtrabackup.

--backup   The XtraBackup backup process is a two stage operation. The first operation with the --backup option performs the physical backup. The second operation with the --prepare option performs an internal crash recovery of the copied tablespace files and accumulated transactional logs to produce a consistent backup that can then be restored in a timely manner.

Using the directory structure of the MySQL installation that was referenced in the LVM section the following syntax will perform a backup. The --datadir parameter should be adjusted accordingly for your MySQL instance.

```
$ sudo su -
$ mkdir -p /mnt/backup/mysql
$ time xtrabackup --backup --datadir=/var/lib/mysql \
   --target-dir=/mnt/backup/mysql/test1
xtrabackup version 2.0.0 for Percona Server 5.1.59 ...
xtrabackup: uses posix_fadvise().
xtrabackup: cd to /var/lib/mysql
xtrabackup: Target instance is assumed as followings.
xtrabackup:   innodb_data_home_dir = ./
xtrabackup:   innodb_data_file_path = ibdata1:10M:autoextend
xtrabackup:   innodb_log_group_home_dir = ./
xtrabackup:   innodb_log_files_in_group = 2
xtrabackup:   innodb_log_file_size - 5242880
xtrabackup: use O_DIRECT
>> log scanned up to (915844705)
[01] Copying ./ibdata1
     to /mnt/backup/mysql/test1/ibdata1
>> log scanned up to (915844705)
>> log scanned up to (915844705)
>> log scanned up to (915844705)
>> log scanned up to (915844705)
[01]        ...done
xtrabackup: The latest check point (for incremental): '915844705'
>> log scanned up to (915844705)
xtrabackup: Stopping log copying thread.
xtrabackup: Transaction log of lsn (915844705) to (915844705) was copied.

real    0m14.428s
user    0m1.400s
sys     0m0.132s
$ ls -ld /mnt/backup/mysql/test1
drwx------ 2 root root 4096 2012-03-08 17:32 /mnt/backup/mysql/test1
$ ls -lh /mnt/backup/mysql/test1
total 435M
-rw-r--r-- 1 root root 434M 2012-03-08 17:32 ibdata1
-rw-r--r-- 1 root root   81 2012-03-08 17:32 xtrabackup_checkpoints
-rw-r--r-- 1 root root 2.5K 2012-03-08 17:32 xtrabackup_logfile
```

--prepare The prepare step of XtraBackup launches the embedded version of InnoDB, performs a crash recovery of the data and accumulated transaction logs, and produces a clean and consistent version that is ready for any recovery requirements.

This step can occur on any server that has the backup files and the same version of XtraBackup installed. This does not need to occur on the machine the backup was taken.

```
$ time xtrabackup --prepare --target-dir=/mnt/backup/mysql/test1
xtrabackup version 2.0.0 for Percona Server 5.1.59 ...
xtrabackup: cd to /mnt/backup/mysql/test1
xtrabackup: This target seems to be not prepared yet.
xtrabackup: xtrabackup_logfile detected: size=2097152, start_lsn=(915844705)
xtrabackup: Temporary instance for recovery is set as followings.
xtrabackup:   innodb_data_home_dir = ./
xtrabackup:   innodb_data_file_path = ibdata1:10M:autoextend
xtrabackup:   innodb_log_group_home_dir = ./
xtrabackup:   innodb_log_files_in_group = 1
xtrabackup:   innodb_log_file_size = 2097152
xtrabackup: Starting InnoDB instance for recovery.
xtrabackup: Using 104857600 bytes for buffer pool (set by --use-memory
parameter)
InnoDB: The InnoDB memory heap is disabled
InnoDB: Mutexes and rw_locks use GCC atomic builtins
InnoDB: Compressed tables use zlib 1.2.3
InnoDB: Warning: innodb_file_io_threads is deprecated. Please use
innodb_read_io_threads and innodb_write_io_threads instead
120308 17:34:27  InnoDB: Initializing buffer pool, size = 100.0M
120308 17:34:27  InnoDB: Completed initialization of buffer pool
120308 17:34:27  InnoDB: highest supported file format is Barracuda.
InnoDB: The log sequence number in ibdata files does not match
InnoDB: the log sequence number in the ib_logfiles!
120308 17:34:27  InnoDB: Database was not shut down normally!
InnoDB: Starting crash recovery.
InnoDB: Reading tablespace information from the .ibd files...
120308 17:34:27 Percona XtraDB (http://www.percona.com) 1.0.17-12.5 started;
log sequence number 915844705

[notice (again)]
  If you use binary log and don't use any hack of group commit,
  the binary log position seems to be:

xtrabackup: starting shutdown with innodb_fast_shutdown = 1
120308 17:34:27  InnoDB: Starting shutdown...
120308 17:34:27  InnoDB: Shutdown completed; log sequence number 915845915

real    0m0.527s
user    0m0.020s
sys     0m0.048s
```

For saving additional time in the recovery process, you can run the --prepare option a second time to prepare clean InnoDB transaction logs. This is not a required step.

NOTE   The xtrabackup command does not create date/time based sub-directories during the backup process.

Backing Up All MySQL Data   As you can see from the XtraBackup commands, only InnoDB specific data is included. To capture all MySQL data, the innobackupex wrapper script packages all the necessary work into a single command. For example:

```
$ time innobackupex --defaults-file=/etc/mysql/my.cnf  \
      --user=root --password=passwd /mnt/backup/mysql

InnoDB Backup Utility v1.5.1-xtrabackup; Copyright 2003, 2009 Innobase Oy
and Percona Inc 2009-2012.  All Rights Reserved.

This software is published under
the GNU GENERAL PUBLIC LICENSE Version 2, June 1991.

120308 17:37:04  innobackupex: Starting mysql with options:
      --defaults-file='/etc/mysql/my.cnf' --user=root --password=xxxxxxxx
      --unbuffered --
120308 17:37:04  innobackupex: Connected to database with mysql child
process (pid=6834)
120308 17:37:10  innobackupex: Connection to database server closed
IMPORTANT: Please check that the backup run completes successfully.
          At the end of a successful backup run innobackupex
          prints "completed OK!".

innobackupex: Using mysql  Ver 14.14 Distrib 5.1.58, for debian-linux-gnu
(x86_64) using readline 6.2
innobackupex: Using mysql server version Copyright (c) 2000, 2010, Oracle
and/or its affiliates. All rights reserved.

innobackupex: Created backup directory /mnt/backup/mysql/2012-03-08_17-37-10
120308 17:37:10  innobackupex: Starting mysql with options:
--defaults-file='/etc/mysql/my.cnf' --password=xxxxxxxx --unbuffered --
120308 17:37:10  innobackupex: Connected to database with mysql
child process (pid=6859)
120308 17:37:12  innobackupex: Connection to database server closed

120308 17:37:12  innobackupex: Starting ibbackup with command: xtrabackup_51
--defaults-file="/etc/mysql/my.cnf" --backup --suspend-at-end
--target-dir=/mnt/backup/mysql/2012-03-08_17-37-10
innobackupex: Waiting for ibbackup (pid=6865) to suspend
innobackupex: Suspend file '/mnt/backup/mysql/2012-03-08_17-37-10/
xtrabackup_suspended'
```

```
xtrabackup_51 version 1.6.5 for MySQL server 5.1.59 unknown-linux-gnu
(x86_64) (revision id: undefined)
xtrabackup: uses posix_fadvise().
xtrabackup: cd to /var/lib/mysql
xtrabackup: Target instance is assumed as followings.
xtrabackup:   innodb_data_home_dir = ./
xtrabackup:   innodb_data_file_path = ibdata1:10M:autoextend
xtrabackup:   innodb_log_group_home_dir = ./
xtrabackup:   innodb_log_files_in_group = 2
xtrabackup:   innodb_log_file_size = 5242880
xtrabackup: use O_DIRECT
>> log scanned up to (0 915844705)
[01] Copying ./ibdata1
     to /mnt/backup/mysql/2012-03-08_17-37-10/ibdata1
>> log scanned up to (0 915844705)
>> log scanned up to (0 915844705)
>> log scanned up to (0 915844705)
>> log scanned up to (0 915844705)
[01]        ...done

120308 17:37:36  innobackupex: Continuing after ibbackup has suspended
120308 17:37:36  innobackupex: Starting mysql with options:
--defaults-file='/etc/mysql/my.cnf' --user=root --password=xxxxxxxx
--unbuffered --
120308 17:37:36  innobackupex: Connected to database with mysql child
process (pid=6874)
>> log scanned up to (0 915844705)
120308 17:37:38  innobackupex: Starting to lock all tables...
>> log scanned up to (0 915844705)
>> log scanned up to (0 915844705)
120308 17:37:48  innobackupex: All tables locked and flushed to disk

120308 17:37:48  innobackupex: Starting to backup .frm, .MRG, .MYD, .MYI,
innobackupex: .TRG, .TRN, .ARM, .ARZ, .CSM, .CSV and .opt files in
innobackupex: subdirectories of '/var/lib/mysql'
innobackupex: Backing up file '/var/lib/mysql/music1/country.frm'
innobackupex: Backing up file '/var/lib/mysql/music1/album_type.frm'
innobackupex: Backing up file '/var/lib/mysql/music1/album.frm'
innobackupex: Backing up file '/var/lib/mysql/music1/db.opt'
innobackupex: Backing up file '/var/lib/mysql/music1/artist.frm'
innobackupex: Backing up file '/var/lib/mysql/music4/country.frm'
innobackupex: Backing up file '/var/lib/mysql/music4/album_type.frm'
innobackupex: Backing up file '/var/lib/mysql/music4/album.frm'
innobackupex: Backing up file '/var/lib/mysql/music4/db.opt'
innobackupex: Backing up file '/var/lib/mysql/music4/artist.frm'
innobackupex: Backing up file '/var/lib/mysql/music2/country.frm'
innobackupex: Backing up file '/var/lib/mysql/music2/album_type.frm'
innobackupex: Backing up file '/var/lib/mysql/music2/album.frm'
innobackupex: Backing up file '/var/lib/mysql/music2/db.opt'
innobackupex: Backing up file '/var/lib/mysql/music2/artist.frm'
innobackupex: Backing up file '/var/lib/mysql/music3/country.frm'
innobackupex: Backing up file '/var/lib/mysql/music3/album_type.frm'
```

```
innobackupex: Backing up file '/var/lib/mysql/music3/album.frm'
innobackupex: Backing up file '/var/lib/mysql/music3/db.opt'
innobackupex: Backing up file '/var/lib/mysql/music3/artist.frm'
innobackupex: Backing up files '/var/lib/mysql/mysql/*.{frm,MYD,MYI,MRG,TRG,TRN,
ARM,ARZ,CSM,CSV,opt,par}'

(69 files)
innobackupex: Backing up file '/var/lib/mysql/music5/country.frm'
innobackupex: Backing up file '/var/lib/mysql/music5/album_type.frm'
innobackupex: Backing up file '/var/lib/mysql/music5/album.frm'
innobackupex: Backing up file '/var/lib/mysql/music5/db.opt'
innobackupex: Backing up file '/var/lib/mysql/music5/artist.frm'
120308 17:37:50  innobackupex: Finished backing up .frm, .MRG, .MYD, .MYI,
 .TRG, .TRN, .ARM, .ARZ, .CSV, .CSM and .opt files

innobackupex: Resuming ibbackup

xtrabackup: The latest check point (for incremental): '0:915844705'
>> log scanned up to (0 915844705)
xtrabackup: Stopping log copying thread.
xtrabackup: Transaction log of lsn (0 915844705) to (0 915844705) was copied.
120308 17:37:52  innobackupex: All tables unlocked
120308 17:37:52  innobackupex: Connection to database server closed

innobackupex: Backup created in directory '/mnt/backup/mysql/2012-03-08_17-37-10'
innobackupex: MySQL binlog position: filename '', position
120308 17:37:52  innobackupex: completed OK!

real    0m48.638s
user    0m1.892s
sys     0m1.652s

$ du -sh /mnt/backup/mysql/2012-03-08_17-37-10
436M    /mnt/backup/mysql/2012-03-08_17-37-10
$ ls -lh /mnt/backup/mysql/2012-03-08_17-37-10
total 435M
-rw-r--r-- 1 root root  357 2012-03-08 17:37 backup-my.cnf
-rw-r--r-- 1 root root 434M 2012-03-08 17:37 ibdata1
drwxr-xr-x 2 root root 4.0K 2012-03-08 17:37 music1
drwxr-xr-x 2 root root 4.0K 2012-03-08 17:37 music2
drwxr-xr-x 2 root root 4.0K 2012-03-08 17:37 music3
drwxr-xr-x 2 root root 4.0K 2012-03-08 17:37 music4
drwxr-xr-x 2 root root 4.0K 2012-03-08 17:37 music5
drwxr-xr-x 2 root root 4.0K 2012-03-08 17:37 mysql
-rw-r--r-- 1 root root   13 2012-03-08 17:37 xtrabackup_binary
-rw-r--r-- 1 root root    1 2012-03-08 17:37 xtrabackup_binlog_info
-rw-r--r-- 1 root root   87 2012-03-08 17:37 xtrabackup_checkpoints
-rw-r--r-- 1 root root 2.5K 2012-03-08 17:37 xtrabackup_logfile
```

This command will automatically place the backup in a date/time defined sub-directory. This can be disabled with the `--no-timestamp` option.

More Information For more information on XtraBackup visit http://www .percona.com/docs/wiki/percona-xtrabackup:xtrabackup:start.

Options Not Discussed

There are several other commands and techniques that are not discussed in detail. These include:

- `mysqlhotcopy` is an included utility that is applicable for MyISAM tables only. This utility should not be used as this is no longer maintained.

- `ibbackup` is the historical name for InnoDB Hot Backup. This has been improved and is now called MySQL Enterprise Backup.

- `mydumper` (http://www.mydumper.org/) is a high performance tool providing many features over `mysqldump` including parallelism, consistency with transactional and non-transactional tables, and binary log management. Refer to Chapter 8 for more information.

- `mt-parallel-dump` is a deprecated Maatkit tool that attempted to perform parallel `mysqldump` commands. The author has recommended this product no longer be used.

- MySQL online backup that was under development in MySQL versions 5.2 and 6.0 was never incorporated into future development.

- Zmanda Recovery Manager for MySQL (http://www.zmanda.com/ backup-mysql.html) provides a user interface and management tool for MySQL backups; however, it does not provide any additional functionality that is not described in this chapter.

- DRBD (Distributed Replicated Block Device) is not discussed as a possible MySQL backup option. DRBD can be used to provide a more highly available system; however, this is not specifically a backup and recovery approach.

CAUTION   Be wary of GUI editors that offer a backup solution or a generic tool that fits all database solutions. A production system requires a production strength backup solution tailored to your business needs and objectives.

Point in Time Requirements

The static backup of a MySQL instance is only the first step of a strategy that will result in a successful recovery. In addition to a backup strategy that provides a backup option to a specific time when the backup was taken, it is generally necessary to perform a point in time recovery to either the most current transactions before a physical disaster, or a time before some human created situation. This is known as a point in time recovery (PITR) that is performed by applying the MySQL binary logs to a recovered snapshot.

Binary Logs

When enabled, the MySQL binary logs record all DML and DDL statements that are performed on a MySQL instance. It is possible for users with appropriate privileges to disable the binary log for individual session statements or globally. This could produce an inconsistent version of data during a recovery process or replication topology. It is important that application users are not given the SUPER permission for this reason.

The binary logs are enabled with the - -log-bin option that is detailed in Chapter 6. The SHOW BINARY LOGS command provides a list of current binary logs managed by MySQL. The SHOW MASTER LOGS command produces the same output.

```
mysql> SHOW BINARY LOGS;
+------------------+-----------+
| Log_name         | File_size |
+------------------+-----------+
| mysql-bin.019662 | 104857736 |
| mysql-bin.019663 | 104857699 |
| mysql-bin.019664 | 104857850 |
...
| mysql-bin.020610 | 104857966 |
| mysql-bin.020611 | 104857679 |
| mysql-bin.020612 | 104857745 |
| mysql-bin.020613 |  51424056 |
+------------------+-----------+
952 rows in set (0.09 sec)
```

These binary log entries match the underlying files defined by the - -log-bin option.

```
$ ls -ltr /var/log/mysql | tail
-rw-rw---- 1 mysql adm 104857848 2011-09-04 22:00 mysql-bin.020607
-rw-rw---- 1 mysql adm 104857953 2011-09-04 22:08 mysql-bin.020608
```

```
-rw-rw----  1 mysql adm 104857739 2011-09-04 22:16 mysql-bin.020609
-rw-rw----  1 mysql adm 104857966 2011-09-04 22:25 mysql-bin.020610
-rw-rw----  1 mysql adm 104857679 2011-09-04 22:33 mysql-bin.020611
-rw-rw----  1 mysql adm 104857745 2011-09-04 22:41 mysql-bin.020612
-rw-rw----  1 mysql adm 104857987 2011-09-04 22:50 mysql-bin.020613
-rw-rw----  1 mysql adm     30432 2011-09-04 22:50 mysql-bin.index
-rw-rw----  1 mysql adm  66904136 2011-09-04 22:56 mysql-bin.020614
```

A high volume system can easily record 500MB per minute of binary logs, and this can have a large impact on available diskspace. The --expire-logs-days option removes these files automatically after the defined number of days. Alternatively, it is important that you use the PURGE BINARY LOGS command to remove these files instead of removing the files from the file system manually, as there is an internal reference between the database and the filesystem.

CAUTION   A system administrator deleting MySQL binary log files via an operating system command is a potential disaster situation. The appropriate MySQL command should always be used to remove binary log files.

Binary Log Position

Depending on the chosen backup option you may also need to capture the current binary log position in order to be able to successfully perform a restoration. The SHOW MASTER STATUS provides the current position. For example:

```
mysql> SHOW MASTER STATUS\G
*************************** 1. row ***************************
            File: mysql-bin.020616
        Position: 63395562
    Binlog_Do_DB:
Binlog_Ignore_DB:
```

This information can be obtained with the --master-data option when using the mysqldump command.

Binary Log Backup Options

The backup of the binary logs is just as important as a backup of your database. Several options exist including filesystem copy, replication, and other disk based technologies.

File Copy

The binary logs are sequential files that can easily be copied to an external server without any impact on ensuring consistency with the running MySQL database. It is possible to perform a remote synchronization of files—for example, with the `rsync` command—on a regular frequency to ensure a secondary copy of the master server binary logs.

Replication

The use of MySQL replication is an easy way to have a copy of the binary log data on a secondary system. When using MySQL replication, a copy of the binary log entries is written to the relay log on the MySQL slave. While this is a copy, there is no accurate reference between the master log file and position and the corresponding relay log file and position. The relay log is not a good way to have a copy of what is in the binary log. Relay log files have a much shorter longevity by default than the master binary logs. The use of `--log-slave-updates` would be a more practical choice. Chapter 4 discusses in more detail various options for understanding the binary logs in a MySQL replication topology.

DRBD

It is possible to easily create a mirrored binary log implementation using additional software including DRBD. This ensures you have a consistent copy of all binary logs on a separate server.

Hardware Considerations

Having available diskspace and network bandwidth are the most important hardware considerations for supporting MySQL backups.

The most likely recovery will be from the most current backup. If you have insufficient diskspace to store this on your primary server, the time for data transfer in a recovery situation may be the most significant portion of time.

If you have insufficient diskspace on your primary server and you store your backup compressed, the time to uncompress your backup may be the most significant component of time.

A common design decision is between using direct attached disk versus a Network Attached Storage device. The choice to use a Storage Area Network (SAN) as a backup solution is not a practical option. In fact, relying solely on SAN is a greater likelihood of a disaster. The use of snapshotting and archiving functionality in addition to SAN usage is necessary for a fully functioning DR plan.

To ensure great network connectivity, using dedicated network connections for application use and internal use ensures copying backup files during peak time does not saturate your network. Network bonding is a further simple hardware option that will reduce the impact of a physical hardware network failure.

Data Source Consistency

Producing a consistent database backup may involve ensuring the consistency of external sources. The design of a database system that stores images in the database is a common argument put forward for ensuring data consistency. This is, however, a classic example where the inclusion of large static objects in the database has a far greater overhead, both in database performance and in database backup and recovery time. The correct design of a disaster recovery (DR) strategy should ensure that images are never stored in the database, as this has a direct effect and is detrimental to an optimal solution.

There are examples for a backup strategy where consistency is not necessary for an entire MySQL instance. The inclusion of backup or copy tables in a MySQL schema is a prime candidate for defining a different schema and excluding this entire schema during a `mysqldump` backup.

The inclusion of large static data or archive data that is managed and updated infrequently can also be separated using an individual schema, for example, when using `mysqldump`. This level of separation may not be applicable for different backup options.

Backup Security

While not discussed in this book, it is an important consideration that your backup files meet applicable security requirements. To obtain important company information, does an intruder need to compromise the security of your production server, or just your backup server?

Conclusion

In this chapter we discussed the primary backup options that are possible for a given MySQL server. Knowing the relative risks of various strategies may alter your plan for how you design a complex system. The use of MySQL replication or other topology options can affect backup options. Knowing and understanding your application, your data, and your rate of data change can also introduce possible optimizations for a hybrid approach.

Producing a suitable backup strategy is only a prerequisite step to the more critical recovery process with considerations for consistency, timeliness, and gradients of data availability. While a full and successful recovery is essential, the time to perform a recovery is one important business requirement that could affect the viability of your entire business. Chapter 3 discusses important business requirements that can affect the technical decisions for choosing the backup and recovery strategy of your MySQL environment.

The SQL statements and web links listed in this chapter can be downloaded from http://effectivemysql.com/book/backup-recovery/.

3

Understanding Business Requirements for Disaster Recovery

"No one cares about your backup; they only care if you can restore."
Adapted from W. Curtis Preston – *Backup & Recovery* (O'Reilly, 2009)

One of the factors in choosing a backup methodology is the business requirements for data recovery. There are businesses where the loss of a single transaction has a substantive impact, and businesses where recovering to last night at midnight meets the business requirements for acceptable loss.

Defining these requirements and classes of data is not strictly a technical problem; however, it is important to prevent very difficult conversations about mismatched expectations.

In this chapter we will discuss:

- Defining requirements

- Determining responsibilities

- Understanding business terminology

- Planning for situations

Defining Requirements

The requirements of the business can dictate how your database backup and recovery strategy is implemented. The business may accept a four hour recovery time, meaning that additional hard drive space is the only additional physical need for an existing system. Or, no downtime may dictate multiple geographically placed servers, many smaller servers rather than fewer larger servers, and with the application designed to support partitioning necessary to satisfy these business requirements.

Being prepared for any level of disaster is just as important as supporting a growing system; however, this never receives the prestige like improving system performance. Many requirements you need to put in place are safety nets that may never be utilized; however, it would be disastrous for your business viability if they were not in place.

Basic hardware redundancies including multiple servers, hard drive RAID configurations, network bonding and duplicate power supplies are basic necessities. Redundancy is designed to prevent a recovery requirement and enable systems to maintain a level of availability, generally in a degraded mode, e.g., a disk failure in a RAID disk, NIC failure in a network bond, or slave failure in a MySQL topology. In these situations the redundancy via either a replication or active/passive usage can ensure seamless operations. The system is considered degraded, as the lack of further redundancy is a point of failure, e.g., 1 disk in RAID 5. Furthermore, additional system load is generally necessary to restore the system failure to full operation.

Advanced considerations include placing servers in different racks to avoid fire, theft, or other serious damage. These decisions could include working with varying external providers adding complexity to the decision making and support processes.

However, it may be impossible to fully consider an explosion that takes out the power supply and backup power options of an entire data center of 10,000 servers. Recently the seizure by FBI agents of servers that were totally unrelated to the original warrant, and upheld by a U.S. district court, showed that physical servers in proximity to alleged illegal activities are not immune to unexpected loss.

Are you prepared? What is important is that you are aware of and consider all of these factors.

What is the cost to downtime? Having an actual figure of $X per hour combined with the potential loss due to reputation is a powerful motivator when requesting the investment of additional servers or other hardware for the implementation of a successful failure strategy.

Determining Responsibilities

This book and the Effective MySQL series provide highly practical and technical content to the reader. This chapter, while one of the least technical sections of any book, is the single most important business information for any system that records information, regardless of the choice of product. Disaster preparedness is too often overlooked in any organization, from a single person startup to Fortune 500 companies.

What is important is that both the business and technical decision makers have clear guidelines and agreement of these guidelines. For example, what does the statement "no downtime" mean in your context? The decision maker may say "no downtime," but what that really means is serving page content and serving ads. This then implies that user management, adding comments, placing orders, and other functions are all services that can afford to have limited outages. These considerations may differ depending on your type of business. A media organization would consider serving of ads critical, while an online store would consider placing orders critical.

The most important component of any business is a disaster recovery (DR) plan. This is especially important when the data you have is your primary business asset. A total loss of data will most likely result in a loss of business viability, including your job and possible reputation. What is the acceptable loss of data, also known as the recovery point objective (RPO)?

Terminology

The following terms are used in defining business requirements for disaster situations.

Term	Description
DR	Disaster recovery (DR) is the plan, including steps, actions, responsibilities, and timelines, that is needed for returning your business to successful operations. The DR plan includes the significant component for the successful and timely recovery of all information, which will depend on a suitable backup strategy.
MTTR	The mean time to recover (MTTR) is the average time taken to successfully recover from failure. This is not a guarantee that a system will be operational within this time. Individual components and types of failure may have very different MTTR values. The replacement of a failed hard drive is different from loss of network connectivity by an upstream provider, or by a denial of service attack.
MTTD	The mean time to detect (MTTD) is often unrepresented in any strategy; however, the time to detect a problem can have a significant impact on the type of recovery and/or the requirements for loss of data.
RPO	The recovery point objective (RPO) is the point in time to which you must recover data as defined by your organization. This is a generated definition of what an organization determines as acceptable loss in a disaster situation. Not all environments require an up to the minute recovery plan. More information at http://en.wikipedia.org/wiki/Recovery_point_objective.
RTO	The recovery time object (RTO) is the acceptable amount of time in the recovery situation to ensure business continuity. This is generally defined in a Service Level Agreement (SLA).
Data classes	Not all data has the same value or net worth. Some information is more important, and this classification can affect how your backup and recovery strategy may operate. In a disaster situation, certain data is more critical. The system may be considered operational without all data available. Defining data classes determines these types of data.
SLA	A Service Level Agreement (SLA) is something to be considered within an existing organization and not just with external suppliers. An SLA should also include both technical and business decision responsibilities in response to any important situation.

Defining a formal SLA within an organization may vary for each system. This may include different values for these terms for each specific system.

Technical Resource Responsibilities

In most significant disasters you will never be given the opportunity to explain the impact, your possible options, or even how hard the solution may be. The questions will be very precise and generally include:

- When will our system be available?
- What information has been lost?
- Why did this happen?

The decision makers will discuss the potential revenue that was lost and the total business impact. Knowing these facts is important in determining what you need to plan and prepare for, how to present confidence at any time, and how to justify additional needs in physical and human resources.

Decision Maker Responsibilities

The role of the decision maker is to ensure the ongoing business viability at your organization. This includes many factors a technical resource may not consider, such as the ongoing media impact, shareholder responsibilities, acquiring additional staff resources, dealing with third party suppliers, and much more. Do you know how to reverse an online transaction, send an e-mail blast, and change the message on your customer support phone system? What is important is that you are prepared to support decisions made. The most likely preparation you can do to provide a level of confidence to your organization includes:

- Have a backup and recovery strategy in place.
- Have actual timings, test results, and daily reports of the success of your strategy freely available for anybody in your organization.
- Consider the extent of possible disaster recovery situations. You may not be able to address all issues; however, be able to think outside of the normal database operations for creative solutions to complex and business threatening conditions.
- Be proactive in providing information to build confidence in advance.

Knowing the decision makers and building a rapport over time is less about technical ability and more about professional development.

Identifying Dependencies

As you will see in the following case study, regardless of the best plans the database administrator has for supporting a disaster, there are dependencies on other resources and operations outside of your control.

Case Study

The following case study of a real world example is used to understand the important technical and business factors for a complex business situation.

The MySQL Topology

Your MySQL topology includes one master server and two slave servers using MySQL replication. This has been implemented because, in the past, several issues about read-scalability and reporting have enabled the justification of additional servers. Your environment supports a dedicated read slave and a dedicated reporting slave.

Your Backup and Recovery Strategy

Your backup strategy involves using one database slave to take a full copy of all of your data. You also realize the importance of the master binary logs for a point in time recovery and you have a secondary process that keeps copies of these at five minute intervals.

The current backup and recovery strategy supports many situations that have occurred in the past.

- You direct reads to your primary slave and reporting to the second slave.
- You can redirect reads to a different slave or the master.
- You can redirect or disable reporting.
- You test your backup. You are confident that a full restore of your system in two to three hours providing necessary hardware is functional.
- You can restore all data to a total loss of five minutes in a multiple database disaster situation and generally you can support data loss to a few seconds.

The current strategy is not perfect. You have some requests in process to support a controlled fail-over using a virtual IP (VIP) rather than a specific domain name; however, this involves implementing application and system changes. These needs do not seem as important as you would wish within your organization.

A Real Life Disaster

Your slave server has stopped applying transactions. There is no error message in replication. Your additional monitoring detects important business metrics and no orders have happened in the past 30 minutes.

Meanwhile on the master server, multiple disk alerts have gone unnoticed and unactioned by the system administrator. As a result the partition holding the MySQL binary logs fills up. This results in the following error in the master error log, which ironically is not actively monitored:

```
[ERROR] mysqld: Disk is full writing '/mysql/binlog/log-bin.000020'
    (Errcode: 28). Waiting for someone to free space... Retry in 60 secs
[ERROR] Could not use /mysql/binlog/log-bin for logging (error 28).
    Turning logging off for the whole duration of the MySQL server process.
    To turn it on again: fix the cause, shutdown the MySQL server and restart it.
```

For more information on the environment conditions that caused this error see http://ronaldbradford.com/blog/never-let-your-binlog-directory-fill-up-2009-07-15/.

Your backup strategy relies on the slave server being up to date, that is, by applying all binary log statements from the master. As this is now disabled, your slave server is missing important business transactions and is inconsistent with your master. You cannot use your primary recovery process, that is, simply restore your last successful static backup and apply the master binary logs for a point in time recovery. Your only option to recover all data is to stop your master database and take a backup, something you have never done on this server.

This new backup also involves having to clean up available disk space to support a copy of the database on this system. You also need to install the latest backup script, as this is not run on this system. Do you risk modifying the backup script and backup across the network to save cleaning up disk-space? How long will that take? Even after this new backup is taken you then have to restore this backup on both slaves.

This late notification and initial investigation has taken two hours to determine the only technical decision to ensure no data loss requires a further six hours to complete just to ensure you have a recoverable situation, and several hours more to complete the recovery of both slave servers. You are required to give regular business updates, to which you have no basis of information for this situation before. The result to the business is no new customer orders for over eight hours.

Your best made plans as a DBA are put to dust by a part time system administrator who is replacing a person on vacation. They did not notice or respond to a disk alert before it was too late. In the past, the DBA group you belong to has requested access to these important system alerts, but the system admin group will not give you access, as that is not your responsibility.

It does not really matter who is to blame—the database was unavailable for eight hours during peak time and you are the highly paid DBA responsible for ensuring the database is operational.

Technical Outcomes

There are many good points to take away from this experience. Your environment has system monitoring in place. Many organizations fail at this most initial step. A MySQL backup and recovery strategy is in place, is tested, documented, and timed. There are multiple MySQL instances to support some situations for failure.

There are some simple technical steps that are not implemented. Open access to all information alerts and the request for implementing using IPs and not using domain names for database connections, both simple technical tasks, but caught up in the bureaucracy of the business and decision makers.

What other options existed that could have been considered if you had more time to investigate or discuss with peers? You could have promoted one of your slaves, the most current, to a master. This would involve changing the MySQL configuration to enable binary logging and modifying your application servers to point to the new server. You could re-configure the second slave server to use this new master. You could have backed up the old master, because you now accept a loss of transactions for the sales during this time. Your downtime is now reduced to three hours; however, you have a mismatch of monies received with the orders defined, and potentially very annoyed customers if they do not get their orders. What is the time to undertake data forensics of the processed orders, then reapplying these orders to the system? There is no easy way because you do not want to double charge customers. What is the additional staff time and greater cost needed? More importantly, do you need to even consider this? We will answer this specific question in the following section.

If you had no idea about your system, and varying options, how could you give multiple options and time estimates to everybody who wants answers?

The mean time to detect (MTTD) is very important in this situation. The mean time to recover (MTTR) is also important. Which is more important may be different with respect to the point of view of responsibilities.

That item on your pending to-do list about having a more documented, tested, and streamlined fail-over process may have been a saving grace. Unfortunately the request to the application team to change the DB connections, the system group to enable a virtual IP (VIP) and necessary MySQL configuration changes are no help.

The Decision Process

As a DBA it is not always your decision about what action to take. That is the decision of the business owner. Who is that in your organization? What is important is how you structure information for the responsible person to make an informed decision.

In this situation, while three hours of downtime is less than eight hours, is this the best decision? Each hour is not just lost revenue, but a loss of business reputation. Will further bad press of being down all day hurt more? Again, it is important to understand the business requirements and to know who is ultimately responsible. In the previous section you considered the additional impacts of the three hour recovery option that accepts data loss from a technical perspective. However, you did not consider the business approach of processing a full refund to all customer orders affected. This functionality already exists to process refunds. The business could also send a specific e-mail apology about the situation and ask customers to re-order, even offering a discount code for the inconvenience. This additional process also already exists. The result would mean no lost data having to be restored and no additional work by physical resources. The only technical requirement would be identifying the customers affected and the details of these now refunded orders.

A disaster is the one thing that an executive of an organization should be kept awake at night worrying about. As a responsible DBA or data architect, your single greatest asset to an organization is to know what to do when something goes wrong, to be prepared. Being proactive and actively simulating and testing disaster recovery situations, documenting, timing, and reporting is the knowledge that separates skilled and technical resources from expert resources with a holistic business view.

Essential External Communication

While communication internally is critical in any disaster scenario, external communication is just as important. Having a public facing status page, a forum, and a feedback loop for customers is essential. It is also critical that information is transparent and open. Previous online disasters where information has been forthcoming promptly reduces additional stresses.

It is critical that the status and feedback options are not part of your primary infrastructure. As detailed with worst case examples in the following section, it is important this infrastructure is in a different data center, and preferably a different host provider.

Planning for the Worst Situation

It is impossible to plan for every possible disaster. Knowing what is possible can help identify how your business may be able to cope, and how it may not. The following are some real life situations that can happen. As a technical resource it is important that you share these situations with decision makers to ensure they are aware of the potential issues. Even the largest companies are not immune to an unexpected disaster. One public failure of the 365 Main data center due to a power incident on July 24, 2007, affected giant Internet sites including Craigslist, GameSpot, Yelp, Technorati, Typepad, and Netflix.

For more supporting information of these real life disasters described in summary here visit http://effectiveMySQL.com/article/real-life-disasters/.

Total SAN Failure

A SAN is not a backup solution. If anything a SAN is a higher likelihood of a larger cascading failure. Losing a single server from multiple hard drive failures (e.g., a RAID 1, RAID 5, and RAID 10 configuration can all operate with a single loss) has far less impact in a hundred server environment than a SAN failing and dropping all mounts for all systems. There are many actual occurrences of SAN failures. With one client, a routine replacement of several failed hard drives and a software upgrade by an employee of a large SAN service provider for a multi-million dollar SAN investment caused an internal panic, which shut down the SAN and 160 different mount points. This resulted in corrupting 30+ database servers and taking the entire website (a top 20 traffic site by Alexa) offline for several days.

In this example, relying on a single SAN for all production servers is a situation that should be avoided.

Power Disruption

Even with backup generators with four days of fuel supply in place, and a DR situation tested and used in the past five years, three out of ten (i.e., 30 percent) backup generators failed to operate when power was lost at a prominent San Francisco data center. The result was 40 percent of customers losing power to equipment. This was a serious disaster causing cascading systems failure.

In this example, hosting your entire infrastructure even with a premier hosting provider with impressive uptime is no guarantee of a total system outage. Using multiple locations is advisable for critical functionality.

Explosion

In June 2008 an electrical explosion at a data center took offline approximately 10,000 servers including the primary web and database server for the author of this book. Under direction from the fire department, due to safety issues and due to the seriousness of the incident, the backup generators located adjacent to the complex were also powered down. This resulted in an outage for several days. The situation was more complicated because the service provider also had their own management servers, domain management, SSL management, client management, and communication tools all in the same location without redundancy.

In this example, knowing your DR plan also includes understanding the DR plan of applicable service providers. An infrastructure for a web presence has many moving parts, some of which you may not consider, in this case, suitable DNS and network fail safes.

This was one example where the host provider managed the situation for customers well. The issue was addressed in a timely manner with regular updates published on a status page and forums. The phone greetings for support also included status information of the problem.

FBI Seizure

In a recent FBI raid for specific hardware, additional servers and important networking equipment were also seized with the same warrant. Much like a serious physical failure, the host provider was given no notice, and unaffected systems were also affected, ultimately leading to a cascading failure. In addition, unlike a physical failure that can be addressed by resources repairing or replacing faulty equipment, this equipment was removed for an undetermined time.

Blackout

Large statewide blackouts are uncommon; however, as a recent incident in September 2011 highlighted, a simple incident with one component (i.e., transformer failure) caused a cascading system failure that resulted in the shutdown of multiple nuclear power plants. In this situation power was lost for 15 hours for a large region across several states leaving entire cities without power. With a high availability solution across data centers, insufficient geographical redundancy could still result in a total loss.

In addition, a loss of power could mean no operation of your customer support telephone system, or facilities for your office staff to operate during the situation. Even with a geographical deployment there may be no way to implement a controlled fail-over, monitor, or update customers easily.

Human Factors

Being hacked, malicious intent by a disgruntled employee, and a failed system wide rollout of software by an employee that disables access to thousands of servers are all very possible situations. For many organizations, the act of changing the keys to your front door, aka the system passwords for your servers, is an important process that needs to be known, documented, tested, and able to be implemented instantly.

Human Resources

In addition to these situations, the impact of human resources may be the most overlooked situation. The case study in this chapter highlighted that less skilled technical resources caused a cascading failure situation. Vacation, sickness, accidents, and even overworked employees are all situations that have to be understood as possible disaster situations.

A commonly overlooked situation is the need for 24/7 support that is required regularly. While key resources may need to be on call for emergency support after hours, if this is always occurring, productively can be significantly impacted. The likelihood of error due to handling issues without appropriate procedures and at constant extended afterhours work are factors not to be avoided.

What is your "red bus" policy? This was a term first heard by the author some 20 years ago when a decision maker was talking about my potential demise. Simply put, what happens when your critical resource is hit by a "red bus"? While this term sounds harsh, this references all possible situations from sickness, vacations, accidents, and even the resignation of critical technical resources. While this is the responsibility of an organization, every individual could be proactive in ensuring your organization has some procedures or contact details for support services, emergency consulting services, or peers to step in.

Developing a Strategic Plan

Defining the requirements and responsibilities as discussed is necessary to determine what is acceptable to the business. In his book *High Availability and Disaster Recovery* (Springer, 2006), Klaus Schmidt describes the two properties important for any failure scenario, the probability of the failure and the damage caused by the failure. The mapping of the types of failure on an XY chart, with Damage on the X-axis and Probability on the Y-axis (pg 83), enables failures to be mapped into three categories: Fault protection or recovery by high availability, fault recovery by disaster recovery, and forbidden zone (pg 84). While the final category may appear inappropriately named, any failure in this category requires a system redesign to remove this limitation in providing a robust solution. This technical approach can be valuable for identifying the risk to the business and contributing to an appropriate strategic plan. In some situations, the addition of applicable redundancy is sufficient to avoid a loss of service situation.

Not discussed in this chapter, but also important in the overall data management plan, are any retention policies for legal or auditing requirements. Your backup plan may require keeping several months of backups on a weekly or monthly cycle.

Conclusion

System failure and disasters are inevitable; however, a catastrophe that affects your business, your own career, and reputation is avoidable. Many disaster situations have far greater business implications than finding and implementing a technical solution. A formal SLA agreement is a driving factor in making well informed decisions during these situations. The Boy Scouts' very simple motto is the most applicable advice for any technologist: Be prepared.

4

Using MySQL Replication

The use of MySQL replication is instrumental in many practical MySQL environments and is generally considered as a primary backup and first viable fail-over option in a higher availability environment. Under normal operating conditions, MySQL replication may be sufficient; however, there are a number of limitations that must be carefully confirmed and verified for replication to be part of a valid backup and recovery strategy. As discussed in Chapter 3, a backup and recovery strategy is critical for ensuring business continuity and meeting the needs of system availability.

In this chapter we will be covering:

- Using replication for backups

- Various replication limitations that can affect backups

- Additional considerations with your backup approach

MySQL Replication Architecture

To understand the features and limitations of MySQL replication for any applicable backup method, it is important to understand the basic mechanics between a MySQL master and slave.

As outlined in Figure 4-1, the following are the key steps in the success of a transaction applied in a MySQL replication environment. This is not an exhaustive list of all data, memory, and file I/O operations performed, rather a high level representation of important steps.

- A MySQL transaction is initiated on the master (1).

- One or more SQL statements are applied on the master (2). The true implementation of the physical result depends on the storage engine used. Generally regardless of storage engine, the data change operation is first recorded within the applicable memory buffer. For InnoDB, the statement is recorded in the InnoDB transaction logs (note that InnoDB data is written to disk by a separate background thread). For MyISAM, the operation is written directly to the applicable table data file.

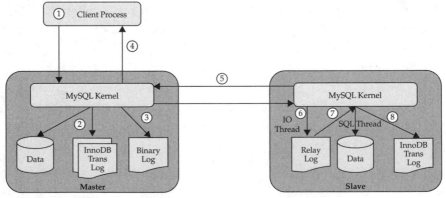

Figure 4-1 *MySQL replication workflow*

- At the completion of the transaction, the master binary log records the result of the DML statement(s) applied (3). MySQL supports varying modes that may record the DML statement or the actual data changes.

- A success indicator is returned to the calling client program to indicate the completion of the transaction (4).

- The slave server detects a change in the master binary log position (5).

- The changes are received (i.e., a pull process) by the slave server and written to the slave relay log by the slave IO thread (6).

- The slave SQL thread reads the relay log and applies all new changes (7 and 8). These changes may be recorded as a statement to be executed, or as a physical row level data modification.

- A success indicator is returned to the slave replication management.

In summary, the SQL transactions are recorded in the master binary log and the change of this log is used as a triggering event for the slave to pull the change. Chapter 2 discussed more information about the operation of the binary log. In Chapter 5, the point in time recovery section provides detailed information on how to review and analyze the master binary log.

MySQL Replication Characteristics

The following are important characteristics of the MySQL implementation of data replication that can impact a backup and recovery strategy:

- Each MySQL slave has only one MySQL master.

- A replication slave pulls new information from the master.

- MySQL replication by default is an asynchronous process [*], i.e., a master does not wait for acknowledgment or confirmation from a slave for a completed and successful transaction on the master.

- A MySQL slave can also be used for read operations, or additional write operations if configured.

- MySQL does not require a slave to be identical to a master. Tables could be stored in a different storage engine or may even contain additional columns. Providing the SQL operation completes without error, replication will not fail.

(*) MySQL 5.5 provides support for semi-sync replication, which is discussed in a following section.

CAUTION *Using MySQL replication for high availability (HA) does not imply you now have a disaster recovery (DR) solution. A MySQL slave may be configured to not include all data on the master or be configured with a different schema structure. While a MySQL slave may include all data, the process of promoting a slave from a read only status, reconfiguring your application to use this slave, and altering other operations designed for the slave are all steps in ensuring a functional DR plan.*

MySQL replication generally exists in a production environment to support scalability, data redundancy, and high availability. These architectural features provide an immediate and viable approach as a backup and recovery strategy option. By combining MySQL replication with the various backup options described in Chapter 2, several problems including locking and availability of the production database can now be avoided.

MySQL Replication Limitations

MySQL replication is not without issues; there are some key limitations for using replication effectively and these can affect a functional database backup and recovery strategy.

Replication Lag

One of the primary issues with a MySQL topology is replication lag. Replication lag can have a significant effect on an up to date backup and on an application that uses replication for read only workloads. The asynchronous nature of MySQL replication implies that a difference between the data on a master and slave is possible at any point in time.

You can determine all information about MySQL replication including lag with the SHOW SLAVE STATUS command on a MySQL instance that is a MySQL slave:

```
mysql> SHOW SLAVE STATUS\G
*************************** 1. row ***************************
              Slave_IO_State: Waiting for master to send event
                 Master_Host: 10.0.0.1
                 Master_User: repl
                 Master_Port: 3306
                   ...
```

```
          Master_Log_File: mysql-bin.001417
       Read_Master_Log_Pos: 52404776
                . . .
    Relay_Master_Log_File: mysql-bin.001417
         Slave_IO_Running: Yes
        Slave_SQL_Running: Yes
                . . .
      Exec_Master_Log_Pos: 51516321
                . . .
    Seconds_Behind_Master: 199
                . . .
```

Replication lag is determined by a non-zero number in `Seconds_Behind_Master`. This number does not represent the actual number of seconds it will take replication to catch up. `Seconds_Behind_Master` displays the time difference between the local time on the slave against the time stamp of the replication event applied on that master and that is currently being processed by the slave SQL.

Replication lag has several causes:

- The volume of concurrent SQL statements performed on a multi-threaded master exceeds the capacity of the single replication IO and SQL threads to process. A high volume production system with an increase of 5 to 10 percent is enough for replication lag to occur and never catch up.

- A DML or DDL statement that takes a long time to execute. As replication is single threaded, subsequent pending statements are further delayed. A good example is an ALTER TABLE statement.

- Replication stopped due to a specific error. The problem was subsequently addressed and replication restarted; however, replication lag now exists.

- MySQL replication supports both local area network (LAN) and wide area network (WAN) connectivity. The use of a slow network with inconsistent transaction throughput or selective connectivity can contribute to lag.

- Replication may be stopped intentionally, for example, a MySQL backup, software upgrade, or a delayed replication implementation.

- Lag can also be the result of a nested replication topology. This can be difficult to correctly determine that the master is indeed a slave of another instance.

NOTE   *It is important to monitor MySQL replication lag to detect and report an increase over time, as this is an indication that replication may not catch up.*

Consistency

It is possible for both the data and schema of a MySQL slave to be different from the applicable MySQL master and replication is operating without errors and/or lag. This is due to the flexibility of a MySQL slave not to be a true read only version of a given master, and the per statement execution of any given SQL statement that can complete without error yet still perform more or less data manipulation than on the master.

A MySQL slave can have different table structures including a change in storage engine and indexes and still support the primary function of executing a successful SQL statement. For example, it is common for a scale-out read architecture to have differing indexes to support SELECT optimizations. A change in table structure does not necessarily mean the data is inconsistent.

There are several basic settings that can be used to limit and/or check schema and data consistency.

Data Consistency

Under normal circumstances the slave should be read only to ensure data consistency. This is enabled with the MySQL configuration option read_only=TRUE. This is an important setting to minimize data manipulation on a MySQL slave when a user connects accidentally or intentionally to a MySQL slave and executes a DML or DDL statement. This will result in the slave having different data or schema structure than the master and may cause future replication errors. Any user connecting to the MySQL slave with the SUPER privilege can override this setting, so it is important to also restrict user permissions accordingly. The slave-skip-error option can also cause inconsistency where these listed errors will not result in a replication failure.

CAUTION   *A MySQL slave that does have a* read_only=TRUE *configuration and has application user access with the SUPER privilege can easily lead to inconsistent data between a master and a slave.*

The use of MySQL triggers and stored procedures may cause inconsistency if any database object definitions differ between the master and the slave.

MySQL replication does not currently provide a checksum of the events recorded in the binary log. There are very isolated situations when corruption from related hardware and network situations may cause a replication error producing a data inconsistency. The current development release of MySQL 5.6 includes the new -binlog-checksum, --master-verify-checksum, and slave-sql-verify-checksum options. More information can be found at http://dev.mysql.com/doc/refman/5.6/en/replication-options-binary-log .html.

The CHECKSUM TABLE command enables you to determine a CRC-32 checksum of all rows in the table. As this reads all rows, different versions of MySQL and even storage engines will produce a different result while the data may actually be identical.

The practical use of CHECKSUM TABLE in a highly concurrent master/ slave environment is limited as it is necessary to ensure a precise comparison at the same point in time within the execution of statements. This command does not have a SQL equivalent syntax to inject within the replication stream. In a low volume environment this command may easily produce a confirmation that tables are identical. When tables do differ, use a read lock with LOCK TABLE <tablename> READ to obtain a more consistent version. This command does read all rows of a table, so for very large tables this may take a significant time to execute.

The MySQL Reference Manual does state that due to the hashing approach it is not guaranteed two tables of differing data may result in the same value. This is true for many hash algorithms. What is important is that using a checksum approach is far more important than assuming your data is consistent following any type of replication error.

The Percona toolkit pt-table-checksum utility available at http:// www.percona.com/software/percona-toolkit/ is an open source tool that can be used for the consistency checking of table data, providing various algorithm options and built-in replication support. This tool replaces the original Maatkit mk-table-checksum utility. This tool can be difficult to understand and operate, as the documentation is not written to be user friendly. The following instructions will provide a simple to use example providing the necessary Perl DBI and DBD::mysql dependencies are already installed.

```
$ wget http://percona.com/get/pt-table-checksum
$ chmod +x pt-table-checksum
$ ./pt-table-checksum --algorithm=BIT_XOR h=localhost,u=user --ask-pass
--replicate=book.checksum --create-replicate-table --databases book
```

A quick explanation of the options used:

- `--algorithm`   This defines the algorithm to use for the table checksum. The most command and useful values include CHECKSUM, BIT_XOR, and ACCUM.

- `--ask-pass`   Prompts the user to specify the user account password.

- `--replicate`   This specifies the `schema.table` where checksum information is stored to support replication comparison.

- `--create-replicate-table`   This option pre-creates the checksum table if it does not exist.

- `--databases`   This defines the schema(s) to perform a checksum for.

When combined with the following SQL query executed on all slave servers, it is possible to detect any data drift and inconsistency between a master and a slave.

```
SELECT db, tbl, chunk,
       IF(this_crc <> master_crc OR
       ISNULL(master_crc) <> ISNULL(this_crc),'YES','NO') AS diff,
       this_cnt-master_cnt AS rowcount_diff
FROM   book.checksum
WHERE  master_cnt <> this_cnt
OR     master_crc <> this_crc
OR     ISNULL(master_crc) <> ISNULL(this_crc);
```

The execution of this utility can have a significant performance overhead on a large database. This utility has many different options including different algorithm selections and determining chunk sizes for data. Refer to the documentation at http://www.maatkit.org/doc/mk-table-checksum.html for more information. Please note that this utility is no longer active as an open source project; however, this is still widely used among the MySQL community. The corporate sponsored Percona toolkit product contains current work.

Schema Consistency

The layman's approach to detecting schema differences is to use the mysqldump utility and to generate the schema only and compare. For example:

```
$ mysqldump --all-databases --no-data --skip-dump-date \
            -u[user] -p -h[master] > master.schema.sql
$ mysqldump --all-databases --no-data --skip-dump-date \
            -u[user] -p -h[slave] > slave.schema.sql
$ diff -u master.schema.sql slave.schema.sql
```

This process is not ideal as there is no guarantee the output is ordered, and the format does differ between MySQL versions; however, this process can be used to confirm that no schema differences exist. In a high volume production system, the additional pruning of AUTO_INCREMENT=N from the CREATE TABLE statement is necessary to produce a clean comparison of the schema only. The following syntax can be added to the previously mentioned commands to produce this output:

```
$ mysqldump ... | sed -e "s/AUTO_INCREMENT=[^\ ] //" > ...
```

The schema sync utility available at http://schemasync.org/ is a Python script that will perform a schema comparison. This tool will also produce a patch script that can be used to bring the two schema definitions into sync. This is a valuable tool to help in the automation of schema correction.

Additional monitoring can be put into place by a DBA to detect a schema change command and then trigger some applicable reporting and verification approach. The MySQL status variables can be used to detect a CREATE, ALTER, or DROP command. For example:

```
mysql> SELECT variable_name, variable_value
    -> FROM INFORMATION_SCHEMA.GLOBAL_STATUS
    -> WHERE variable_name LIKE 'COM_ALTER%'
    -> OR variable_name LIKE 'COM_DROP%'
    -> OR variable_name LIKE 'COM_CREATE%';
+----------------------+----------------+
| variable_name        | variable_value |
+----------------------+----------------+
| COM_ALTER_DB         | 0              |
| COM_ALTER_DB_UPGRADE | 0              |
| COM_ALTER_EVENT      | 0              |
| COM_ALTER_FUNCTION   | 0              |
| COM_ALTER_PROCEDURE  | 0              |
| COM_ALTER_SERVER     | 0              |
| COM_ALTER_TABLE      | 0              |
| COM_ALTER_TABLESPACE | 0              |
```

```
| COM_CREATE_DB          | 1 |                |
| COM_CREATE_EVENT       | 0 |                |
| COM_CREATE_FUNCTION    | 0 |                |
| COM_CREATE_INDEX       | 0 |                |
| COM_CREATE_PROCEDURE   | 0 |                |
| COM_CREATE_SERVER      | 0 |                |
| COM_CREATE_TABLE       | 2 |                |
| COM_CREATE_TRIGGER     | 0 |                |
| COM_CREATE_UDF         | 0 |                |
| COM_CREATE_USER        | 2 |                |
| COM_CREATE_VIEW        | 0 |                |
| COM_DROP_DB            | 0 |                |
| COM_DROP_EVENT         | 0 |                |
| COM_DROP_FUNCTION      | 0 |                |
| COM_DROP_INDEX         | 0 |                |
| COM_DROP_PROCEDURE     | 0 |                |
| COM_DROP_SERVER        | 0 |                |
| COM_DROP_TABLE         | 0 |                |
| COM_DROP_TRIGGER       | 0 |                |
| COM_DROP_USER          | 0 |                |
| COM_DROP_VIEW          | 0 |                |
+-----------------------+----------------+
```

This SQL statement shows the number of statements that have been executed in total since the server was restarted. You can use this information to perform regular difference checks between previously recorded values. Alternatively you can use the `mysqlbinlog` command to filter and parse the MySQL binary logs for any CREATE, ALTER, or DROP commands. Neither of these options is ideal nor provides an absolute guarantee to capture the occurrence of a schema modification.

Object Consistency

It is also important that triggers and stored procedures are consistent between the master and the slave. You can leverage the same trick with comparing the master and slave object definitions using `mysqldump` with the additional `--routines` option. For example:

```
$ mysqldump --all-databases --no-data --no-create-info --routines \
            --skip-dump-date -u[user] -p -h[master] > master.routines.sql
$ mysqldump --all-databases --no-data --no-create-info --routines \
            --skip-dump-date -u[user] -p -h[slave] > slave.routines.sql
$ diff -u master.routines.sql slave.routines.sql
```

All routine definitions and other metadata are held in the INFORMATION_SCHEMA database. It is possible to use SQL to perform a quick sanity check. For example:

```
mysql> SELECT ROUTINE_SCHEMA,ROUTINE_NAME, ROUTINE_TYPE,
    -> LENGTH(ROUTINE_DEFINITION) AS size,
    -> MD5(ROUTINE_DEFINITION) AS checksum
    -> FROM INFORMATION_SCHEMA.ROUTINES;
```

This statement will produce a list of all routines, the size, and a checksum. This output can be recorded daily and a comparison performed to verify any object changes. For example:

```
+-------+-----------------+-----------+------+----------------------------------+
| SCHEMA| ROUTINE_NAME    | ROUTINE_TY| size | checksum                         |
+-------+-----------------+-----------+------+----------------------------------+
| mem   | fill_numbers    | PROCEDURE |  305 | 9e1277913061ce8e33506406c542d2c9 |
| mem   | run_numbers     | PROCEDURE |  153 | 2cb170ca0a892dbfd5ea0d3a1edc9fb3 |
| sakila| film_in_stock   | PROCEDURE |  204 | 96c55b0e83fdeb23a314c3200e10f49c |
| sakila| film_not_in_stoc| PROCEDURE |  208 | e78efc824bce8b7015ef8733043fbc10 |
| sakila| get_customer_bal| FUNCTION  | 1120 | e84c6e0df8d5f1472fb34e0aaf1d649d |
| sakila| inventory_in_sto| FUNCTION  |  490 | 0ffc09cb3deb5dd8a5ec1097ddad504f |
| sakila| rewards_report  | PROCEDURE | 1246 | a0a99e101af1a5c6cbf9d051d87facc0 |
| wp    | clean_install   | PROCEDURE |  260 | c7ab3d30f866c0782a2040d6d8fd61ba |
| wp    | create_author   | FUNCTION  | 1310 | c934451b02bc8107c1dd24824c655a66 |
| wp    | create_post_keyw| FUNCTION  |  909 | 98161d4a03ed8feef741640ee0c2e68b |
| wp    | create_post_term| FUNCTION  |  909 | 2a9f0a466d62b4dee2b31b6a73aab929 |
+-------+-----------------+-----------+------+----------------------------------+
```

Completeness

MySQL binary logging can be affected by several configuration options including `binlog-do-db` and `binlog-ignore-db`. This can result in DML and DDL statements not being logged to the binary log. The relay log application on a MySQL slave can further be affected by several configuration options including `replicate-do-db`, `replicate-ignore-db`, `replicate-wild-do-table`, `replicate-wild-ignore-table`, and `replicate-rewrite-db`.

Combined with the ability to disable individual SQL statements by the `SET SQL_LOG_BIN=0` command with applicable privileges, there is no guarantee that all successful SQL statements applied with your master data will be applied on a given MySQL slave.

When combined with a more complex MySQL replication topology, ensuring that the schema and data are consistent is not enough to determine that the slave used for a backup strategy contains all data.

For a detailed list of MySQL replication options and variables refer to the MySQL Reference Manual at http://dev.mysql.com/doc/refman/5.5/en/replication-options-table.html.

Replication Design Considerations

Several MySQL configuration options can have an effect on the design of your MySQL replication.

Binary Log Row Format

Starting with MySQL 5.1, it is possible to alter the binary log format from the historic and default value of STATEMENT, to either ROW or MIXED by using the `binlog_format` variable. The STATEMENT format, as the name suggests, records the actual SQL statements, which are then applied on the slave. This is known as statement-based replication (SBR). The ROW format provides a binary representation of each table row after modification of the data on the master, which is subsequently applied precisely on the slave. This is known as row-based replication (RBR).

Several configuration operations or statements may lend themselves to requiring or requesting a different row format. For example, altering the transaction isolation variable `tx_isolation` from the default setting of REPEATABLE_READ will require a MIXED or ROW format to be used. MySQL will provide the following error message in this situation:

```
mysql> CREATE SCHEMA IF NOT EXISTS book;
mysql> USE book;
mysql> DROP TABLE IF EXISTS t1;
mysql> CREATE TABLE t1(c1 INT);
mysql> INSERT INTO t1 VALUES (1);
mysql> SET SESSION tx_isolation='READ-COMMITTED';
mysql> INSERT INTO t1 VALUES (2);
ERROR 1665 (HY000): Cannot execute statement: impossible to write to
binary log since BINLOG_FORMAT = STATEMENT and at least one table
uses a storage engine limited to row-based logging. InnoDB is limited
to row-logging when transaction isolation level is READ COMMITTED or
READ UNCOMMITTED.
```

Unsafe Statements

MySQL may determine a SQL statement as unsafe with SBR. The updating or deleting of a limited number of rows with the LIMIT statement will produce a warning. Statements that contain system functions, nondeterministic functions, user defined functions (UDFs), and auto-increment changes are also considered unsafe. For example:

```
mysql> USE book;
mysql> DELETE FROM t1 LIMIT 1;
Query OK, 1 row affected, 1 warning (0.19 sec)
mysql>  SHOW WARNINGS\G
*************************** 1. row ***************************
  Level: Note
   Code: 1592
Message: Unsafe statement written to the binary log using statement format
since BINLOG_FORMAT = STATEMENT. The statement is unsafe because it uses
a LIMIT clause. This is unsafe because the set of rows included cannot be
 predicted.
```

A full list can be found in the MySQL Reference Manual at http://dev
.mysql.com/doc/refman/5.5/en/replication-rbr-safe-unsafe.html.

Trigger Operation

MySQL triggers operate differently for the binary log formats. With SBR,
triggers executed on the master are also executed on the slave. The definition
of triggers and stored procedures may also differ between the master and a
slave, which can further cause potential data inconsistency. For RBR, triggers
are not executed on the slave. The row changes on the master resulting from
any trigger action are applied directly.

Statement-based Replication (SBR)

This format has been the default since the earliest versions of MySQL starting with 3.23. The advantages of this format include, in general, less data is
written to the binary log. A DML statement that alters thousands of rows is
reflected only as a single SQL statement. The slave has to perform the same
amount of work that occurred on the master. An expensive statement needs
to be repeated on all slaves. The binary log can be analyzed with mysqlbinlog
to produce an audit of all SQL DML and DDL statements.

Row-based Replication (RBR)

With this new format, there is an improved safety of data changes. This is
especially applicable for several operations that are considered unsafe. In
general, more data is written to the binary log to reflect a change for every
row, which can affect disk performance. Starting with MySQL 5.6.2 this can
be adjusted with the binlog_row_image configuration option. Less locking is required on the slave for INSERT, UPDATE, and DELETE statements.
The binary log is also unable to provide details of SQL statements executed.

In MySQL 5.6.2 you can use the `binlog_rows_query_log_events` configuration option to provide this information.

Semi-synchronous Replication

Starting with MySQL 5.5, it is possible to improve the asynchronous nature of MySQL replication by enabling semi-synchronous functionality. In this mode, the master waits for an acknowledgment from a configured slave where the transaction has been successfully written and flushed before returning a success indicator to the client. Semi-synchronous replication must be configured and enabled on both the master and the slave for this to occur.

The production master performance is impacted due to the additional slave acknowledgment; however, the benefit is a better guarantee of data integrity.

Semi-synchronous replication in described in greater detail in Chapter 3 of *Effective MySQL: Advanced Replication Techniques*. More information is also available from the MySQL Reference Manual at http://dev.mysql.com/doc/refman/5.5/en/replication-semisync.html.

Replication Backup Considerations

Understanding that MySQL replication provides a copy of the primary database and with listed limitations including lag, schema, and data consistency, you can leverage a replication topology for an effective backup option.

It is possible to stop MySQL replication temporarily to provide better consistency for an optimized backup. This includes control for stopping either the IO or SQL thread separately depending on your needs. These options do not affect your primary master database when performing operations (except when using semi-synchronous replication); however, the time replication is stopped has downstream effects depending on the use of the MySQL slave instance in question.

You can stop the applying of data changes to your MySQL replication environment with the STOP SLAVE SQL_THREAD command. When correctly configured as a read slave this enables a consistent version of data, for example, with the `mysqldump` command independently of varying storage engines and locking strategies used.

By stopping the IO thread and ensuring all data is flushed, you are providing an environment where there are no physical file system changes. This can be of benefit for providing a more consistent snapshot view.

Additional Prerequisite Checks

Before using a backup option described in Chapter 2, there are several checks that affect a consistent backup that should be considered.

Checking Replication Lag

A small amount of replication lag is acceptable, This lag time is identical for replaying the master binary logs during a point in time recovery. A larger replication lag will result in a longer recovery time, which may be unacceptable. Your backup script that uses a MySQL slave should perform a precheck similar to the following:

```
TMP_FILE=/tmp/slave-status.tmp"
# Capture all output for later messaging if necessary
mysql -e "SHOW SLAVE STATUS\G" > ${TMP_FILE}
# Get seconds behind master value
SECONDS=`grep Seconds_Behind_Master ${TMP_FILE} | awk -F': ' '{print $2}'`
# Error checking
[ ${SECONDS} = "NULL"  o ${SECONDS} -gt 60 ] && \
echo "ERROR: Replication is stopped or lagging" && exit 1
```

MySQL Temporary Tables

The use of MySQL temporary tables on the master has an impact on ensuring a successful database recovery using a slave. Due to the per session nature, a temporary table can span multiple transactions; however, if a backup is performed while temporary tables are in use, these will not be present during a point in time recovery process that processes the replication stream. This issue also exists when using temporary tables during a MySQL slave instance restart and can result in a SQL error.

You can determine if a MySQL slave SQL thread has open temporary tables using the INFORMATION_SCHEMA or SHOW command. This check should be performed both before and after a STOP SLAVE SQL_THREAD command. Should a non-zero value be returned, the backup process should re-try and ensure this condition before commencing.

```
mysql> SELECT variable_value
    -> FROM INFORMATION_SCHEMA.GLOBAL_STATUS
    -> WHERE variable_name='SLAVE_OPEN_TEMP_TABLES';
+----------------+
| variable_value |
+----------------+
| 1              |
+----------------+
```

or

```
mysql> SHOW GLOBAL STATUS LIKE 'Slave_open_temp_tables';
+------------------------+-------+
| Variable_name          | Value |
+------------------------+-------+
| Slave_open_temp_tables | 1     |
+------------------------+-------+
```

The design of SBR can help in some circumstances to overcome this loss of data with temporary table use. SBR provides a copy of the actual data change, not a statement that will cause the data change. The interaction of temporary table use and a backup approach is very dependent on the specific application design. In general, it is best to ensure there are no open temporary tables to avoid a potential situation that you do not test for.

When intermediate data is required within your application there are several techniques that can be implemented to overcome this situation.

InnoDB Background Threads

Stopping the SQL thread is not sufficient to ensure a consistent version of the underlying MySQL data on the filesystem. While this stops the application of data changes, internally InnoDB manages flushing of data from the InnoDB Buffer pool to disk by background IO threads. When performing a file copy, inconsistency between different data files will result, as a file copy is a sequential process. When using a filesystem snapshot utility, all underlying database files will be consistent at the time of the snapshot. When restored, the MySQL database will still need to perform a consistency check and statements in the InnoDB transaction log may be applied. This occurs as part of an automatic recovery process. There is no way with the current version of official MySQL binaries to produce a clean state without shutting down the server.

Cold Backup Options

Stopping a MySQL slave instance has no impact to operations on a master system. However, it is important to ensure any application using the MySQL slave for additional purposes, including handling read scalability and/or reporting, will be affected. Generally the procedure is to ensure the server is removed from application access accordingly during the backup. By default, a MySQL slave instance, when started, will automatically connect to the master and start the process of synchronizing. The configuration option `skip-slave-start` will disable the slave from automatically commencing replication on startup. Depending on the time the slave instance is unavailable it may take minutes to hours before the slave is consistent.

mysqldump Options

Using `mysqldump` of a production database with the `--master-data` option and combined with the master binary logs enables a full point in time recovery option. When using a MySQL slave, the `--master-data` option does not provide the position of the master. At best, this option will produce an error message; at worst, it will record the position of the master binary log on the slave, if the slave is also configured as a master. The following examples show both conditions:

```
$ mysqldump --master-data --no-data --no-create-info mysql
...
mysqldump: Error: Binlogging on server not active
```

A MySQL slave may be configured to record a binary log using the `-log-bin` option and optionally the `-log-slave-updates` option. This means the MySQL slave is actually configured as a master for additional slaves. This is known as chaining where a replication environment may have three or more levels (e.g., a grandfather, father, and child). In this situation the `--master-data` option would result in information; however, this is the position of the binary log of this slave, not the master of the slave.

Using the MySQL Sandbox tool available at http://mysqlsandbox.net/ is an excellent way to quickly test and verify different replication situations. To highlight this specific condition we create a standard master and two slave sandbox replication environments:

```
# NOTE: A newer version may exist, check https://launchpad.net/mysql-sandbox
$ wget http://launchpad.net/mysql-sandbox/mysql-sandbox-3/

        mysql-sandbox-3/+download/MySQL-Sandbox-3.0.21.tar.gz
$ tar xvfz MySQL-Sandbox-3.0.21.tar.gz
$ cd MySQL-Sandbox-3.0.21
# Download a version of MySQL for your architecture
$ ./make_replication_sandbox /path/to/mysql/binary
```

We can then look at the specific `mysqldump` output for a given slave in this replication topology:

```
# Depending on your MySQL version this directory will differ
$ cd $HOME/sandbox/rsandbox_5_5_15/node1
$ mysqldump --defaults-file=my.sandbox.cnf --master-data --no-data \
            --no-create-info mysql
...
CHANGE MASTER TO MASTER_LOG_FILE='mysql-bin.000001', MASTER_LOG_POS=178;
...
```

As described in the earlier point, the position described is not the actual position of the master for this slave, but rather the position of the binary log on this slave, which is also acting as a master. This can be confirmed with:

```
slave2 [localhost] {msandbox} ((none)) > SHOW MASTER STATUS\G
*************************** 1. row ***************************
            File: mysql-bin.000001
        Position: 178
    Binlog_Do_DB:
Binlog_Ignore_DB:
slave2 [localhost] {msandbox} ((none)) > SHOW SLAVE STATUS\G
*************************** 1. row ***************************
               Slave_IO_State: Waiting for master to send event
                  Master_Host: 127.0.0.1
                  Master_User: rsandbox
                  Master_Port: 19570
                Connect_Retry: 60
              Master_Log_File: mysql-bin.000001
          Read_Master_Log_Pos: 10589
               Relay_Log_File: mysql_sandbox19572-relay-bin.000002
                Relay_Log_Pos: 3015
        Relay_Master_Log_File: mysql-bin.000001
...
           Exec_Master_Log_Pos: 2869
```

By stopping the MySQL slave and capturing the SHOW SLAVE STATUS, it is possible to create a backup of the MySQL slave, and use this in conjunction with the master binary logs to perform a successful point in time recovery.

Starting with MySQL 5.5 the `--dump-slave` option provides the correctly formatted output you would expect:

```
$ mysqldump --defaults-file=my.sandbox.cnf --dump-slave --no-data \
            --no-create-info mysql
...
CHANGE MASTER TO MASTER_LOG_FILE='mysql-bin.000001', MASTER_LOG_POS=2869;
...
```

CAUTION   The use of MySQL replication requires careful consideration for correctly identifying the position of the master when using a static backup of a slave and the master binary log files for point in time recovery.

The `--apply-slave-statements` option can also be used to stream-line the use of a `mysqldump` file for automated recovery. This option adds the STOP SLAVE and SLAVE START commands to the output produced.

Filesystem Snapshot Options

The stopping of the MySQL SQL slave thread prior to performing a FLUSH TABLES WITH READ LOCK can reduce the pending wait time of this command. The optional stopping of the MySQL IO thread will provide a consistent file system copy of the relay logs; however, this is not necessary with any filesystem snapshot technology.

The replication position is also recorded on the filesystem in the file defined by the `relay_log_info_file` system variable. Using the MySQL replication environment configured in the previous section with MySQL Sandbox this can be verified. For example:

```
slave2> SHOW GLOBAL VARIABLES LIKE 'relay_log_info_file';
+---------------------+----------------+
| Variable_name       | Value          |
+---------------------+----------------+
| relay_log_info_file | relay-log.info |
+---------------------+----------------+
$ cat data/relay-log.info
./mysql_sandbox19572-relay-bin.000002
3015
mysql-bin.000001
2869
```

MySQL Enterprise Backup (MEB) Options

The MEB product has an additional option when used with a MySQL slave server:

- `--slave-info`   This option creates the `meta/ibbackup_slave_info` file containing the necessary CHANGE MASTER command to restore the backup to produce an identical slave server.

CAUTION   *An important change to the use of the* --slave-info *option was introduced in the most recent version of MEB version 3.7.1 regarding the synchronizing of data between the slave SQL thread and slave I/O thread.*

XtraBackup Options

The XtraBackup utility manages MySQL slave specific instances using these options:

- --slave-info   This option creates the xtrabackup_slave_info file containing the necessary CHANGE MASTER command for recovery.

- --safe-slave-backup   This option stops the SQL thread and waits until there are no temporary tables in use.

Using the syntax for XtraBackup from Chapter 2, these two options are added for a backup of a MySQL slave:

```
$ innobackupex --defaults-file=/mysql/etc/my.cnf –no-timestamp  \
               --slave-info --safe-slave-backup /backup/mysql/slave
```

This produces the necessary SQL for use during recovery with the defined MySQL master:

```
$ more /backup/mysql/slave/xtrabackup_slave_info
CHANGE MASTER TO MASTER_LOG_FILE='mysql-bin.000001', MASTER_LOG_POS=17342
```

For more information see http://www.percona.com/doc/percona-xtrabackup/innobackupex/replication_ibk.html.

Architecture Design Considerations

When knowing the strengths and weaknesses of MySQL replication you may consider alternative approaches when designing your scalable architecture. While replication is well known for read scalability, other options that leverage improvements in data manageability, backup, recovery, and caching are possible. This could include the separation of write once data or batch managed data from more general read/write data.

The use of MySQL replication may also impact these design needs. Understanding data availability differently for write, read, and cached needs combined with read and write scalability, MySQL replication may be implemented and used in many different ways.

For example, if you have 30 years of financial data that is added to daily, however, each year of data is completely static, the separation of data into a static table of the first 29 years of data and a dynamic table of growing data could enable a vastly different backup and recovery strategy. This would improve caching options; however, it would add programming complexity to your application to support this level of manual partitioning. This one architecture decision could reduce daily backup operations of time and volume by 90 percent. Recovery may also be five to ten times faster. The complexity is now two different database environments with different caching strategies, different backup and recovery approaches, and the appropriate application overhead.

MySQL provides functionality for several different approaches towards addressing this specific example. MySQL partitioning and the ARCHIVE storage engine provide different advantages for functionality and should be evaluated in combination with the merits of applicable backup and recovery for these choices.

Improving your schema design for intermediate processing of data and temporary tables, enabling a specific database schema to be ignored for binary logging and replication may greatly improve replication performance. This in turn minimizes potential limitations.

Upcoming Replication Functionality

The current development version of MySQL 5.6 includes numerous replication improvements which address some of the identified backup concerns. In summary these improvements include:

- Binary log checksums
- Removing the row format before image
- Logging SQL statements in addition to row format
- Delayed replication
- Logging binary log and relay log positions using tables as well as files
- Multi-threading support on slaves supporting parallel transactions per database schema

More information about MySQL 5.6 features can be found in the MySQL Reference Manual at http://dev.mysql.com/doc/refman/5.6/en/mysql-nutshell.html and http://dev.mysql.com/doc/refman/5.6/en/news-5-6-x.html. These options are also discussed in *Effective MySQL: Advanced Replication Techniques*.

Conclusion

MySQL replication is an essential component for any high availability and scale out MySQL environment. Understanding how MySQL replication can be used for a backup and recovery strategy can be beneficial for designing a suitable MySQL topology to support both HA and DR requirements.

The backup approach is only the first component of a successful backup and recovery strategy. Applying the various options in Chapter 2, with MySQL replication considerations and with the business needs detailed in Chapter 3, it is now possible in the following chapter to fully evaluate the successful recovery of your valuable business information.

The SQL statements and web links listed in this chapter can be downloaded from http://effectivemysql.com/book/backup-recovery/.

5

Using Recovery Options

A backup is only as good as the ability to correctly recover and then use your data. A successful recovery is both the verification step of your backup procedures, and the peace of mind for your business sustainability. It is important that you test your entire recovery process from end to end regularly, practicing, verifying, refining, and most importantly, timing. In the event of a disaster after knowing recovery is possible, knowing how long this will take is an important business consideration.

In this chapter we will be covering:

- The different types of MySQL recovery
- Review of the recovery option for each backup type
- The importance of testing and verification

A Word About Testing

Backups become regular daily operations after initially configured. Recovery is rarely routine; they happen at any time, and generally require immediate action with the quickest response possible to resolve the problem. Testing of the recovery process to ensure that the backups are indeed valid and functional, and that the recovery process is known, documented, and verified, is an ideal practice to master.

This information may sound like repetition, and it is because this is the single most important process not to perform. As a consultant, every disaster engagement involving recovery has been in a situation that the client had not considered, or indeed tested. In many situations these were the common occurrences of the most obvious cases as discussed throughout this book.

A memorable quote found on the Internet regarding backup and recovery is, "Only two types of people work here, those who do backups [and restores] and those who wish they had."

NOTE   There is a common misconception that testing is about ensuring your software works correctly. Testing is really a process for trying to find ways to break your software, and then applying improvements to address these failures. Many testing practices are flawed because this correct approach is not used. The backup and recovery process of a MySQL ecosystem requires the same due diligence. As with many real world life situations, your successes are never publicly applauded; you are remembered by your failures.

Determining the Type of Recovery Necessary

While you have a backup approach in place, the primary purpose for this is for a full data recovery. Is this necessary to restore production operations in every situation? As described in Chapter 3, the business may accept a certain amount of data loss depending on the total recovery time. A data recovery process may also be necessary for a system crash or corruption and may not require a full restore from backup. This chapter will cover a variety of crash situations and possible recovery requirements.

MySQL Software Failure

The underlying MySQL process mysqld may fail. The following options discuss the primary operations in the event of a MySQL crash. The cause of failure may include a physical hardware problem, a MySQL bug, the process failing due to an exhausted memory or disk resource, or the process being intentionally terminated. For example:

```
110128 12:54:28 - mysqld got signal 11;
This could be because you hit a bug. It is also possible that this binary
or one of the libraries it was linked against is corrupt, improperly built,
or misconfigured. This error can also be caused by malfunctioning hardware.
We will try our best to scrape up some info that will hopefully help diagnose
the problem, but since we have already crashed, something is definitely wrong
and this may fail.

key_buffer_size=6442450944
read_buffer_size=104853504
max_used_connections=1984
max_connections=5500
threads_connected=813
It is possible that mysqld could use up to
key_buffer_size + (read_buffer_size + sort_buffer_size)*max_connections
 = 1132669413 Kbytes of memory
Hope that's ok; if not, decrease some variables in the equation.

thd=0x171a7870
Attempting backtrace. You can use the following information to find out
where mysqld died. If you see no messages after this, something went
terribly wrong...
Cannot determine thread, fp=0x480040d0, backtrace may not be correct.
Stack range sanity check OK, backtrace follows:
(nil)
New value of fp=0x171a7870 failed sanity check, terminating stack trace!
Please read http://dev.mysql.com/doc/mysql/en/using-stack-trace.html
and follow instructions on how to resolve the stack trace. Resolved
stack trace is much more helpful in diagnosing the problem, so please do
resolve it
Trying to get some variables.
Some pointers may be invalid and cause the dump to abort...
thd->query at 0x170bd740 = select ...
thd->thread_id=256
The manual page at http://www.mysql.com/doc/en/Crashing.html contains
information that should help you find out what is causing the crash.

Number of processes running now: 0
110128 12:54:28  mysqld restarted
```

Depending on the storage engine used, no further action may be required to ensure a functioning and accessible database. The MySQL error log will generally provide information about this situation, as described in the following section. However, it is important to determine why this has occurred and to prevent the situation from recurring.

NOTE   *In a low volume Linux production system you may not detect that MySQL has even crashed unless you review the MySQL error log. Under default operations, the* mysqld *process will automatically restart through the wrapper daemon* mysqld_safe. *If your application does not use persistent connections, this can occur without any obvious application effect.*

Crash Recovery

When using the InnoDB transactional storage engine, crash recovery is performed after a system failure. This process will detect a difference between the InnoDB data files and the InnoDB transactional logs and perform a necessary roll forward to ensure data consistency if applicable. Depending on the size of your InnoDB transaction logs, that can take some time to complete.

The MySQL error log will provide detailed information of the InnoDB crash recovery when performed.

```
InnoDB: Log scan progressed past the checkpoint lsn 0 188755039
100624 16:37:44  InnoDB: Database was not shut down normally!
InnoDB: Starting crash recovery.
InnoDB: Reading tablespace information from the .ibd files...
InnoDB: Restoring possible half-written data pages from the doublewrite
InnoDB: buffer...
InnoDB: Doing recovery: scanned up to log sequence number 0 193997824
InnoDB: Doing recovery: scanned up to log sequence number 0 195151897
InnoDB: 1 transaction(s) which must be rolled back or cleaned up
InnoDB: in total 105565 row operations to undo
InnoDB: Trx id counter is 0 18688
100624 16:37:45  InnoDB: Starting an apply batch of log records to the
database...
InnoDB: Progress in percents: 2 3 4 5 6 7 8 9 10 11 12 13 14 15 16 ... 99
InnoDB: Apply batch completed
InnoDB: Last MySQL binlog file position 0 12051, file name ./binary-log.000003
InnoDB: Starting in background the rollback of uncommitted transactions
...
```

The InnoDB crash recovery process performs the following specific steps:

1. Detects if the underlying data on disk is not consistent by comparing the checkpoint LSN with the recorded redo log LSN.

2. Applies any half written data pages that were first written to the doublewrite buffer.

3. Applies all committed transactions in the InnoDB transaction redo logs.

4. Rolls back any incomplete transactions.

In addition, during a crash recovery the insert buffer merge and the delete record purge are performed. These steps are also performed in general background operations on a working MySQL instance and are not specific to the crash recovery process.

More recent versions of MySQL have greatly improved the final stage of InnoDB crash recovery when applying the redo log, starting with MySQL 5.1.46 (InnoDB plugin 1.07) and MySQL 5.5.4. In the past, one consideration was to have smaller InnoDB transaction logs due to possible long recovery time. For more information on the specific improvement see http://blogs .innodb.com/wp/2010/04/innodb-performance-recovery/.

Testing InnoDB Crash Recovery

Testing of InnoDB crash recovery on a loaded system is important to determine if this process completes in a few minutes or can take more than one hour.

Additional information about steps to undertake when MySQL is crashing can be found at http://ronaldbradford.com/blog/mysql-is-crashing-what-do-i-do-2010-03-08/ and http://ronaldbradford.com/blog/how-to-crash-mysqld-intentionally-2010-03-05/.

TIP   *Testing a crash recovery of MySQL is as simple as executing a kill -9 on the* `mysqld` *process.*

Under normal circumstances when MySQL is stopped correctly, InnoDB crash recovery is not needed. However, as part of starting MySQL you should always check the error log. In this example, while MySQL was stopped gracefully, the error log shows crash recovery was always being performed. As the data set was small (< 1GB) the client was assuming the extended startup time was normal.

Shutdown log information:

```
$ cat /var/log/mysql/error.log
110426 14:05:53 [Note] /usr/sbin/mysqld: Normal shutdown
110426 14:05:53 [Note] Slave I/O thread killed while reading event
110426 14:05:53 [Note] Slave I/O thread exiting, read up to log
'mysql-bin.000031', position 16313924
110426 14:05:53 [Note] Event Scheduler: Purging the queue. 0 events
110426 14:05:53 [Note] Error reading relay log event: slave SQL thread was killed
110426 14:05:56  InnoDB: Starting shutdown...
```

Startup log information:

```
$ cat /var/log/mysql/error.log
110426 14:05:59 [Note] Plugin 'FEDERATED' is disabled.
InnoDB: Log scan progressed past the checkpoint lsn 6 2726373466
110426 14:05:59  InnoDB: Database was not shut down normally!
InnoDB: Starting crash recovery.
...
```

Monitoring InnoDB Crash Recovery

Monitoring the amount of recovery is possible if existing MySQL monitoring includes regular logging of the SHOW ENGINE INNODB STATUS information. The LOG section provides the Log Sequence Number (LSN) position. This can be compared with the reported LSN in the MySQL error log during a crash recovery. This information is also useful for general monitoring of internal InnoDB operations and should be part of proactive administration of any production system.

```
mysql> SHOW ENGINE INNODB STATUS;
...
---
LOG
---
Log sequence number 0 195151897
Log flushed up to   0 195141979
Last checkpoint at  0 188755039
```

Chapter 7 will discuss advanced techniques diagnosing and correcting an InnoDB crash recovery when this process fails. This is generally required when there is additional corruption of the InnoDB data and transaction log files.

MyISAM Table Recovery

When using the MyISAM storage engine, the default engine for all MySQL versions prior to MySQL 5.5, crash recovery, if necessary, is generally a manual process. Detection of possible corruption can also be more complex.

This is because there may be no advance notification until a corrupt MyISAM table is accessed via an index.

A problem can be detected with the CHECK TABLE or `myisamchk -c` command; however, this is impractical in a large database, as this operation can take a long time to determine if a problem exists. When MySQL does detect a problem, the MySQL error log will report a problem requiring further attention. For example:

```
100126 22:44:35 [Warning] Checking table:    './db1/tb1'
100126 22:44:35 [ERROR] /var/lib/mysql5/bin/mysqld: Table './db1/tb1'
is marked as crashed and should be repaired
100126 22:44:35 [Warning] Checking table:    './db1/tb2'
100126 22:44:35 [ERROR] /var/lib/mysql5/bin/mysqld: Table './db1/tb2'
is marked as crashed and should be repaired
```

Alternatively you may see an error such as:

```
100322 11:42:50  mysqld started
100322 11:42:54  InnoDB: Started; log sequence number 1447 3027352095
100322 11:42:54 [Note] /usr/libexec/mysqld: ready for connections.
Version: '5.0.88-rs-log'  socket: '/var/lib/mysql/mysql.sock'  port: 3306
100322 12:01:35 [ERROR] /usr/libexec/mysqld: Table './db1/tb1'
is marked as crashed and last (automatic?) repair failed
100322 12:01:35 [ERROR] /usr/libexec/mysqld: Table './db1/tb2'
is marked as crashed and last (automatic?) repair failed
```

NOTE   *Data for a MyISAM table (the* `.MYD` *file) is always flushed to disk for each DML statement. The error message actually references that the underlying B-tree index (the* `.MYI` *file) is inconsistent with the data. The MyISAM recovery process is the rebuilding of the indexes for a given table. This helps with the understanding that the reporting of a MyISAM table as crashed may not occur at system startup, rather when the table data is accessed via a given index.*

The MySQL configuration variable `myisam-recover` can help in some situations where the MySQL process will attempt MyISAM crash recovery. The recommended settings are:

```
#my.cnf
[mysqld]
myisam-recover=FORCE,BACKUP
```

TIP   *The* `myisam-recover` *configuration option can offer some crash safe properties for MyISAM tables.*

Chapter 7 will provide more information on managing MyISAM crash recovery.

Other Storage Engines

MySQL offers a number of additional default storage engines as well as third party pluggable engines. The following list provides a summary of recovery capabilities of popular engines.

Included Default Engines

Storage Engine	Recovery Considerations
ARCHIVE	NONE
MERGE	The MERGE storage engine is actually a meta-definition of multiple underlying MyISAM tables. This results in the same recovery issues as detailed for MyISAM.
BLACKHOLE	This storage engine actually stores no data so recovery time is immediate. The data, however, was lost at insertion time, as the statements or blocks are only logged to the binary log.
MEMORY	As the name suggests, this storage engine does not persist data. After a crash recovery no data recovery is possible.

Popular Third Party Engines

Storage Engine	Recovery Considerations
Percona XtraDB	This fork of the InnoDB storage engine is identical in operation to InnoDB auto-recovery.
Tokutek TokuDB	TokuDB provides a full ACID compliant auto-recovery storage engine.
Akiban AKIBANDB	AKIBANDB provides a full ACID compliant auto-recovery storage engine.
Schooner SQL	Schooner SQL provides a full ACID compliant auto-recovery storage engine.

This is not a full list of MySQL storage engines. You should refer to the individual storage engine vendors for specific crash recovery details.

Table Definition Recovery

For every table in a MySQL instance, regardless of storage engine used, there is an underlying table definition file, represented by a corresponding .frm file. There are circumstances where these files may become corrupt or inconsistent with a storage engine's additional table meta-information. For example:

```
111227 14:48:04 [ERROR] mysqld: Incorrect information in file:
'./test/empty.frm'
```

and

```
110222 23:46:48 [ERROR] Cannot find or open table demo/tbl from
the internal data dictionary of InnoDB though the .frm file for the
table exists. Maybe you have deleted and recreated InnoDB data
files but have forgotten to delete the corresponding .frm files
of InnoDB tables, or you have moved .frm files to another database?
or, the table contains indexes that this version of the engine
doesn't support.
See http://dev.mysql.com/doc/refman/5.1/en/innodb-troubleshooting.html
how you can resolve the problem.
```

and

```
120413 16:03:34 [ERROR] Table db/results contains 8 indexes inside InnoDB,
which is different from the number of indexes 7 defined in the MySQL
```

This may require a different approach to obtaining this file and the matching data depending on the type of error.

NOTE   An unexpected MySQL restart has an additional impact on performance. The primary memory buffers including the InnoDB buffer pool and the MyISAM key cache are empty. These must be re-populated when data is requested, causing additional disk I/O. Internally, MySQL does not store statistics for InnoDB tables, and these have to be re-calculated when tables are first accessed.

Performing a Static Recovery

The performing of a static recovery involves a number of clearly defined steps independent of the type of backup option used. These steps are:

1. Necessary software requirements

2. Static data recovery

3. Data verification

4. Point in time recovery (if applicable)

5. Data verification

MySQL Software Installation

The recovery of, and use of, recovered MySQL data are not possible without a functioning MySQL installation. Chapter 2 does not describe in any detail the various approaches for managing the MySQL software. It is beneficial in a disaster recovery situation to minimize risk by using the same version of MySQL, installed via the same procedures—for example, via system packaging or binary distribution—and placing all important MySQL components in the same directory structures.

The use of automated installation and deployment tools can ensure a repeatable approach to MySQL software management. Popular runtime configuration management tools include Puppet, Chef, and CFEngine. These tools can ensure the current MySQL configuration is available before a restore process.

MySQL Configuration

It is important that the MySQL configuration is in place before a data recovery process begins when performing a SQL restore. Important global memory settings, including the `innodb_buffer_pool_size` and `key_buffer_size`, are critical for efficient data recovery via SQL execution. Depending on the memory usage of the machine and normal database concurrency, you could choose to adjust these values to utilize as much system memory as possible during recovery.

CAUTION   If the physical hardware used for a database recovery does not match the hardware source of the MySQL configuration, it is possible the configuration may cause MySQL to fail to start or not operate optimally.

You may also elect to optimize or adjust the configuration during the recovery process. If the server uses binary logging with the `log-bin` option, disabling this will aid in the reloading of data via a SQL file for a static backup and point in time recovery. Altering the InnoDB transaction logging with `innodb_flush_log_at_trx_commit` and `sync_binlog` can also reduce some disk I/O during a data restore.

Depending on the recovery process used, you should also disable any replication with the `skip_slave_start` option.

Alternatively, disabling the query cache with `query_cache_type=0` and disabling external network access with `skip_networking` are common additional steps that can make a small improvement as well as restrict unwanted access during the recovery time. The `init_file` and `init_connect` options may also include steps that should be disabled during the recovery process.

It is critical that the application is disabled from accessing data during the restore process, especially if some important settings for data integrity are altered. The verification process would also require the correction and restarting of the MySQL instance with the correct configuration before application access is permitted. Restriction processes may include `skip_networking` as mentioned, firewall rules to restrict external access to the MySQL TCP/IP port, normally 3306, or changing the MySQL user privileges to deny SQL access.

CAUTION   *Removing external access during a database restore by enabling* `skip_networking` *does not stop any batch or cron jobs that are executed on the local machine. These may affect the data restore process. It is important you know all data access points when performing a database restore.*

MySQL Data

The restore of MySQL data will depend on the backup approach used. Using the backup approaches defined in Chapter 2, we cover each option.

Filesystem Copy

A cold filesystem copy or file snapshot restore is the installation of all MySQL data and configuration files. This has to be performed when the MySQL installation is not running. It is important that the MySQL configuration is correctly restored to match the copied files, as several parameters will cause MySQL to fail to start correctly, or may disable important components, for example, the InnoDB storage engine. For example, any change in the file size with the `innodb_data_file_path` and `innodb_log_file_size` configuration settings will cause InnoDB not to be enabled or may stop the MySQL instance from starting.

SQL Dump Recovery

A SQL dump recovery requires a correctly configured, running MySQL installation. The restore uses the `mysql` command line client to execute all SQL statements in the dump file. For example:

```
$ time mysql -u[user] -p < dump1.sql > dump1.out 2>&1; echo $?
real     14m13.817s
user     1m6.960s
sys      0m1.516s
0
$ ls -l dump1.out
-rw-rw-r-- 1 uid gid 0 2012-04-08 04:07 dump1.out
```

This example syntax requires the dump file to include necessary create database schema commands. These are included by default with `mysqldump` when using the `--all-databases` option to create the backup. The backup file will include the following syntax, for example:

```
CREATE DATABASE /*!32312 IF NOT EXISTS*/ `book` /*!40100
DEFAULT CHARACTER SET latin1 */;
```

If you dump an individual schema with `mysqldump` this is not included by default. The `--databases` option is necessary to generate this SQL syntax within the backup file.

By default, `mysqldump` will not drop database schemas. To include this syntax to enable a clean restore for a MySQL instance when existing data may be present, use the `--add-drop-database` option.

The restore of a `mysqldump` generated file is a single threaded process. Some benefit may be obtained by multi-threading this process; however, this requires a means to create parallel files and monitoring of resources for any bottlenecks. Chapter 8 will discuss a number of options for considering a more optimized recovery approach.

The use of per table dump files, particularly in a known format, may be significantly faster to load using the LOAD DATA statement rather than individual INSERT SQL statements generated by `mysqldump`. There is a trade-off between the complexity to generate these files consistently, the additional scripting for restoring data, and point in time recovery capabilities. Chapter 8 will discuss situations when using the per table dump approach can speed up data access during a recovery procession.

For more information on all possible options with the `mysqldump` command, refer to the MySQL Reference Manual at http://dev.mysql.com/doc/refman/5.5/en/mysqldump.html.

SQL Dump Recovery Monitoring   There is no easy means of determining where the database recovery process is or how long the process will actually take; however, there are several tricks that can be used to view the recovery process. There is no substitute for testing and timing the recovery process to have an indicator of the expected time. This will change over time as your database grows in size.

You can use the SQL statement being executed, as shown by the SHOW PROCESSLIST command, to determine how much of the `mysqldump` file has been processed. You can compare this line with the total number of lines in the dump file. This can provide a rough approximation.

Recording table sizes and row counts in a daily audit process will greatly assist in calculation of the approximate table size. This can be easily determined via the INFORMATION_SCHEMA. For example:

```
SELECT  table_schema, table_name,
        engine,row_format AS format, table_rows,
        avg_row_length AS avg_row,
        ROUND((data_length+index_length)/1024/1024,2) AS total_mb,
        ROUND((data_length)/1024/1024,2) AS data_mb,
        ROUND((index_length)/1024/1024,2) AS index_mb,
        CURDATE() AS today
FROM    INFORMATION_SCHEMA.tables
WHERE   table_schema NOT IN
        ('mysql','information_schema','performance_schema')
ORDER BY table_schema, table_name;
```

NOTE   *Depending on the type of storage engine, some information provided by this SQL statement is only an estimate. For example, with the InnoDB storage engine, the data and index size information are accurate; the number of rows is only an estimate.*

Including this information with the backup process is of benefit for later analysis and verification.

MySQL Enterprise Backup (MEB) Recovery
The restoration of a static backup from MEB is a simple command. It is necessary to perform some prerequisite steps to ensure a successful restore.

- Stop the MySQL instance.

- Remove any existing data directory.

- Create a clean data directory, or enable permissions for the user to create the data directory.

- Run mysqlbackup copy-back.

For example:

```
$ sudo su - mysql
$ sudo service mysql stop    # Ubuntu
$ sudo rm -rf /var/lib/mysql # or applicable data directory
$ sudo mkdir -m /var/lib/mysql
$ sudo chown mysql:mysql //var/lib/mysql
$ time /opt/meb/bin/mysqlbackup --defaults-file=/etc/mysql/my.cnf \
  --backup-dir=/mysql/backup/meb/first \
  --innodb-log-files-in-group=2 copy-back
MySQL Enterprise Backup version 3.7.0 [2011/12/19]
Copyright (c) 2003, 2011, Oracle and/or its affiliates. All Rights Reserved.
...
120408 02:08:49 mysqlbackup: INFO: Starting to copy back files
120408 02:08:49 mysqlbackup: INFO: in '/mysql/backup/meb/first/datadir'
directory
120408 02:08:49 mysqlbackup: INFO: back to original data directory
'/var/lib/mysql'
120408 02:08:49 mysqlbackup: INFO: Copying back directory '/mysql/backup/meb/
first/datadir/book2'
120408 02:08:49 mysqlbackup: INFO: Copying back directory '/mysql/backup/meb/
first/datadir/employees'
120408 02:08:49 mysqlbackup: INFO: Copying back directory '/mysql/backup/meb/
first/datadir/musicbrainz'
120408 02:08:49 mysqlbackup: INFO: Copying back directory '/mysql/backup/meb/
first/datadir/mysql'
120408 02:08:49 mysqlbackup: INFO: Copying back directory '/mysql/backup/meb/
first/datadir/sakila'
120408 02:08:49 mysqlbackup: INFO: Copying back directory '/mysql/backup/meb/
first/datadir/world_innodb'
120408 02:08:49 mysqlbackup: INFO: Copying back directory '/mysql/backup/meb/
first/datadir/world_myisam'
 mysqlbackup: INFO: Starting to copy back InnoDB tables and indexes
in '/mysql/backup/meb/first' back to original InnoDB data directory:
 /var/lib/mysql
 mysqlbackup: INFO: Copying back file '/mysql/backup/meb/first/datadir/ibdata1'
120408 02:11:36 mysqlbackup: INFO: Starting to copy back InnoDB log files
in '/mysql/backup/meb/first/datadir' back to original InnoDB log directory
 '/var/lib/mysql'
 mysqlbackup: INFO: Copying back file
 '/mysql/backup/meb/first/datadir/ib_logfile0'
 mysqlbackup: INFO: Copying back file
'/mysql/backup/meb/first/datadir/ib_logfile1'
120408 02:11:44 mysqlbackup: INFO: Finished copying backup files.
mysqlbackup completed OK!
```

```
real     2m55.449s
user     0m1.392s
sys      0m22.137s
$ sudo service mysql start
$ tail -50 /var/log/mysql/error.log
```

When MySQL is restarted the following messages may occur. This is expected:

```
120408  2:12:04  InnoDB: Initializing buffer pool, size = 4.9G
120408  2:12:05  InnoDB: Completed initialization of buffer pool
InnoDB: The log file was created by ibbackup --apply-log at
InnoDB: ibbackup 120407 21:29:50
InnoDB: NOTE: the following crash recovery is part of a normal restore.
InnoDB: The log sequence number in ibdata files does not match
InnoDB: the log sequence number in the ib_logfiles!
120408  2:12:05  InnoDB: Database was not shut down normally!
InnoDB: Starting crash recovery.
InnoDB: Reading tablespace information from the .ibd files...
InnoDB: Restoring possible half-written data pages from the doublewrite
InnoDB: buffer...
InnoDB: Last MySQL binlog file position 0 5555, file name ./mysql-bin.000017
120408  2:12:06  InnoDB: Started; log sequence number 1 2234524172
120408  2:12:06  [Note] Event Scheduler: Loaded 0 events
120408  2:12:06  [Note] /usr/sbin/mysqld: ready for connections.
Version: '5.1.61-0ubuntu0.11.10.1-log'  socket: '/var/run/mysqld/mysqld.sock'
  port: 3306  (Ubuntu)
```

CAUTION   *The current MEB version 3.7.0 requires the specification of the* `innodb-log-files-in-group` *configuration variable to operate correctly. If this is not defined in your MySQL installation, this must be specified on the command line.*

Generally the MySQL data directory is owned by the `mysql` user; however, the parent directory does not provide sufficient permissions to create. If the directory is removed, the following error may occur:

```
$ time /opt/meb/bin/mysqlbackup --defaults-file=/etc/mysql/my.cnf \
    --backup-dir=/mysql/backup/meb/first --innodb-log-files-in-group=2 \
    copy-back
MySQL Enterprise Backup version 3.7.0 [2011/12/19]
Copyright (c) 2003, 2011, Oracle and/or its affiliates. All Rights Reserved.
...
mysqlbackup: Can't create directory '/var/lib/mysql' (Errcode: 13)
  mysqlbackup: ERROR: Could not create directory for server repository;
  Creation of datadir failed.
```

MEB does not perform any of the pre-checks as noted in these instructions. MEB can perform a successful recovery with a running MySQL installation; however, this will not produce the results you would expect. Chapter 7 provides an example of the level of inconsistency and errors that occur.

CAUTION   MySQL Enterprise Backup does not perform any checks on whether MySQL is running, or whether the existing data directory exists. While a restore may complete successfully, this will cause an inconsistency and possible errors.

XtraBackup Recovery

The XtraBackup restore process is a simple command. XtraBackup also requires several prerequisite steps. The XtraBackup was created with the commands:

```
$ time innobackupex --defaults-file=/etc/mysql/my.cnf --user=root \
    --password=passwd --no-timestamp /mysql/backup/xtrabackup/first
$ time innobackupex --apply-log /mysql/backup/xtrabackup/first
```

Before restoring an XtraBackup you must first stop MySQL, and you must ensure the existing data directory exists and is empty. XtraBackup will not check that MySQL is not running. Common errors are:

```
Original data directory is not empty! at /usr/bin/innobackupex line 503.
```

and

```
Original data directory does not exist! at /usr/bin/innobackupex line 499.
```

The restore is a single command:

```
$ time innobackupex --copy-back /mysql/backup/xtrabackup/first/
InnoDB Backup Utility v1.5.1-xtrabackup; Copyright 2003, 2009 Innobase Oy
and Percona Inc 2009-2012.  All Rights Reserved.
...
innobackupex: Starting to copy files in '/mysql/backup/xtrabackup/first'
innobackupex: back to original data directory '/var/lib/mysql'
innobackupex: Copying file '/var/lib/mysql/ib_logfile0'
innobackupex: Copying file '/var/lib/mysql/xtrabackup_binlog_pos_innodb'
innobackupex: Copying file '/var/lib/mysql/xtrabackup_checkpoints'
innobackupex: Copying file '/var/lib/mysql/ib_logfile1'
innobackupex: Creating directory '/var/lib/mysql/sakila'
innobackupex: Copying file '/var/lib/mysql/actor_info.frm'
...
innobackupex: Starting to copy InnoDB system tablespace
innobackupex: in '/mysql/backup/xtrabackup/first'
```

```
innobackupex: back to original InnoDB data directory '/var/lib/mysql'
innobackupex: Copying file '/mysql/backup/xtrabackup/first/ibdata1'
innobackupex: Starting to copy InnoDB log files
innobackupex: in '/mysql/backup/xtrabackup/first'
innobackupex: back to original InnoDB log directory '/var/lib/mysql'
innobackupex: Finished copying back files.
120408 02:46:18  innobackupex: completed OK!

real    3m19.643s
user    0m0.404s
sys     0m17.981s
```

It is important to check the file and directory permissions after the Xtra-Backup restore. In the previous example performed by the root OS user, starting MySQL would result in an error similar to:

```
$ /etc/init.d/mysqld start
Timeout error occurred trying to start MySQL Daemon.
Starting MySQL:                                      [FAILED]
$ tail -20  mysqld.log
120108 18:05:07  InnoDB: Operating system error number 13 in a file operation.
InnoDB: The error means mysqld does not have the access rights to
InnoDB: the directory.
InnoDB: File name ./ibdata1
InnoDB: File operation call: 'open'.
InnoDB: Cannot continue operation.
120108 18:05:07  mysqld ended
```

Innobackupex has a lot of verbose information, but no message at the end stating that permissions should be set. The following is required to correctly start MySQL following an XtraBackup restore with the root OS user:

```
$ chown -R  mysql:mysql /var/lib/mysql
$ /etc/init.d/mysqld start
```

More information on XtraBackup recovery options is available in the documentation at http://www.percona.com/doc/percona-xtrabackup/.

Chapter 8 will discuss more advanced XtraBackup options including streaming, compressing, filtering, and parallel operations.

XtraBackup Manager   The XtraBackup Manager (XBM) project provides additional wrapper commands and database logging for XtraBackup. This is written in PHP. See http://code.google.com/p/xtrabackup-manager/wiki/QuickStartGuide for detailed instructions in getting started.

Performing a Point in Time Recovery

Regardless of the static recovery approach used, a point in time recovery is the application of MySQL master binary logs from the time of the backup, to a given time, generally all possible data. A point in time recovery can also be performed to a particular time or binary log position if necessary.

There are two mechanisms for using the master binary logs; these depend on the use of the restored MySQL environment in relation to MySQL replication. If the server is standalone, the extraction of SQL statements from the binary log and application via the mysql command line client is performed. If the server is a slave in a MySQL topology, the replication stream can be used to perform this automatically, levering the binary logs that exist on the MySQL master.

Both options require the correct position and corresponding binary log for a successful recovery.

Binary Log Position

The current position at the time of the database backup is necessary to apply binary log statements.

Using mysqldump

With mysqldump, the use of the --master-data on the master server, or --dump-slave on the slaver server, will generate the following SQL statement with the output:

```
CHANGE MASTER TO MASTER_HOST='10.0.0.1',
                 MASTER_USER='repl',
                 MASTER_PASSWORD='******',
                 MASTER_LOG_FILE='mysql-bin.000146',
                 MASTER_LOG_POS=810715371;
```

The referenced information will be used in later examples.

By default the CHANGE MASTER TO statement is applied during the data recovery. If a value of 2 was specified for either of these options, for example, --master-data=2, then this SQL statement is only a comment and must be manually applied during the recovery process. For older style backup approaches, the CHANGE MASTER syntax can be generated via the SHOW SLAVE STATUS output.

```
$ mysql -uroot -p -e 'SHOW SLAVE STATUS\G' > slave.status
$ cat slave.status | awk '/Master_Log_File/ { LOG=$2 } /Exec_Master_Log_Pos/ \
{ POS=$2; printf "CHANGE MASTER TO MASTER_LOG_FILE=\"%s\", \
MASTER_LOG_POS=%s;SHOW SLAVE STATUS\\G",LOG,POS}'
```

Filesystem Copy or Filesystem Snapshot

Depending on the other backup approaches used, the position is held in the underlying `master.info` file and will be defined when the data is restored via a filesystem approach.

MySQL Enterprise Backup (MEB)

MySQL Enterprise Backup has this information in the `meta` sub-directory of the backup. For example:

```
$ grep binlog meta/backup_variables.txt
binlog_position=mysql-bin.000017:5555
```

XtraBackup

XtraBackup has this information in the backup directory. For example:

```
$ cat xtrabackup_binlog_info
mysql-bin.000001    37522
```

Standalone Recovery

Following a successful static recovery, the application of the MySQL binary logs requires the use of the `mysqlbinlog` command to translate the information into SQL statements that can be applied by the `mysql` command.

Using the details of the master position as shown in the previous CHANGE MASTER example, we know the binary log file is **'mysql-bin.000146'** and the position is **810715371.**

```
$ mysqlbinlog /path/to/mysql-bin.000146 --start-position=810715371 \
 | mysql -uroot -p
```

It is likely additional binary log files are also required for a point in time recovery to the most current transaction.

```
$ mysqlbinlog /path/to/mysql-bin.000147 /path/to/mysql-bin.00148 ... etc\
 | mysql -uroot -p
```

NOTE *A trick with managing the binary logs is to perform a FLUSH LOGS command during the backup process. This produces a new binary log file at the time of the backup, and can reduce the complexity necessary to determine the start position with binary logs to be applied.*

You can also use the `mysqlbinlog` command to retrieve selected SQL transactions for a more specific period via time or position using the `--start-datetime`, `--stop-datetime`, `--start-position`, and `--stop-position` options, respectively. These options can be used to perform a point in time recovery to a date or position before the end of the binary log, generally to undo a human generated data error such as an accidental deletion of data. These options are particularly beneficial for data analysis of a binary/relay log when an error has occurred.

Analysis of the binary log using an unknown start position or unknown end position can result in misleading information. The following shows an error in processing the binary log; however, this not a result of the contents of the actual binary log:

```
$ mysqlbinlog relay-log.007112 --start-position=650000 --stop-position=700000
...
ERROR: Error in Log_event::read_log_event(): 'read error',
data_len: 538976288, event_type: 32
ERROR: Could not read entry at offset 650000: Error in log format or read error.
...

$ mysqlbinlog relay-log.007112 --start-position=640000 --stop-position=700000

...
ERROR: Error in Log_event::read_log_event(): 'Event too big',
data_len: 1414677843, event_type: 110
ERROR: Could not read entry at offset 640000: Error in log format or read error.
...
```

When using correctly aligned event boundaries, no error occurs.

```
$ mysqlbinlog relay-log.007112 --start-position=616063 --stop-position=616413
# at 616063
#100605  0:48:23 server id 1   end_log_pos 616220 Query   thread_id=5331
      exec_time=0
      error_code=0
use blog/*!*/;
SET TIMESTAMP=1275713303/*!*/;
UPDATE `wp_options` SET `option_value` = '18784' WHERE `option_name` =
'akismet_spam_count'
/*!*/;
# at 616220
#100605  0:48:23 server id 1   end_log_pos 616413 Query   thread_id=5331
```

```
      exec_time=0
        error_code=0
SET TIMESTAMP=1275713303/*!*/;
DELETE FROM wp_comments WHERE DATE_SUB('2010-06-05 04:48:23',
INTERVAL 15 DAY) > comment_date_gmt AND comment_approved = 'spam'
/*!*/;
DELIMITER ;
```

For more information on the full options for the `mysqlbinlog` command refer to the MySQL Reference Manual at http://dev.mysql.com/doc/refman/5.5/en/mysqlbinlog.html.

Leveraging the Replication Stream

If the server is the slave of an existing and functioning MySQL master within a replication topology, the normal replication stream can be leveraged providing the position of the master binary log is correctly defined for the slave. Depending on the data backup and static recovery process, this may or may not be already defined for the recovered data.

When using the `--master-data` or `--dump-slave` option you will observe in the `mysqldump` output file a CHANGE MASTER statement that will set the correct position. If using the output information from a SHOW SLAVE STATUS command you can construct the correct syntax as shown in the previous section.

Following this command you should run SHOW SLAVE STATUS in order to verify settings, then START SLAVE to start processing the replication stream. You should review the SHOW SLAVE STATUS output a second time for any errors including invalid permissions and other errors. The following is a command error:

```
mysql> SHOW SLAVE STATUS\G
...
            Slave_IO_Running: No
           Slave_SQL_Running: Yes
...
                  Last_Errno: 0
                  Last_Error:
...
               Last_IO_Errno: 1236
               Last_IO_Error: Got fatal error 1236 from master when
reading data from binary log: 'Could not find first log file name in
binary log index file'
              Last_SQL_Errno: 0
              Last_SQL_Error:
```

This shows that the master no longer has the required binary log files necessary to replay all SQL statements via the replication stream.

For more information about the SHOW SLAVE STATUS command, refer to the MySQL Reference Manual at http://dev.mysql.com/doc/refman/5.5/en/mysqlbinlog.html.

Binary Log Mirroring

A new feature of the current 5.6 DMR version is the ability to read the binary logs of a remote system, rather than having to copy the binary logs to process. In addition, a new option is also provided to read a remote binary log and produce an exact copy in binary format. This feature can also allow for binary log mirroring.

The `--read-from-remote-server` option tells `mysqlbinlog` to connect to a server and request its binary log. This is similar to a slave replication server connecting to its master server. The `--raw` option produces binary output, and the `--stop-never` option enables the process to remain open and continue to read new binary log events as they occur on the master. For example:

```
$ mysql -h10.0.0.1 -e "SHOW MASTER LOGS"
+------------------+-----------+
| Log_name         | File_size |
+------------------+-----------+
| mysql-bin.000001 |       125 |
| mysql-bin.000002 |       125 |
| mysql-bin.000003 | 104878834 |
| mysql-bin.000004 | 142853798 |
| mysql-bin.000005 | 156100014 |
| mysql-bin.000006 | 110673964 |
| mysql-bin.000007 | 945009860 |
| mysql-bin.000008 | 192498500 |
| mysql-bin.000009 | 109169248 |
| mysql-bin.000010 | 853187461 |
| mysql-bin.000011 | 186417244 |
| mysql-bin.000012 |     17154 |
| mysql-bin.000013 |     13064 |
| mysql-bin.000014 |       149 |
| mysql-bin.000015 |       149 |
| mysql-bin.000016 |       149 |
| mysql-bin.000017 |      8328 |
+------------------+-----------+
$ mysqlbinlog -h10.0.0.1 --read-from-remote-server mysql-bin.000012
...
```

```
# at 4
#120402 23:56:13 server id 1  end_log_pos 106  Start: binlog v 4,
server v 5.1.61-0ubuntu0.11.10.1-log created 120402 23:56:13
BINLOG '
nTx6Tw8BAAAAZgAAAGoAAAAAAAQANS4xLjYxLTB1YnVudHUwLjExLjEwLjEtbG9nAAAAAAAAAAAA
AAAAAAAAAAAAAAAAAAAAAAAAEzgNAAgAEgAEBAQEEgAAUwAEGggAAAAICAgC
'/*!*/;
# at 106
CREATE TABLE IF NOT EXISTS mysql.backup_progress( ...
/*!*/;
# at 501
...
INSERT INTO mysql.backup_history(backup_id, tool_name, ...)
VALUES(13334239375677869,'/opt/meb/bin/mysqlbackup --user=root
--backup-dir=/mysql/backup/meb/second-compressed --compress backup ',
'2012-04-03 03:32:17','2012-04-03 03:36:59',...)
/*!*/;
...
# at 17135
#120403  4:32:26 server id 1  end_log_pos 17154      Stop
DELIMITER ;
# End of log file
ROLLBACK /* added by mysqlbinlog */;
/*!50003 SET COMPLETION_TYPE=@OLD_COMPLETION TYPE*/;
```

You can produce a copy of the master binary log with:

```
$ mysqlbinlog -h10.0.0.1 --read-from-remote-server \
  --raw mysql-bin.000012  > mysql-bin.000012
$ ls -al mysql-bin.000012
-rw-rw-r-- 1 uid gid 17154 2012-04-07 22:19 mysql-bin.000012
# Same number of bytes as in SHOW MASTER LOGS
```

You can also obtain content from all binary logs from a given file with:

```
$ mysqlbinlog -h10.0.0.1 --read-from-remote-server --to-last-log mysql-bin.000013
```

Analysis of the output provides the following to see the change in file-names:

```
$ mysqlbinlog -h10.0.0.1 --read-from-remote-server --to-last-log \
  mysql-bin.000013 | grep Rotate
#700101  0:00:00 server id 1  end_log_pos 0     Rotate to mysql-bin.000013
#120404  6:25:04 server id 1  end_log_pos 13064 Rotate to mysql-bin.000014
#700101  0:00:00 server id 1  end_log_pos 0     Rotate to mysql-bin.000014
#120405  6:25:02 server id 1  end_log_pos 149   Rotate to mysql-bin.
#700101  0:00:00 server id 1  end_log_pos 0     Rotate to mysql-bin.000015
#120406  6:25:01 server id 1  end_log_pos 149   Rotate to mysql-bin.000016
#700101  0:00:00 server id 1  end_log_pos 0     Rotate to mysql-bin.000016
#120407  6:25:02 server id 1  end_log_pos 149   Rotate to mysql-bin.000017
#700101  0:00:00 server id 1  end_log_pos 0     Rotate to mysql-bin.000017
```

TIP *Even if your production environment is not running MySQL 5.6, you can install this MySQL version on another server and use these commands connecting to an older server version, as shown in these examples connecting to a MySQL instance running MySQL 5.1.*

For more information see http://dev.mysql.com/doc/refman/5.6/en/mysqlbinlog-backup.html.

Recovery Verification

The successful recovery of a MySQL environment is not complete until verification is performed. This can be difficult to determine as the various reasons for requiring a recovery may affect the ability to calculate verification results.

The checking of applicable restore command(s) error status, log files, and MySQL error log is a mandatory initial step. While this appears obvious, this author has experienced DBA resources not performing this most basic of steps, so this is mentioned for completeness.

The first obvious data check is to look at the size of your database. This can be as simple as an INFORMATION_SCHEMA query. While this step is not a confirmation of success, this will confirm no obvious import or restore failure. This can indicate no more time consuming validation is required when a failure is immediately detected. This check can be performed after both the static recovery and point in time recovery steps. It is important to also check the number of database objects, including tables, routines, and triggers, in a similar fashion.

The second check is to confirm a likely most recent transaction. This could be as simple as looking at the last order, status update, or log entry in a given table. When your system performs hundreds of INSERT or UPDATE statements per second and there is a recorded insert or update timestamp or AUTO_INCREMENT primary key, there is an easy comparison of the last reported database modification. Again, this check is not a confirmation of success, rather an indicator of obvious failure or highlighting of potential or expected data loss. This can be performed after both the static recovery and point in time recovery steps.

When a complete point in time recovery process is performed, the reported binary log position from SHOW SLAVE STATUS can be verified with the applicable master binary log position, recorded as part of the backup, the current file size of the last imported binary log, or the current SHOW MASTER STATUS information.

The most conclusive agnostic approach is to perform a table checksum to compare the actual data. The CHECKSUM TABLE command or the Percona Toolkit `pt-table-checksum` utility can be used. This is impractical in a large database due to the time to read all data to calculate. It may be practical only to check certain tables with this detailed analysis. A more simplified check of the number of rows, or sum of an important column, for example, and order table invoice amount can provide an initial check.

With all these steps, data verification is generally complex because the restored data source cannot be accurately compared with an active and ever changing production environment. Given this situation and knowing these limitations, adding additional checks during the backup process can be critical in reducing risk. By recording a checksum, count, sum, or some other calculation on the database at the time of a static backup, an applicable check can be made after the static recovery step.

Using the same data checksum approach for the schema definition and all stored routines and trigger code is also highly recommended. See Chapter 4 for examples on data and object consistency.

The importance of database verification is to detect any problem before it becomes a real issue. If data is lost or incomplete further application use may compound this problem; a database recovery may not be possible in 12 hours' time. Difficult and time consuming data analysis may then be needed to address any data corruption, loss, or creep.

Important business metrics are generally the first indicator of a likely problem. The amount of verification is proportional to the important value of the data. It may be critical to ensure that all data is consistent for customer orders, and less important for a review of a product, for example.

During the verification process application access to the underlying database should never occur. It is very important this step is adequately catered for during the recovery process. This is often overlooked when a full end-to-end test is not performed. After any disaster it is advisable to perform a backup as soon as possible.

The Backup and Recovery Quiz

In response to several organizations failing to have applicable production resilience the following checklist was created in early 2010 to poll what procedures existed.

1. Do you have MySQL backups in place?

2. Do you back up ALL your MySQL data?

3. Do you have consistent MySQL backups?

4. Do you have backups that include both static snapshot and point in time transactions?

5. Do you review your backup logs EVERY SINGLE day or have tested backup log monitoring in place?

6. Do you perform a test restore of your static backup?

7. Do you perform a test restore to a point in time?

8. Do you time your backup and recovery process and review over time?

9. Do you have off-site copies of your backups?

10. Do you back up your primary binary logs to a different server?

This is not an exhaustive checklist of all requirements, only the first ten items necessary for ensuring adequate minimal procedures. If you do not score eight or better in this checklist for your business, you are at higher risk of some level of data loss in a future disaster situation. If you are an owner/ founder/executive this should keep you awake at night if you are not sure of your business viability following a disaster.

Source:http://ronaldbradford.com/blog/checked-your-mysql-recovery-process-recently-2010-02-15/

Other Important Components

This chapter has discussed the recovery of MySQL software, configuration, and data. This is the primary purpose of this book. Any operational production database system generally includes much more than just MySQL software and data. While not discussed it is important that as a database administrator, any additional database and system related features are included in a total backup solution. For example:

- Cron job entries
- Related scripts, run via cron, via batch or manually
- Application code
- Additional configuration files (e.g., SSH, Apache, logrotate, etc.)
- System password and group files
- Monitoring scripts or monitoring plugins
- Backup and restore scripts
- Any system configuration files (e.g., /etc)
- Log files

Conclusion

Your business viability and data management strategy are only as good as your ability to successfully recover your information after any level of disaster. In this chapter we have discussed the essential steps in the process for a successful data recovery and the importance of data verification. Chapter 7 will extend these essential foundation steps with a number of disaster scenarios to highlight further advanced techniques in ensuring an adequate MySQL backup and recovery strategy. Chapter 8 provides more examples of recovery options for various advanced backup options.

The SQL statements and web links listed in this chapter can be downloaded from http://effectivemysql.com/book/backup-recovery/.

6

MySQL Configuration Options

MySQL 5.5 supports over 300 configurable system variables. A number of these variables have a direct effect on how MySQL will operate when dealing with a database backup and crash recovery situation. Understanding what system variables do and how they change the behavior of the MySQL server will help define how your backup and recovery system will act when you need it the most.

In this chapter we will discuss:

- Data management system variables
- Replication system variables
- Recovery system variables

Data Management

In this section we will cover data locations, consistency, and binary logging system variables. Having a homogeneous system setup is the preferred way to run an environment, especially at scale. Knowing where your data is located on a file system is a tremendous help when troubleshooting a system along with automation and other tasks. Enabling the right system variables for data consistency driven by your Service Level Agreement (SLA) and knowing when to use certain binary logging options are all part of system design, and, in the end, how your system will recover from disaster.

Data Locations

The following options define the physical filesystem locations of important data stored in MySQL. It is important to note that these locations are often overlooked when running recoveries from server to server. Keeping your data locations homogeneous throughout your system will lessen confusion during recovery especially if your system is sharded. This means keeping all of the MySQL data, tmp, and base directories the same throughout your environment. Other considerations would be keeping the InnoDB data file path and InnoDB log file sizes the same throughout your environment. Here you will find a more detailed list of system variables that need to be the same from master to slave and from shard to shard:

- `datadir` The `datadir` is, by default, the directory where all databases, tables, InnoDB data, server logs, and binary log files are located on the filesystem. Directories within the `datadir` represent databases. Tables within the databases are represented by files, which can differ depending on storage engine and server configuration. InnoDB tablespace(s) and transaction logs will also be stored here unless defined by other variables. The same can be said about server logs like the slow query log and error log along with binary and relay log files. For Linux distributions this, by default, is /var/lib/mysql.

- basedir The basedir is the filesystem location of the MySQL installation directory. It is a good idea to have this directory located in your PATH for easy access to the MySQL server and client utilities. Keep in mind that the basedir, by default, is /usr on Linux and will probably be different from company to company. In this case you should put the $basedir/bin inside your PATH so you do not require the full path to the MySQL server and client utilities.

- innodb_data_file_path This variable defines the location to individual InnoDB data files, also known as tablespaces, along with their sizes and behavior. The size limit of individual files will be determined by your operating system; however, the sum of the files, by default, has to be a minimum of 10MB. InnoDB files can also be set to autoextend. In this case, these InnoDB files grow, if the data exceeds the initially defined size and "auto-extend" is enabled. Please note that these files are currently required by InnoDB to function and are considered system tablespace(s). This includes when InnoDB is set to run with innodb_file_per_table.

- innodb_data_home_dir If you are not using absolute paths to define your shared tablespaces in the innodb_data_file_path system variable you can use innodb_data_home_dir to specify where all common InnoDB data files will be located on the filesystem. Like innodb_data_file_path, this variable does not affect the location of per-file tablespaces when innodb_file_per_table is enabled. The default value for this variable is the MySQL datadir.

- innodb_file_per_table When innodb_file_per_table is enabled all tables that are created with the InnoDB storage engine will create their own tablespace. The per-table tablespace created is represented as tablename.ibd in the corresponding database directory. The .ibd file is where data and indexes are stored. If innodb_file_per_table is disabled, the default, all data and indexes will be stored in the system tablespace. Innodb_file_per_table must be enabled if you choose to use newer InnoDB file formats starting with Barracuda.

CAUTION The `innodb_file_per_table` *variable should be set before creating any database objects. It is not possible to have a hybrid model. The only means to safely convert from a system tablespace to a per-table tablespace is to dump all data, drop all objects, and re-create database objects and reload all data.*

Data Consistency

These configuration options affect how MySQL writes and flushes data to disk. MySQL provides options that produce a tradeoff between write performance and durability (i.e., D of ACID) for all transactions. The combination of varying disk hardware configurations such as Battery Backed Write Cache (BBWC) RAID controllers also can affect consistency.

- `sync_binlog` When the value of `sync_binlog` is set to one (1), the safest setting, events sync to the binary log after every commit, which provides, at most, one statement lost in the event of a `mysqld` crash if auto-commit is enabled. Setting `sync_binlog` to a value greater than the default, zero (0), allows MySQL to sync events at a much slower rate (allowing the disk to not work as much). Although setting `sync_binlog` to 1 is the slowest setting it can also be sped up with the use of a Battery Backed Write Cache.

  As stated earlier, setting `sync_binlog` to a value of 1 is the slowest but safest setting. This is because InnoDB will sync to the log files after every commit, which, in turn will increase the amount of I/O on your system. SSD (Solid State Drives) drives are becoming less expensive and more prevalent in many installations. When using SSDs on your system you may not notice any performance degradation when setting `sync_binlog` to a value of 1.

- `innodb_flush_log_at_trx_commit` By default the value of `innodb_flush_log_at_trx_commit` is 1, meaning that the log buffer is written out to the InnoDB log files after every commit and a flush disk operation is performed on the log file. Setting the value of `innodb_flush_log_at_trx_commit` to 2 will flush the log buffer to the InnoDB log file at a loose interval of once per second. It is not recommended you use the value of 0.

CAUTION   *Setting* `innodb_flush_log_at_trx_commit` *to 1 does not ensure full ACID compliance. Also, setting this variable to 1 is one of the most performance hindering aspects of replication. For more information please see, http://dev.mysql.com/doc/refman/5.5/en/innodb-parameters.html#sysvar_ innodb_flush_log_at_trx_commit.*

- `innodb_support_xa`   This option enables InnoDB to run two-phase commits for XA transactions and is enabled by default. This variable is essential for systems that are using binary logging and have more than one thread changing InnoDB data in XA transactions. Although enabling `innodb_support_xa` causes an extra disk flush for transaction preparation it is necessary to ensure that transactions are placed into the binary log in the correct order. The only times you should disable this variable is when your system only uses one (1) thread to add and modify data or you are not using replication.

TIP   *Disabling or setting* `innodb_support_xa` *to 0 could be beneficial, performance wise, when restoring a SQL backup and* `log-bin` *is enabled. This will remove the need for an extra fsync(). For faster overall performance you can disable* `innodb_support_xa`*; however, you must gauge the risk of possibly having inconsistent data with performance.*

- `innodb_doublewrite`   InnoDB performs a sequential write and sync of all data pages that are being flushed by the InnoDB I/O thread before writing the data pages to the appropriate random data file positions. If a MySQL crash occurs, the buffer can be used during crash recovery to obtain a correct copy of data pages. This variable is enabled by default (value of 1). The InnoDB doublewrite buffer guarantees page recoverability and reduces the amount of fsync to disk.

  When this variable is enabled a chunk of pages is written to the doublewrite buffer followed by an fsync, then pages are written to the tablespace followed by an fsync. If `innodb_doublewrite` is disabled each page that is written would need to be fsync'ed.

- `innodb_flush_method`   There are three valid values, O_DSYNC and O_DIRECT, along with the default value of fdatasync. The overall goal for this variable is to modify the behavior of synchronizing I/O.

POSIX offers different variants to synchronize I/O, which are O_SYNC, O_DYSNC, O_RSYNC, and O_DIRECT.

Linux implements O_SYNC, but glibc maps O_DSYNC and O_RSYNC to the same value as O_SYNC. O_SYNC semantics require all meta-data updates of a write to on disk when returning to userspace. O_DSYNC requires only the file data and meta-data necessary to access it again to be on disk by the time the system call returns. O_DIRECT minimizes cache effects of the I/O to and from a file and makes an effort to transfer data synchronously but gives no guarantees that data and necessary meta-data are transferred.

If the value of `innodb_flush_method` is set to O_DSYNC InnoDB will use O_SYNC for the logs files and fsync to flush data files. When innodb_flush_method is set to O_DIRECT InnoDB uses O_DIRECT to open data files and fsync to flush both data and log files. By default, InnoDB uses fsync to flush both data and log files.

Given that InnoDB has its own caching, i.e., `innodb_buffer_pool`, setting `innodb_flush_method` to O_DIRECT may help avoid double buffering between the buffer pool and the filesystem cache when you are running with hardware RAID and Battery Backed Write Cache. In any case you will need to benchmark your particular environment to see what setting works best with your load.

- `innodb_fast_shutdown` Changing the behavior of InnoDB upon shutdown is nice to have but can be dangerous. `innodb_fast_shutdown` has three valid values, 0, 1 (the default), and 2. When the value is set to 0, InnoDB performs a slow shutdown, meaning a full purge and an insert buffer merge before shutdown. With a value of 1, InnoDB skips the purge and merge and does a fast shutdown, making the shutdown process faster but still safe. When the value is set to 2, the most dangerous, InnoDB flushes its logs and shuts down cold, like a crash. Although no committed transactions are lost, an InnoDB crash recovery will occur during the next startup and may take more time for the instance to come online.

- `default_storage_engine` Sometimes the ENGINE of the table can differ from environment to environment (i.e., Dev, Test, QA, and Production). It is important to set the `default_storage_engine` through all parts of the environment identically to ensure the correct behavior of the table throughout all points of the product life cycle. In MySQL versions from 3.23 to 5.5.4 the default value is MyISAM. In version 5.5.5 and higher the default value is now InnoDB.

Binary Logging

These initial options are mandatory settings for the configuration of MySQL binary logging. These options are necessary to ensure that a point in time recovery (PITR) is possible. These settings are also necessary to enable replication on a master.

- `server_id` With the current implementation of replication, MySQL needs to know that it is executing statements on unique servers so as to not duplicate work. Setting the `server_id` to a unique value for every slave in your MySQL topology will ensure that replicated data is applied correctly. If duplicate server ids are noticed in a MySQL topology a few errors can occur. Replication will not start and the slave will throw an error stating the master and slave hosts have the same `server_id`. If there is more than one slave host your error may fill up with the following note:

```
[Note] Slave I/O thread: Failed reading log event, reconnecting to retry, log
'mysql-bin.000729' at position 1047954349
[Note] Slave: received end packet from server, apparent master shutdown:
```

A good practice is to set the `server_id` to an integer based off of the IP address of the server. The integer address of the IP 192.168.0.1 is 3232235521 and can be set as the value of `server_id` as long as the integer is less than or equal to 4294967295. For example:

```
mysql> SELECT INET_ATON('192.168.0.1');
+--------------------------+
| INET_ATON('192.168.0.1') |
+--------------------------+
|               3232235521 |
+--------------------------+
1 row in set (0.01 sec)
```

- `log_bin` This enables the binary log and is absolutely necessary if you want to replicate data and/or have point in time backups. It is a good practice to set an absolute path and basename for the value of `log_bin` to control the name of the binary logs. If no basename is given

MySQL will place the binlogs in the `datadir` with "host_name-bin" as the basename.

- `log_bin_index` The `log_bin_index` file holds the names of binary logs acting as an index. Again, if you do not specify the filename and omit the basename in `log_bin` MySQL will use "host_name-bin.index" as the default filename.

- `binlog_format` With this variable you will be able to control the type of binary logging that MySQL uses. Setting the value to STATEMENT, the default, will cause MySQL to use pure statement based replication where all statements are recorded to the binlog. Setting the value to ROW will cause MySQL to use pure row based replication and log changed blocks to the binary log. Finally, if you set `binlog_format` to MIXED, both statements and blocks can be inserted into the binary log.

- `binlog_do_db` & `binlog_ignore_db` These variables are used on the master host. When `binlog_do_db` is specified and using statement based replication, the only statements that will be logged to the binary log are those that are preceded by the USE `database_name` statement. If more than one database is needed you will need to use multiple lines in the `my.cnf` file because database names can contain commas. Keep in mind that cross-database statements will not be logged while a different database is set as default or no database is selected. When using row based replication only changes belonging to the database name are made regardless if the USE statement is used. Adversely, you can use `binlong_ignore_db` to exclude databases from the binary log on the master host.

  If you do choose to use these variables it can change the way backups and recovery are performed. There are certain situations or setups that these variables are good for; however, you should be aware that it is possible to have data inconsistencies when used.

- `binlog_cache_size` If a MySQL host has binary logging enabled, transactional storage engines are being used (i.e., InnoDB) and you are using large transactions, you can increase the value of `binlog_cache_size` to possibly increase performance. This cache is used to hold changes to the binary log during a transaction.

By checking the value of the server status variable, `binlog_cache_use`, you can determine the number of transactions that used the binary log cache. The `binlong_cache_disk_use` is another server status variable to check that indicates the number of transactions that used the binary log cache but exceeded the value of `binlog_cache_size` and used temporary files to store changes.

- `binlog_stmt_cache_size`   This variable specifies the size of the cache for the binary log to hold non-transactional statements during transactions on a per client basis. Again, if you are using large non-transactional statements within transactions you may benefit from increasing the value on `binlog_stmt_cache_size`. Also, this variable only matters if binary logging is enabled.

  The server status variable, `binlog_stmt_cache_use`, specifies the number of non-transactional statements that used the binary log statement cache.

- `binlog_row_event_max_size`   The value is represented in bytes with a default value of 1024 and should be a multiple of 256. This variable represents the maximum size of a row based binary log event.

MySQL Replication

MySQL replication is crucial in systems that have a good backup and recovery plan. There are a few variables that affect the way MySQL replication behaves. Whether a slave host is set to only replicate certain databases, skip certain errors, and or is set up in a unique chain topology, it is important to know how the following will affect your setup.

- `relay_log`   MySQL uses a numbered set of files called relay logs to hold replicated database changes before the SQL thread applies them to the slave. These files are located on the slave host directly and are only active on the "master" host when `log_slave_updates` is active. The relay log files are numbered in sequence starting from 000001 and are accompanied by what is referred to as the relay index file, which contains the names of all relay files currently being used. Relay log files are in the same format as MySQL binary logs, making them easy to read using the `mysqlbinlog` client utility.

Like the binary log, relay log positions are represented by byte offsets, so if the `Relay_Log_Pos` is `671` and the `Relay_Log_File` is `mysqld-relay-bin.000002` then MySQL has read up to `671` bytes of the corresponding file. The naming conventions for the relay log file can be altered with the `relay-log=[file_name]` and `relay-log-index=[file_name]` options in the `my.cnf` file. If either of the preceding is absent in the `my.cnf` file the relay logs will take their naming convention from the `pid-file` option, if specified. For example, when a PID is specified in the `my.cnf` and the `relay-log` and `relay-log-index` are omitted, the relay logs will be `mysql_3306-relay-bin.index` and `mysql_3306-relay-bin.000001`. If `relay-log`, `relay-log-index`, and `pid-file` are not specified, the relay logs will default to `host_name-relay-bin.nnnnnn` and `host_name-relay-bin.index`, where `host_name` is the server host and `nnnnnn` represents the sequential file numbering.

- `relay_log_index` The `relay_log_index` system variable holds the names of all the relay logs for quick lookup.

- `replicate_do_db` & `replicate_ignore_db` These variables are used on the slave host and act much like `binlog_do_db` and `binlog_ignore_db` do on the master host. If a slave is set up using `replicate_do_db` and using statement based replication only, statements that have a preceding USE database_name statement will be applied to the slave host. If row based replication is used, a statement with a qualifying database_name.table_name will be applied to the slave host. Adversely, if you specify `replicate_ignore_db`, all transactions relating to the database specified will not be applied to the slave host.

- `slave_skip_errors` Replication error codes can be skipped automatically when `slave_skip_errors` is specified. Normally replication will stop when the SQL thread encounters an error; however, this variable will cause the SQL thread to skip those errors listed in the variable value.

It is important to mention that it is not always a good idea to specify a value for `slave_skip_errors`, given the implications of data drift and/or data integrity.

- slave_exec_mode   There are two valid values for slave_exec_ mode, IDEMPOTENT and STRICT. This variable is used for replication conflict resolution and error checking. If the value is set to IDEMPOTENT (default for NDB), the slave will not error out during duplicate key or no key found errors. The IDEMPOTENT value is useful with a system that is set up in a multi-master or circular replication fashion. When the value is set to STRICT, the default, replication will stop on duplicate key and no key found errors.

- log_slave_updates   When log_slave_updates is set to true and binary logging is turned on, the slave host will write all replicated changes to its own binary log. This option is used to chain multiple nodes together through replication. For example, if you have three servers (A, B, and C) and want to connect them in a chain you would use log_slave_updates on B. B would replicate from A, and C from B, forming a chain, (A -> B -> C).

Recovery

InnoDB has provided the ability to auto recover after a crash or detecting errors. In later releases, version 5.0, MyISAM is now able to run check and recover automatically when an error or crash is detected. There are four system variables that need to be in every administrator's arsenal when dealing with InnoDB or MyISAM corruption.

- innodb_force_recovery   One would use innodb_force_ recovery to recover InnoDB tables that have been corrupted on the page level. Setting this variable to a value greater than 0 (the default) will allow an administrator to start the MySQL server and run a SELECT ... INTO OUTFILE or mysqldump. Corruption may cause InnoDB to crash, assert, or roll forward recovery to crash from InnoDB background threads or when issuing a SELECT * FROM table_name statement. Innodb_force_recovery is used to prevent InnoDB background operations from running so you are able to start the server and dump out your data.

  There are seven different levels of innodb_force_recovery, 0 – 6; however, it should be noted that when setting the value past 4, most of your data might be irrecoverable. InnoDB prevents INSERT, UPDATE, and DELETE operations when the value of innodb_force_recovery is greater than 0. The following is a list of what the different levels accomplish.

- (DEFAULT)   A normal startup without a forced recovery.

- (SRV_FORCE_IGNORE_CORRUPT)   Allows the server to run even if it detects a corrupt page. This will allow InnoDB to jump over corrupt index records and pages when running SELECT * FROM table_name.

- (SRV_FORCE_NO_BACKGROUND)   If a crash occurs during the purge operation, setting the value to 2 would prevent the main thread from running.

- (SRV_FORCE_NO_TRX_UNDO)   Ensures that transaction rollbacks do not occur after recovery.

- (SRV_FORCE_NO_IBUF_MERGE)   Table statistics are not calculated and no insert buffer merge operations occur.

- (SRV_FORCE_NO_UNDO_LOG_SCAN)   Skips looking at InnoDB undo logs upon startup and treats incomplete transactions as committed.

- (SRV_FORCE_NO_LOG_REDO)   Ensures that the log roll-forward is not run in connection with recovery.

- myisam_recover   There are four values you can use for myisam_recover: DEFAULT, BACKUP, FORCE, and QUICK. Furthermore you can use any combination of the preceding values if you separate them by commas. If myisam_recover is enabled MySQL will check if a MyISAM table is marked as crashed or was not closed properly every time the table is opened. The following is a list describing what each of the values does:

  - DEFAULT   Recover without backup, forcing, or quick checking.

  - BACKUP   Run a backup of the table if the data file was changed during recovery. In this case a backup of table_name.MYD will be saved as table_name-datetime.BAK.

- FORCE   Runs a recovery even if more than one row of data would be lost from the .MYD file.

- QUICK   If there are no deleted blocks, rows in the table will not be checked.

When using MyISAM and you want to recover from most problems automatically, you should use the options BACKUP, FORCE as the values for myisam_recover. It is important to note that the server will write a note to the error log before the server automatically repairs the table.

- myisam_max_sort_file_size   The default setting for myisam_max_sort_file_size is 2GB and represents the max allowed file size when re-creating a MyISAM index during a REPAIR TABLE, ALTER TABLE, or LOAD DATA INFILE. If the size of the index is greater than the value of myisam_max_sort_file_size the key cache is used instead. Keep in mind that the space must be available on the filesystem where the original index file is located.

- myisam_sort_buffer_size   This setting specifies the size of the buffer that is allocated when sorting MyISAM indexes during a REPAIR TABLE or when creating indexes. The max value on 32 bit systems is 4GB but can be greater on 64 bit systems.

Conclusion

As stated at the beginning of the chapter, there are over 300 different configuration variables. It is very important to know how a MySQL server has been configured in order to streamline backups and recovery; furthermore, it is important to know how the MySQL server will act in the event of a crash given the storage engine(s) used. Given all the aforementioned variables the correct settings can only be determined by the load of your unique system. That said, please make sure to benchmark with your particular load and make sure to practice disaster recovery on a regular basis so, when the time comes, you and your business know what to expect.

7

Disaster Scenarios

"Disaster is inevitable. Total failure is avoidable."

Ronald Bradford & Paul Carlstroem – 2011

Disaster happens. This is generally when you are not expecting or prepared. Having an idea of what sort of problems may occur that require a level of recovery will help you understand how your backup and recovery strategy plan will succeed. Understanding these various situations and the many other possible cases can help in the testing and verification steps implemented for your business information. Disaster recovery (DR) is a requirement in the planning for a high availability (HA) solution. In many environments clear procedures and architectural design is in place enabling growth more seamlessly.

Unfortunately the same is not said for disaster preparedness, the poor cousin. Improving, refining, and testing various disaster recovery situations are often left to a crisis situation where costly mistakes can occur.

In this chapter we will cover several situations including:

- Actual business ending disaster situations
- Common MySQL disaster situations
- MySQL recovery tool options
- Managing the human factor

Handling a MySQL Disaster

A backup is only as good as the ability to perform a successful recovery. Unfortunately performing a recovery in a controlled situation is never the case. The need to perform a disaster recovery is always at an unpredictable time and often includes other factors or cascading failures. An action in one situation may be critical to protect against further data loss, while the same action in a different situation will lead to permanent data loss. There is no instruction manual for every situation; foreknowledge of a wide range of situations and practice of these is your best asset in the decision making process. The following examples showcase some typical and less typical disasters. A number of common and less common disaster situations are provided to enable the preparation and testing for these situations. Some of these disaster situations are completely avoidable with pre-emptive procedures.

With over 20 years of IT experience, the author has been involved in averting serious business loss in a number of situations and varying technologies. He is also not immune to having caused a few minor disasters as a result of human error. Learning from the mistakes of others is a critical step in a database administrator (DBA) or system administrator (SA) mastering their respective fields. This book hopes to outline the tools for creating an appropriate backup and recovery strategy for your specific environment and provide invaluable tips and information to avoid making the mistakes others have encountered.

In fact, during the final production stage of this book, two different disasters were encountered working with two separate clients on consecutive days. Both situations were then added to this chapter as unique examples. In both cases the final outcome was positive, but the risk of not being prepared is that your business may suffer a serious if not fatal situation. You never want this to occur on your watch and be a line item you try to avoid mentioning on your resume for the next job opportunity.

Notable MySQL Disasters

For every disaster that is discussed in this chapter, many more exist that are not known or spoken of. Rarely do organizations advertise a data failure that resulted in loss of revenue, users, creditability, or that resulted in a total failure of the business. The following are a few very public examples of situations with varying levels of disaster and outcome.

DISCLAIMER: The author of this book is repeating knowledge that is provided and generally available online. These examples demonstrate possible situations and results regardless of the validity of the information in the source story.

Magnolia

Ma.gnolia.com was a social bookmarking site that shut down due to a MySQL data disaster in 2009. The public information about the problem includes a one-man operation, limited equipment redundancy, a faulty backup system, a hard drive failure, and an apparent inability for a specialist to recover any data.

A quote from a listed reference, "A clear lesson for users is not to assume that online services have lots of staff, lots of servers and professional backups, and to keep your own copies of your data, especially on free services," highlights that you should not assume your data is safe. If you have the ability to obtain a copy of your own recorded data, then do it. In the case with Magnolia they provided APIs to download all of your recorded personal data.

From a different reference is the comment "Outsource your IT infrastructure as much as possible (e.g., AWS, AppEngine, etc.)." This is not a wise practice to blindly trust your information with a third party. How are you sure their practices are fully functional, secure, and result in a timely recovery? You should always keep your important and critical data close to physical control. The loss of control is a potential career limiting move if your responsibility is to ensure the integrity and availability of information.

CAUTION *Any organization that provides third party services for your backup and recovery strategy and that states certain characteristics of data availability and recovery is not a guarantee until it can be proven and verified.*

The following lessons can be learned from this experience:

1. Adequate hardware redundancy is important.
2. Testing the backup and recovery process is important.
3. A particular hardware failure may not mean all data is lost.
4. If data you store on an external website is important, make your own backup.
5. Being upfront with your customers during a situation is a sound business practice.

References

- http://www.datacenterknowledge.com/archives/2009/02/19/magnolia-data-is-gone-for-good/
- http://www.wired.com/epicenter/2009/01/magnolia-suffer/
- http://www.transparentuptime.com/2009/02/magnolia-downtime-saas-cloud-trust.html

Couch Surfing

The information obtained from the shutdown of Couch Surfing reads like a story that should be told to every database administrator and decision maker for any company that cares about their data. The TechCrunch article title sums the risk to any organization, "CouchSurfing Deletes Itself, Shuts Down."

This environment contained both MyISAM and InnoDB data. There was apparently no binary logging enabled, and the backup procedure, which had been failing for over a month, was not performing a remote sync of all important MySQL data files. Even if the rsync backup process was operating correctly, a restore process would still result in a corrupted database, as the rsync of a running database is not a consistent view of all MySQL data. It took a hard drive crash for the situation of an incomplete backup process to become apparent and destroy the dream of an entrepreneur who had contributed over three years to this project.

The following lessons can be learned from this experience:

1. Disaster is inevitable; be prepared.

2. Any level of sane production system availability in MySQL starts with two servers. This uses MySQL replication, and the all important binary logging.

3. Daily verification of your backup process should be one of the top daily tasks of your administrator. Simple metrics such as the size of your database, and the size of your backup, and a check of change over time are simple red flags.

4. Test and verify.

References

- http://techcrunch.com/2006/06/29/couchsurfing-deletes-itself-shuts-down/

- http://forums.mysql.com/read.php?28,99328,99328#msg-99328

Journal Space

In 2009, a six-year-old blog hosting website ceased operations due to all data being destroyed and with no appropriate backup in place.

Information from articles indicates that data was managed on a RAID-1 configuration. While RAID-1 provides a level of disk mirroring to support a hardware failure in one of two drives, this is not a total backup solution. Disk mirroring supports one situation when there is a failure of one drive. Due to the hardware or software implementation of RAID-1, an action applied on one disk is mirrored to the second disk under normal operating procedures. If a system administrator physically removed the database either intentionally or unintentionally, the deletion is applied to the mirrored disk. The purpose of mirroring is to have an identical copy of the original on the same server host. An attempt to recover the data that was apparently deleted was also unsuccessful. Data recovery in this situation is usually possible providing information is not overwritten.

CAUTION *RAID is not a data backup solution. RAID provides a level of redundancy for only one type of physical disk failure. RAID is an important first step in data protection only.*

While backups apparently existed for the application code base, this is useless without an underlying source of data held in the database.

The following lessons can be learned from this experience.

1. Hardware redundancy is not an adequate backup strategy.

2. Secure offsite backups are necessary if your data is critical for business viability.

3. Data loss and corruption can easily occur as a result of human factors.

4. If the data you store on an external website is important, make your own backup.

References

- http://blog.backblaze.com/2009/01/05/journal-space-shuts-down-due-to-no-backups/

- http://blog.bismuth.com/?p=275

- http://idm.net.au/blog/006734-blogging-community-destroyed-lack-backup

Percona

Even industry leaders in the field of MySQL are not immune to a disaster scenario. Percona, the largest independent organization that provides MySQL support services, reported a "catastrophic failure of three disks on our primary web server" in 2011. As mentioned in an earlier example, being open with your customers regarding the recovery process is as important as correcting the problem. A cascading series of issues including a disk failure, a disk controller failure, and then data corruption due to configuration highlight that being prepared for more than one situation is always necessary. The delay in the recovery time was also attributed to staff changes.

As reported, "no customer data was compromised," and some services, including customer service activities, were not affected. These references indicate that sound architectural practices for a system failure of varying components do not necessarily result in total system unavailability.

This example is included to indicate that compounding problems do occur and that there are ways to address potential problems. The article also highlights that due to a configuration setting, data corruption occurred after a series of unexpected events.

CAUTION   *A disaster does not always match your prepared disaster recovery situations when one component or system fails. A disaster can easily result in multiple cascading failures causing unexpected effects.*

The outcome of any disaster is an acknowledgment for an organization to learn from the experience. The following quote is an important message that describes the business decisions resulting from this experience and is a great lesson for all readers. "The recovery lessons learned for us have been considerable and will be incorporated into our internal processes. Availability and performance of all of our websites is a top priority."

The following lessons can be learned from this experience:

1. A disaster can easily lead to more than one problem occurring at one time.

2. A documented process and knowledge by additional resources are important for timely resolution.

3. Disaster preparedness is a continual improvement process.

Reference

- http://www.mysqlperformanceblog.com/2011/07/19/server-outages-at-percona/

Other Notable Data Disasters

For additional reference material in the type of disasters that can occur, the following non-MySQL specific examples show failures with cloud based technologies, open source providers, and even a bank.

The Sidekick/Microsoft Data Loss

Disasters happen with large organizations. Danger, a $500 million acquisition by Microsoft, had no backups for the users of the Sidekick phone. All information about contacts, photos, calendars, etc., for potentially hundreds of thousands of devices was stored in the cloud. Official statements of a serious failure included "likely lost all user data that was being stored on Microsoft's servers due to a server failure... Microsoft/Danger is describing the likelihood of recovering the data from their servers as extremely low." Later reports claimed that the company failed to make a backup before a Storage Area Network (SAN) upgrade, and when this was botched, the result was loss of all data.

An important question in this situation is not "Why was there no backup?", but why executive management did not ask "What confirmation do we have in our business that our data is safe?" Executives should also be asking in any business "How do we recover from a disaster?" and "When was the last time we did this?"

TIP   *A decision maker of any organization should be paranoid with what could occur during a data loss situation while having full knowledge of what procedures, practices, and drills are in place to protect data from ever being lost.*

References

- http://techcrunch.com/2009/10/10/t-mobile-sidekick-disaster-microsofts-servers-crashed-and-they-dont-have-a-backup/

- http://www.zdnet.com/blog/btl/the-t-mobile-microsoft-sidekick-data-disaster-poor-it-management-going-mainstream/25777

- http://gizmodo.com/5378805/t+mobile-sidekick-outrage-your-datas-probably-gone-forever

Github

One of the most popular repositories of source code version control for open source projects and many commercial companies suffered a severe database failure. Using references from the official blog post: "Due to the configuration error GitHub's production database was destroyed then re-created. Not good" and "Worse, however, is that we may have lost some data from between the last good database backup and the time of the dele-tion. Newly created users and repositories are being restored, but pull request state changes and similar might be gone" we get a picture that adequate backup and recovery procedures were not in place.

However, the true cause of the problem was actually a configuration er-ror. This was due to a test environment co-located on a production environ-ment, and most likely a lack of appropriate user security settings that should be different between environments. The result, a perfectly normal test prac-tice of dropping and re-creating the database, worked as designed; it was just never designed to be executed on a production situation.

TIP   *Do not run development or test environments on the same machine as your production environment. A production environment should always have a different user account and password for management than non-production environments.*

Reference

- https://github.com/blog/744-today-s-outage

TD Bank

Of all the industries, you would expect that banks would have iron clad pro-cedures for management of customers' bank account information. In this botched upgrade, when two systems were merged into one, customers found out the frustration of not having accurate information and not being able to access their cash. System interruptions and inaccessible accounts were pro-longed for days and were compounded by batch processing operations caus-ing additional data corruption. This upgrade failure shows that adequate backups before an upgrade, and an executable recovery process in the event of a failed upgrade, are simple steps that can be tested before a production migration.

References

- http://www.zdnet.com/blog/btl/td-bank-botches-it-system-consolidation-customer-havoc-ensues/25321

- http://www.bizjournals.com/philadelphia/stories/2009/09/28/daily30.html

- http://www.olegdulin.com/2009/10/this-weeks-tdbank-debacle-and-takeaways-for-it-leaders.html

- http://www.nbcphiladelphia.com/news/business/Computer-Glitch-Causes-Problems-at-TD-Bank-63103572.html

General MySQL Disaster Situations

The lack of basic MySQL configuration requirements is a common cause of avoidable disasters. These situations that will be discussed include:

1. Not using MySQL binary logging
2. Using a single MySQL server in production
3. Using appropriate MySQL security

Other types of common and avoidable disasters are the result of a human resource deleting something. What do you do in these situations?

1. Deleting MySQL data
2. Deleting the MySQL InnoDB data file
3. Deleting MySQL binary logs

Binary Logging Not Enabled

Using MySQL in a production system with only nightly backups and not point in time capabilities is not a sound business practice. With a particular customer's e-commerce operation that included sales of several million dollars daily and large transactions exceeding $100,000, a loss of any successful transaction would have a business impact. A loss of all data from the last successful backup would have a significant and serious business effect.

If any data was accidentally deleted, if the server had any hardware failure that simply resulted in downtime of the website for a day, or any serious disk failure resulting in data loss occurs, it would have resulted in serious financial loss. Under any of these situations, the lack of binary logging makes it impossible to retrieve critical lost information.

For any production system, binary logging is critical to enable the possible recovery of any data following a nightly backup. While not adequate to support different types of disaster, the lack of this essential setting is a common failure for a new business.

Chapter 2 describes the MySQL configuration settings necessary to enable MySQL binary logging.

NOTE   *No binary logging means no point in time recovery, period.*

A Single Server

A single MySQL database with nightly backups and binary logging is a sound business practice that can provide adequate data recovery. Unfortunately, in a production situation even with the ability to perform a successful recovery, the absence of access to data such as in a read only mode, or access to hardware to perform a recovery, is a primary loss of credibility with your existing customers while your site is unavailable.

Every minute of time taken to provision or re-purpose a server and install and configure the necessary technology stack is loss of business reputation and business sales.

Any MySQL infrastructure in a production system should always start with two database servers. MySQL replication is very easy to set up and configure. The MySQL Reference Manual provides a detailed guide at http://dev.mysql.com/doc/refman/5.5/en/replication-howto.html. Chapter 4 describes the benefits of replication for backup and recovery. The next book in the Effective MySQL series titled *Advanced Replication Techniques* will also cover replication in greater detail.

Appropriate MySQL Security

The greatest cause of system administrator related problems with MySQL is a lack of appropriate security permissions on underlying MySQL data. It is recommended that the MySQL data directory, as defined by datadir, and the binary log directory, as defined by log-bin, have permissions only for the `mysqld` process, generally the `mysql` OS user. For a common Linux distribution installation, the following permissions would be used for optimal security:

```
$ chown mysql:mysql /var/lib/mysql
$ chown 700 /var/lib/mysql
```

Depending on the installation, the MySQL data directory may not reside in `/var/lib/mysql`.

CAUTION   Some distributions place the socket file in the data directory. This has to be moved to a world readable directory in order for MySQL to function normally with a secure data directory.

Application Security

The greatest cause of application developer related problems with MySQL is the lack of appropriate permissions and privileges for user accounts that can modify data, structure, or configuration settings. A MySQL environment where an application user is given ALL PRIVILEGES on all objects (i.e., *.*) can, for example, disable binary logging, which would affect any MySQL slaves, and then possibly your defined backup and recovery strategy. There are many additional reasons why this blanket privilege can cause issues in a production environment.

More information on the effects of GRANT ALL ON *.* can be found at http://ronaldbradford.com/blog/why-grant-all-is-bad-2010-08-06/.

Appropriate MySQL Configuration

Several MySQL configuration settings can lead to data integrity issues that can cause undesirable situations with production data.

Read Only Replication Slaves

The most common problem is not setting a MySQL slave to read only with the `read_only` configuration option. Without this option, an application that incorrectly connects to a replicated copy of the data has the ability to modify this data. The first impact is data inconsistency, also referred to as data drift. The second impact may cause MySQL replication to fail in the future, which can lead to further complications for data correction and slave usage.

To reiterate the point in the previous section regarding the importance of applicable application security, the following example demonstrates the potential disastrous effects.

Two MySQL users are defined, a user with the appropriate permissions for an application, and then a user with all privileges. These users are defined on a replication slave that is correctly configured as read only.

```
mysql> CREATE USER goodguy@localhost IDENTIFIED BY 'sakila';
mysql> GRANT SELECT,INSERT,UPDATE,DELETE ON appdb.* TO goodguy@localhost;

mysql> CREATE USER superman@'%';
mysql> GRANT ALL ON *.* TO superman@'%';
$ mysql -ugoodguy -psakila appdb
mysql> INSERT INTO test1(id) VALUES(1);
ERROR 1290 (HY000): The MySQL server is running with the --read-only option
 so it cannot execute this statement

$ mysql -usuperman appdb
mysql> INSERT INTO test1(id) VALUES(1);
Query OK, 1 row affected (0.01 sec)
```

This one example should highlight the importance of appropriate user privileges for application users.

SQL Server Modes

The lack of an appropriate SQL server mode with the `sql_mode` configuration option can easily cause data integrity issues that when not adequately monitored by the application can result in disastrous results that may not be detected for some time. The following are simple examples to show that data loss can occur without error in MySQL when operating with default SQL server mode settings:

```
mysql> CREATE TABLE person (
    -> first_name  VARCHAR(10) NOT NULL)
    -> ENGINE=InnoDB;
mysql> INSERT INTO  person (first_name) VALUES('stephanie');
mysql> INSERT INTO  person (first_name) VALUES('angeline');
mysql> INSERT INTO  person (first_name) VALUES('jacqueline');
mysql> INSERT INTO  person (first_name) VALUES('christopher');

mysql> SELECT * FROM person;
+------------+
| first_name |
+------------+
| stephanie  |
| angeline   |
| jacqueline |
| christophe |
+------------+
```

Everything may appear correct; however, the final name was actually silently truncated by MySQL without producing an error.

```
mysql> CREATE TABLE portfolio(
    -> stock_price DECIMAL(6,2))
    -> ENGINE=InnoDB;

mysql> INSERT INTO portfolio(stock_price) VALUES (25.5);    -- 25 1/2
mysql> INSERT INTO portfolio(stock_price) VALUES (25.75);   -- 25 3/4
mysql> INSERT INTO portfolio(stock_price) VALUES (25.875);  -- 25 7/8

mysql> SELECT * FROM portfolio;
+-------------+
| stock_price |
+-------------+
|       25.50 |
|       25.75 |
|       25.88 |
+-------------+
```

In this example, the 0.005 rounding error could be great for your portfolio, as it rounded up:

```
mysql> CREATE TABLE birth (
    -> birth_date   DATE NOT NULL)
    -> ENGINE=InnoDB;

mysql> INSERT INTO birth (birth_date) VALUES ('1965-02-29');
mysql> INSERT INTO birth (birth_date) VALUES ('1968-06-00');

mysql> SELECT * FROM birth;
+-------------+
| birth_date  |
+-------------+
| 0000-00-00  |
| 1968-06-00  |
+-------------+
```

In this example, an invalid date is modified causing the data that was entered to be lost, and a zero data value is permissible.

Fortunately, setting a correct SQL server mode within MySQL can easily solve these data integrity issues. For example:

```
mysql> SET sql_mode='STRICT_ALL_TABLES,NO_ZERO_IN_DATE,NO_ZERO_DATE';
mysql> INSERT INTO  person (first_name) VALUES('christopher');
ERROR 1406 (22001): Data too long for column 'first_name' at row 1
mysql> INSERT INTO birth (birth_date) VALUES ('1965-02-29');
ERROR 1292 (22007): Incorrect date value: '1965-02-29' for column
'birth_date' at row 1
mysql> INSERT INTO birth (birth_date) VALUES ('1968-06-00');
ERROR 1292 (22007): Incorrect date value: '1968-06-00' for column
'birth_date' at row 1
```

TIP   *One of the greatest sources of creeping data corruption that goes undetected and is almost impossible to recover is due to the MySQL default SQL server mode. One configuration option, when set at the creation of a new MySQL instance, can provide great relief for future data integrity.*

CAUTION   *The modification of the SQL server mode on an existing production system will generally result in unexpected errors, especially with date management. When using certain recommended date settings, issues may also not present as problems until table alterations are applied.*

Deleting MySQL Data

"I have deleted all the data in a table. What do I do now?" In this situation with a single server, a database recovery is generally needed. In a MySQL replicated environment it is likely the destructive statement has affected all slaves. If detected immediately, it may be possible to stop replication execution on a slave to preserve the data that was deleted. This is only likely if your slave is lagging adequately, not a usual situation in a production situation.

However, depending on certain conditions, data may be recoverable via other means. The following is an actual customer example of a successful data recovery provided by Johan Idrén from the SkySQL support team and reproduced with permission.

The customer has executed a rather devastating "DELETE   FROM table_a;" command. The only backup available was made several hours after the erroneous statement, so what we had left to work with was the underlying table_a.idb file. Based on the underlying file size of the individual tablespace for this InnoDB table, most of the data may be still recoverable. This was a job suited for the Percona InnoDB data recovery tool.

The first requirement is to obtain the table definition from the customer. The output of the SHOW CREATE TABLE command provides this. After creating an identical table on a local MySQL server, the create_defs.pl script is used to create a necessary table_defs.h file.

```
$ ./create_defs.pl --host=localhost --user=root --db=test --table=table_a \
  > table_defs.h
```

With this definition, it is possible to build a binary to extract data from the available table data file. Execution appeared to work well, providing output consistent with the table definition provided.

```
$ ./constraints_parser -5 -f table_a.idb > table_a.tsv
$ head table_a.tsv
table_a 1 John Doe
table_a 2 Sakila Dolphin
...
```

A suitable LOAD DATA INFILE statement was used to process the generated data file:

```
mysql> LOAD DATA INFILE '/path/to/table_a.tsv'
    -> REPLACE INTO TABLE table_a
    -> FIELDS TERMINATED BY '\t'
    -> OPTIONALLY ENCLOSED BY '"'
    -> LINES STARTING BY 'table_a\t'
    -> (id, firstname, lastname);
```

After initial testing some additional work was needed to remove some duplicate rows and garbage data in the generated data file. The end result was that all data was recovered and the customer was happy, a great success!

What caused this recovery process to go relatively easy?

1. The InnoDB storage engine was used.

2. No further DML statements were run on the table.

3. The `innodb_file_per_table` configuration option makes the use of the InnoDB recovery tool a lot simpler, as this only has to process the individual tablespace file and not the common tablespace, which supports all InnoDB tables.

The closing comment by Johan echoes all this reference stands for. "The moral of the story? Backup, backup, backup."

NOTE   *In some conditions, data recovery from a DELETE FROM TABLE command is possible.*

References

- http://blogs.skysql.com/2011/05/innodb-data-recovery-success-story.html

- https://launchpad.net/percona-data-recovery-tool-for-innodb

- http://www.chriscalender.com/?p=49

--i-am-a-dummy Configuration Option

An additional configuration option that could have averted this situation is the `--i-am-a-dummy` variable. While you may laugh, this is a valid configuration alias for the `--safe-updates` option. This option disables table level delete and update operations as described in the following example:

```
mysql> SET SESSION sql_safe_updates=TRUE;

mysql> DELETE FROM portfolio;
ERROR 1175 (HY000): You are using safe update mode and you tried to update
a table without a WHERE that uses a KEY column
```

For more information refer to the MySQL Reference Manual at http://dev .mysql.com/doc/refman/5.5/en/mysql-command-options.html#option_ mysql_safe-updates.

Deleting the InnoDB Data File

The circumstances for how data has been deleted matters. For example, if the InnoDB tablespace file (e.g., `ibdata1`) is deleted while MySQL is running on a Linux operating system, it is possible to recover your MySQL data but only if the MySQL server has not been stopped.

On a test system, the following is performed to demonstrate this situation:

```
$ cd /var/lib/mysql
  ls -lh ib*
-rw-rw---- 1 mysql mysql 274M 2012-02-06 15:17 ibdata1
-rw-rw---- 1 mysql mysql 128M 2012-02-06 15:17 ib_logfile0
-rw-rw---- 1 mysql mysql 128M 2011-09-07 19:36 ib_logfile1
$ rm ibdata1
$ ls -lh ib*
-rw-rw---- 1 mysql mysql 128M 2012-02-06 15:17 ib_logfile0
-rw-rw---- 1 mysql mysql 128M 2011-09-07 19:36 ib_logfile1
$ mysqldump -uroot -p --all-databases --no-data | grep InnoDB | wc -l
44
$ cd /backup/dir
$ time mysqldump -uroot -p --all-databases > backup.sql
```

As you can see there were 44 tables that were defined as InnoDB tables. If the `mysqldump` of data was not performed before the MySQL instance was stopped, that data is lost without performing a full data recovery.

```
$ service mysql stop
$ service mysql start

120206 17:11:09 [Note] /usr/sbin/mysqld: Normal shutdown
120206 17:11:09 [Note] Event Scheduler: Purging the queue. 0 events
```

```
120206 17:11:09  InnoDB: Starting shutdown...
120206 17:11:14  InnoDB: Shutdown completed; log sequence number 0 383854662
120206 17:11:14 [Note] /usr/sbin/mysqld: Shutdown complete

120206 17:11:25 [Note] Plugin 'FEDERATED' is disabled.
120206 17:11:25  InnoDB: Initializing buffer pool, size = 300.0M
120206 17:11:26  InnoDB: Completed initialization of buffer pool
InnoDB: The first specified data file ./ibdata1 did not exist:
InnoDB: a new database to be created!
120206 17:11:26  InnoDB: Setting file ./ibdata1 size to 10 MB
InnoDB: Database physically writes the file full: wait...
InnoDB: Error: all log files must be created at the same time.
InnoDB: All log files must be created also in database creation.
InnoDB: If you want bigger or smaller log files, shut down the
InnoDB: database and make sure there were no errors in shutdown.
InnoDB: Then delete the existing log files. Edit the .cnf file
InnoDB: and start the database again.
120206 17:11:26 [ERROR] Plugin 'InnoDB' init function returned error.
120206 17:11:26 [ERROR] Plugin 'InnoDB' registration as a STORAGE ENGINE failed.
120206 17:11:26 [ERROR] Aborting
```

This situation for possible data recovery after deleting the InnoDB tablespace file is because the mysqld process retains the file inode link until the process terminates. In this situation it is possible to extract the data using mysqldump.

Any online advice that states to shut down the MySQL process if data is deleted may or may not be the correct advice. Knowing the situation that caused the disaster is necessary information before making any decision, as shown in this example.

In this situation, as indicated in the error log, it is necessary to also remove the InnoDB transaction logs to enable the MySQL instance to start before performing a data recovery.

Deleting MySQL Binary Logs

A common problem is the disk partition holding the MySQL data directory filling up. While many situations include the case where no monitoring is in place to detect a full filesystem, a common action is a system administrator detects a filesystem at 80% or 90% full and then acts to delete files rather than consulting the database administrator or considering the ramifications of a database system, not a filesystem. Allowing a system administrator to remove MySQL binary log files causes multiple problems.

The best file to consider removing to reclaim space in a MySQL installation is the binary log. These can grow in size; in a large production system these can be as much as 500MB per minute. The first problem when removing files manually is the reference to this file in MySQL is not removed. The correct approach to remove binary log files is with the PURGE MASTER command. This will remove the physical file and the internal definition.

Removing the binary logs also affects your disaster recovery possibilities and your MySQL replication topology. If a MySQL slave has stopped for some reason and is one day behind the master, removing the binary logs on the master that are older than six hours will render the slave useless and will have to be fully recovered. A full recovery involves using a backup (for example, from last night), and then the application of the binary logs until the current point in time. If those binary logs the system administrator so wisely deleted to ensure the disk does not fill up have not been backed up during the day—for example, if that only happens daily or even every 12 hours—your environment is not recoverable with existing backups. A different approach including an immediate backup is needed.

The final problem is common when the binary log files and the MySQL data are found in the same directory. This is the default configuration for the popular RedHat/CentOS/Oracle Linux and Ubuntu distribution installations. An over-zealous system administrator running a smart find command that is used for cleanup on other filesystems can easily remove files in the MySQL data directory that are important and can easily crash or corrupt a MySQL installation.

TIP   A well configured MySQL installation should clearly separate the MySQL data directory, the MySQL binary log, and MySQL relay log directories for better system administration.

A final frustrating example is when a client performs a volume test in preparation for a production deployment and the result of the test fills up the partitions for the data and/or binary logs. The action of the experienced DBA to reduce the amount of logs kept with by setting the expire_logs_days configuration option to 1, or the proactive removal of the master binary logs during the test is not a wise practice. The purpose of a volume test is to prove a production situation. Are you going to proactively remove important files necessary for any level of disaster recovery? Would considering that the defined (and organizational standard) filesystem structures are inappropriate for this deployment be a more applicable action?

TIP   The purpose of testing is to break your software, and then correct discovered issues so these situations are avoided in the future within a production environment.

Existing Backup and Recovery Procedure Disasters

The following examples are where an existing MySQL backup approach was in place; however, the recovery encountered situations where the process was insufficient in some way.

- Does your backup work after a software upgrade?
- Does MySQL still perform after a restart?
- Handling MyISAM corruption.
- Missing schema data in backup.
- Restoring a backup on a running server.

MySQL Software Upgrades

Running a MySQL backup and ensuring this completed successfully and that backup files exist are not enough. In the Chapter 5 quiz one important step is "Do you review your backup logs EVERY SINGLE day or have tested backup log monitoring in place?"

This is what was found when reviewing a backup log for a client:

```
mysqldump: Got error: 1142: SELECT,LOCK TABL command denied to user
 'root'@'localhost' for table 'cond_instances' when using LOCK TABLES
mysqldump: Got error: 1142: SELECT,LOCK TABL command denied to user
 'root'@'localhost' for table 'cond_instances' when using LOCK TABLES
```

The backup script was completing, and backup files were in place (and were listed in the log file output); however, these errors were occurring. Some data was potentially not being included in the backup due to this error.

This server was running multiple MySQL instances and recently one instance was upgraded from MySQL 5.1 to MySQL 5.5; however, the call to `mysqldump` was not. This error was the result of running a version 5.1 `mysqldump` against a version 5.5 MySQL instance. By changing the hard coded path in the backup the error message went away.

In this example, a backup process was in place and historically operated without error. The greater problem is teaching people to understand the importance of the verification process.

Operating System Security Patch Upgrade

Backing up the MySQL configuration file can be as important as the MySQL data.

A production MySQL system was upgraded to include new operating system security patches. This resulted in the Linux distribution also updating MySQL 5.0 to a new point release. The correct process of taking a database backup before the upgrade was performed; however, following the upgrade, application performance was seriously degraded. It was reported by the client that it was not possible to undo the software upgrade.

Discussion and analysis determined that no application changes were applied, the system load was much higher, and the application was now taking 10 times longer to perform basic tasks. The client believed only the MySQL upgrade could be the cause. The system had been running over 150 days without any similar issues.

The first observation is that MySQL has been restarted. This has three significant effects on performance.

1. The first is time taken to refresh the applicable memory caches of data and indexes over time as they are first accessed from disk. In some situations there is a benefit in pre-caching important data on a system restart.

2. The second situation is the need for InnoDB to recalculate the table statistics for the query optimizer. This occurs when a table is first opened and requires random dives of accessing index information, initially having to read from disk. MySQL 5.6 includes a new feature to save and load these table statistics for faster restarts.

3. The third effect is less obvious but important. MySQL will read the configuration from the applicable filesystem files, e.g., my.cnf. This means that any dynamic changes made to the previously running system that were not applied to the configuration file are lost. If this was not documented, the previous running system could have improvements in performance that were not persisted during the restart.

The simple solution is to record the running values of all MySQL configuration variables by adding this to the daily backup process. A further verification of running values with the filesystem values in the default MySQL configuration file can be performed.This information can be obtained in the following ways:

```
$ mysqladmin variables
```

or

```
mysql> SHOW GLOBAL VARIABLES;
```

With the runtime configuration of a number of system variables, the system was able to improve performance. The review of the worst offending SQL statements and the creation of additional indexes also made a significant improvement. While a minor upgrade should not affect the performance of SQL statements, it is always a good practice to run important SQL statements without using the query cache, capturing execution time and execution plan details before and after any upgrade.

Handling MyISAM Corruption

The following scenario is a detailed explanation of a MyISAM corruption situation that recently occurred and the steps to triangulate a possible recovery and the ultimate solution. The environment was a single MySQL production server with binary logging (that was disabled prior in the day). There was no MySQL replication server in place.

The Call for Help

While checking my inbox at breakfast the following e-mail draws attention:

```
From: Existing client
Subject: Emergency
Are you around? My production system is crashed, I'm travelling, and have
an emergency.
```

NOTE   *Disaster does not care if you are on vacation.*

The Confirmation of a Serious Problem

I immediately contact the client, determine that the situation appears serious, and connect to a running production system finding the following errors in the MySQL error log:

```
120320  5:57:01 [ERROR] Got error 127 when reading table './cust/tbl1'
120320  5:57:01 [ERROR] Got error 127 when reading table './cust/tbl1'
120320  6:01:59 [ERROR] Got error 127 when reading table './cust/tbl1'
120320  6:01:59 [ERROR] Got error 127 when reading table './cust/tbl1'
120320  6:10:48 [Note] Retrying repair of: './cust/tbl1' with keycache
120320  6:10:48 [Note] Retrying repair of: './cust/tbl1' failed. Please
try REPAIR EXTENDED or myisamchk
120320  6:12:22 [ERROR] /var/lib/mysql5/bin/mysqld: Table './cust/tbl1'
is marked as crashed and last (automatic?) repair failed
120320  6:12:41 [ERROR] /var/lib/mysql5/bin/mysqld: Table './cust/tbl2'
is marked as crashed and should be repaired
120320  6:12:41 [Warning] Checking table:    './cust/tbl2'
```

This is the first obvious sign of MyISAM corruption. This generally occurs when the MySQL instance crashes or is not cleanly shut down. A quick review confirms that three minutes earlier this occurred. It is always recommended to try and find the cause to ensure this is understood in future situations.

```
120320  5:54:21 - mysqld got signal 11;
This could be because you hit a bug. It is also possible that this binary
or one of the libraries it was linked against is corrupt, improperly built,
or misconfigured. This error can also be caused by malfunctioning hardware.
We will try our best to scrape up some info that will hopefully help diagnose
the problem, but since we have already crashed, something is definitely wrong
and this may fail.

key_buffer_size=629145600
read_buffer_size=131072
max_used_connections=8
max_connections=500
threads_connected=7
It is possible that mysqld could use up to
key_buffer_size + (read_buffer_size + sort_buffer_size)*max_connections
= 1702396 K
bytes of memory
Hope that's ok; if not, decrease some variables in the equation.

thd=0x87d9d68
Attempting backtrace. You can use the following information to find out
where mysqld died. If you see no messages after this, something went
terribly wrong...
Cannot determine thread, fp=0xb, backtrace may not be correct.
Bogus stack limit or frame pointer, fp=0xb, stack_bottom=0x1e0000,
 thread_stack=196608, aborting backtrace.
Trying to get some variables.
Some pointers may be invalid and cause the dump to abort...
thd->query at 0x87e4a60 = SELECT * FROM ...
thd->thread_id=6
The manual page at http://www.mysql.com/doc/en/Crashing.html contains
information that should help you find out what is causing the crash.

Number of processes running now: 0
120320 05:54:21  mysqld restarted
```

```
120320  5:54:21 [Note] /var/lib/mysql5/bin/mysqld: ready for connections.
Version: '5.0.51a-log'  socket: '/tmp/mysql.sock'  port: 3307
MySQL Community Server (GPL)
```

The First Resolution Attempt

In this situation it is best to shut down MySQL and perform a myisamchk of
underlying MyISAM data. Depending on the size of your database, this can
take some time. By default, myisamchk with no options will perform a check
only.

```
$ sudo /etc/init.d/mysqld stop
$ sudo su - mysql
$ cd /var/lib/mysql
$ myisamchk cust/*.MYI
```

This output is good:

```
Checking MyISAM file: /var/lib/mysql/cust/tblX.MYI
Data records:        0   Deleted blocks:        0
- check file-size
- check record delete-chain
- check key delete-chain
- check index reference
- check data record references index: 1
- check data record references index: 2
- check record links
```

This output is not good:

```
Checking MyISAM file: /var/lib/mysql/cust/tblY.MYI
Data records:      68384   Deleted blocks:        0
- check file-size
- check record delete-chain
- check key delete-chain
- check index reference
- check data record references index: 1
- check data record references index: 2
- check data record references index: 3
- check data record references index: 4
- check data record references index: 5
- check record links
myisamchk: error: Found wrong record at 1644072
MyISAM-table '/var/lib/mysql/cust/tblY.MYI' is corrupted
Fix it using switch "-r" or "-o"
```

To perform a repair on a MyISAM table the -r option is required. For
example:

```
$ myisamchk -r /var/lib/mysql/cust/tblY.MYI
- recovering (with sort) MyISAM-table '/var/lib/mysql/cust/tblY.MYI'
Data records: 68384
- Fixing index 1
```

```
myisamchk: Duplicate key for record at 315344 against record at 315296
myisamchk: Duplicate key for record at 312272 against record at 312224
- Fixing index 2
- Fixing index 3
- Fixing index 4
- Fixing index 5
Data records: 68382
myisamchk: warning: 2 records have been removed
```

This shows a successful repair. The following shows an unsuccessful repair:

```
$ myisamchk -r /var/lib/mysql/cust/tblZ.MYI
- recovering (with sort) MyISAM-table '/var/lib/mysql/cust/tblZ.MYI '
Data records: 22528
- Fixing index 1
- Fixing index 2
Wrong bytesec:  2- 0- 38 at     386620; Skipped
MyISAM-table '/var/lib/mysql/cust/tblZ.MYI' is not fixed because of errors
Try fixing it by using the --safe-recover (-o), the --force (-f) option
or by not using the --quick (-q) flag
```

This following error on the client's largest and most important table is that classic WTF moment:

```
$ myisamchk -r /var/lib/mysql/cust/tbl1.MYI
- recovering (with sort) MyISAM-table '/var/lib/mysql/cust/tbl1.MYI '
Data records: 584
- Fixing index 1
Key 1 - Found wrong stored record at 14541448
Found wrong packed record at 14542372
Wrong aligned block at 109106305
Delete link points outside datafile at 109106305
Key 1 - Found wrong stored record at 18204008
Found block with too small length at 18204228; Skipped
Key 1 - Found wrong stored record at 18205160
...
Several hundred more lines
...
Found block with too small length at 109330004; Skipped
Wrong bytesec: 14- 0- 25 at    65272324; Skipped
Key 1 - Found wrong stored record at 114760168
Key 1 - Found wrong stored record at 114761084
Segmentation fault
```

As a side note, if myisamchk fails to complete, a temporary file is actually left behind. (First time experienced by the author.)

```
$ myisamchk -r /var/lib/mysql/cust/tbl1.MYI
- recovering (with sort) MyISAM-table '/var/lib/mysql/cust/tbl1.MYI '
Data records: 584
myisamchk: error: Can't create new tempfile: '/var/lib/mysql/cust/tbl1.TMD'
/var/lib/mysql/cust/tbl1.MYI ' is not fixed because of errors
```

```
Try fixing it by using the --safe-recover (-o), the --force (-f) option
or by not using the --quick (-q) flag
```

The Second Resolution Attempt

One of the benefits of MyISAM is that the underlying data and indexes are simply flat files. These can be copied around between database schemas with the appropriate table definition file (i.e., .frm). The following steps were used to simulate a new table.

1. Obtain the table definition from a backup file or SHOW CREATE TABLE command.

2. Create a new table in a different schema with the table definition and all indexes removed.

3. Copy the existing .MYD file over the newly created table .MYD file. The new table does not need to be the same name as the old table; however, the .MYD name must match the new name.

4. Repair table (requires MySQL instance to be stopped).

5. Confirm the data is accessible.

```
$ /etc/init.d/mysqld stop
Shutting down MySQL                                          [  OK  ]
$ myisamchk -r test/newtbl1.MYI
- recovering (with keycache) MyISAM-table ': test/newtbl1.MYI'
Data records: 0
Wrong bytesec:    4-  1- 68 at    4299268; Skipped
Key 1 - Found wrong stored record at 4303188
Key 1 - Found wrong stored record at 14541448
Key 1 - Found wrong stored record at 14542180
...
Hundreds of more errors
...
Key 1 - Found wrong stored record at 114760168
Key 1 - Found wrong stored record at 114761084
Data records: 461981
$ /etc/init.d/mysqld start
```

As you can see, a repair of the table this time did not produce a core dump. A further confirmation defines data is accessible.

```
mysql> SELECT * FROM newtbl1 limit 10;
+---------+-----------+-----------+----------------+-----
| id      | fk_id     | xxx       | xxxx           | name
+---------+-----------+-----------+----------------+-----
| 1739461 |      7847 | NULL      |           5806 | Merc
| 1739460 |      7867 | NULL      |           5265 | Ford
```

```
| 1739459 |        7894 | NULL       |                5321 | Ford
| 1739458 |        7875 | NULL       |                5105 | Ford
| 1739457 |        7979 | NULL       |                5670 | Linc
| 1739456 |        7871 | NULL       |               18726 | Merc
| 1739455 |        8113 | NULL       |               18131 | Ford
| 1739454 |        7908 | NULL       |               18626 | Merc
| 1739453 |        7877 | NULL       |                5801 | Merc
| 1739451 |        8064 | NULL       |                5171 | Ford
+---------+------------+------------+----------------+-----
```

At this time an attempt to re-create the indexes on the table is performed to enable this table and index structure to be copied back to the production schema.

```
mysql> ALTER TABLE newtbl1 ADD PRIMARY KEY (id);
ERROR 1194 (HY000): Table 'newtbl1' is marked as crashed and should be repaired
mysql> CHECK TABLE newtbl1;
+--------------+-------+-----------+-----------------------------+
| Table        | Op    | Msg_type  | Msg_text                    |
+--------------+-------+-----------+-----------------------------+
| test.newtbl1 | check | error     | Found wrong record at 1891772 |
| test.newtbl1 | check | error     | Corrupt                     |
+--------------+-------+-----------+-----------------------------+
2 rows in set (0.10 sec)
```

It is clear that the table does not want to be repaired.

The Third Resolution Attempt

At this time, the decision to continue or to pursue data recovery or a restore from the previous night's backup is considered, and both options are undertaken in parallel. A more detailed recovery is performed using initially the −o option for the older recovery method, and then with −e option for an extended recovery. It should be noted that the myisamchk documentation states *"Do not use this option if you are not totally desperate."*

The table is confirmed as crashed again.

```
$ myisamchk tbl1.MYI
Checking MyISAM file: tbl1.MYI
Data records:   434956   Deleted blocks:        0
myisamchk: warning: Table is marked as crashed and last repair failed
- check file-size
- check record delete-chain
- check key delete-chain
- check index reference
- check record links
myisamchk: error: Wrong aligned block at 3159939
MyISAM-table 'tbl1.MYI' is corrupted
Fix it using switch "-r" or "-o"
```

A successfully reported repair is performed.

```
$ myisamchk -r tbl1.MYI
- recovering (with keycache) MyISAM-table 'tbl1.MYI'
Data records: 434956
Key 1 - Found wrong stored record at 3158440
Wrong aligned block at 3159939
Wrong bytesec:   0-  3-  0 at     3159939; Skipped
Wrong bytesec:   4-  0-217 at     3160780; Skipped
Key 1 - Found wrong stored record at 3161408
Key 1 - Found wrong stored record at 3162608
...
Hundreds of more messages
...
Key 1 - Found wrong stored record at 63449568
Found link that points at 3514223880326435700 (outside data file)
at 63449688
Key 1 - Found wrong stored record at 63450556
Data records: 461818
```

However, the table is still considered corrupt.

```
$ myisamchk tbl1.MYI
Checking MyISAM file: tbl1.MYI
Data records:   461818    Deleted blocks:        0
- check file-size
- check record delete-chain
- check key delete-chain
- check index reference
- check record links
myisamchk: error: Found wrong record at 2209068
MyISAM-table 'tbl1.MYI' is corrupted
Fix it using switch "-r" or "-o"
```

A more extensive recovery is performed.

```
$ myisamchk -ro tbl1.MYI
- recovering (with keycache) MyISAM-table 'tbl1.MYI'
Data records: 461818
Key 1 - Found wrong stored record at 2209068
Found wrong packed record at 2209288
Delete link points outside datafile at 2210372
Key 1 - Found wrong stored record at 2211256
Key 1 - Found wrong stored record at 6095384
...
Hundreds of more messages
...
Key 1 - Found wrong stored record at 93394632
Key 1 - Found wrong stored record at 93395436
Data records: 461709
```

The number of data records has decreased from 461,818 to 461,709.

```
$ myisamchk -re tbl1.MYI
- recovering (with keycache) MyISAM-table 'tbl1.MYI'
Data records: 461564
Found link that points at 3480506256749577327 (outside data file) at 4784
Found link that points at 3478534832401433711 (outside data file) at 6860
Found link that points at 3482475482076759406 (outside data file) at 13572
...
...
Tens of thousands of more messages
...
Found block that points outside data file at 108557672
Found block that points outside data file at 108558168
Found block that points outside data file at 108558668
Data records: 461523
```

The number of data records has decreased again from 461,818 originally to 461,523, an indication that perhaps corrupted data has been removed.

At this time, the best approach is to try and obtain as much data as possible by extracting data.

```
$ mysqldump -u -p cust tbl1 > dump.sql
mysqldump: Error 1194: Table 'tbl1' is marked as crashed and should be
repaired when dumping table 'tbl1' at row: 9378
```

This more in-depth approach to try and recover data has also failed.

A Failed Database Backup

There is now no other option than to perform a database restore from the previous night's backup. This, however, failed with the following problems:

```
gunzip: cust1_20120319.sql.gz: invalid compressed data--crc error
gunzip: cust1_20120319.sql.gz: invalid compressed data--length error
gunzip: cust2_20120319.sql.gz: invalid compressed data--length error
 incomplete literal tree
gunzip: cust3_20120319.sql.gz: invalid compressed data--format
violated
gunzip: cust4_20120319.sql.gz: invalid compressed data--length error
 incomplete distance tree
```

Some 25% of individual schema backup files failed to uncompress on both the production server and a remote server containing the backup files. What was interesting was the variety of different error messages. The customer was now forced with considering an older backup.

TIP   Testing your backup on an external system is important to ensure corruption is not occurring at the time of your backup.

Detecting Hardware Faults

In isolated situations and when other plausible explanations are exhausted, faulty hardware can be the issue. During this data restore process other symptoms of slow performance, especially compressing the original data, and some of the unexplained outcomes shown indicated a possible hardware error. The system log showed no indication of problems to validate this hypothesis; however, in previous situations the end result has been hardware.

During the process of taking additional filesystem backups of the current data and configuration files for contingency, the system failed with a kernel panic. At this time the client was left with no production server, no current backup of data or binary logs, and an uneasy time as the host provider system engineers looked into the problem.

Almost an hour passes before the system is accessible again, and the host provider reports a fault memory error on the console. MySQL is restarted, a myisamchk is performed on the entire database, and several tables require a recover process—all occur without further incident. Another hour later, the database is in what is considered a stable state. A backup is then performed. The client is now convinced of the importance of the need for the process.

NOTE   *Any organization without an adequate backup and recovery process is at risk for serious business disruption. In this actual example, luck was on their side.*

Conclusion

This client backup process had two important flaws. The first was the backup was not checked for any type of error. The uncompressing of backup files was producing errors.

The second flaw was that the binary logs were not being stored on a separate system. If the hardware failure was a disk and not memory, data recovery may have not been possible. Not mentioned in any detail in this example is an additional restore issue where the binary log position was not recorded during the backup.

This is a good working example of the various approaches to attempting to correct a MyISAM database failure. All of these steps were performed with a client that had an emergency and no plan. If you do not have access to expert resources attempting to resolve this type of problem, the likelihood of not exhausting all options increases.

Missing Database Schemas

A client needed to perform a restore from the previous night's backup. When verifying the recovery process using the most recent customer that had been created, the application was completely crashing when viewing customer information. What happened was one transaction that recorded the customer was included in the backup, and new data for the customer was not included.

The cause was in not understanding that mysqldump does not produce a consistent static backup. Using mysqldump with--all-databases and the implied--lock-tables does not provide a consistent backup. For this disaster, the application would create a new schema for a software as a service model. The first step is recording the new customer in a central master database, then creating a new customer database, starting with the letter c followed by a three letter hash, and finally reporting this has successfully completed.

When mysqldump got to the backup of the master schema, all tables were locked, and the data extracted, including a reference to the new customer schema, was not included in the backup because database schemas are processed sequentially, and locking only occurs on a per schema basis. To better understand the cause, the following example is a look at the actual SQL statements of a mysqldump of the example database environment in Chapter 8. You can capture all SQL statements using the general query log.

```
mysql> SET GLOBAL general_log=1;

$ time mysqldump --all-databases > dump.sql
$ more /var/lib/mysql/`hostname -s`.log
...
44 Query      SHOW DATABASES
44Init DB     book2
44 Query      SHOW CREATE DATABASE IF NOT EXISTS `book2`
44 Query      show tables
44 Query      LOCK TABLES `album` READ /*!32311 LOCAL */,`album_type`
READ /*!32311 LOCAL */,`artist` READ /*!32311 LOCAL */,`country`
READ /*!32311 LOCAL */,`track` READ /*!32311 LOCAL */
44 Query      show table status like 'album'
44 Query      SET OPTION SQL_QUOTE_SHOW_CREATE=1
44 Query      SET SESSION character_set_results = 'binary'
44 Query      show create table `album`
44 Query      SET SESSION character_set_results = 'utf8'
44 Query      show fields from `album`
44 Query      SELECT /*!40001 SQL_NO_CACHE */ * FROM `album`
...
44 Query      UNLOCK TABLES
44Init DB     employees
44 Query      SHOW CREATE DATABASE IF NOT EXISTS `employees`
```

```
44 Query      show tables
44 Query      LOCK TABLES `departments` READ /*!32311 LOCAL */,`dept_emp`
READ /*!32311 LOCAL */,`dept_manager` READ /*!32311 LOCAL */,`employees`
READ /*!32311 LOCAL */,`salaries` READ /*!32311 LOCAL */,`titles`
READ /*!32311 LOCAL */
...
```

A further error was in the application where it was not correctly handling the error of a non-existing database table for a given customer. It was assumed that if the customer could log in, confirming credentials from the master database, that the underlying per customer schema objects already existed.

Restoring a Backup on a Running MySQL Instance

For all restore options except using `mysqldump`, the process requires the MySQL instance to not be running. When using MySQL Enterprise Backup (MEB), no check is performed to ensure the instance is not running, and it is therefore possible to perform a restore on a running instance. This is likely to result in inconsistent data and a potentially corrupt database. The following occurred while documenting the recovery options described in Chapter 5. This type of problem can also occur with other backup and restore products.

The steps taken were:

1. A backup was performed.

2. A new schema was created (`before_restore`), an existing schema was dropped (`employees`), and an individual table was dropped (`book2.artist`).

3. A restore was performed on a running instance.

```
mysql>SHOW SCHEMAS;
+--------------------+
| Database           |
+--------------------+
| information_schema |
| book2              |
| employees          |
| musicbrainz        |
| mysql              |
| sakila             |
| world_innodb       |
| world_myisam       |
+--------------------+
```

```
mysql>DROP TABLE book2.artist;
mysql>SHOW TABLES FROM book2;
+-----------------+
| Tables_in_book2 |
+-----------------+
| album           |
| album_type      |
| country         |
| track           |
+-----------------+
mysql>DROP SCHEMA employees;
mysql>CREATE SCHEMA before_restore;
mysql>SHOW SCHEMAS;
+--------------------+
| Database           |
+--------------------+
| information_schema |
| before_restore     |
| book2              |
| musicbrainz        |
| mysql              |
| sakila             |
| world_innodb       |
| world_myisam       |
+--------------------+
```

A `mysqlbackup copy-back` as described in Chapter 5 was performed. The following initial SQL statements were run after to initially verify the recovery:

```
mysql> SHOW SCHEMAS;
+--------------------+
| Database           |
+--------------------+
| information_schema |
| before_restore     |
| book2              |
| employees          |
| musicbrainz        |
| mysql              |
| sakila             |
| world_innodb       |
| world_myisam       |
+--------------------+
mysql> SHOW TABLES FROM book2;
+-----------------+
| Tables_in_book2 |
+-----------------+
| album           |
| album_type      |
| artist          |
| country         |
| track           |
+-----------------+
```

As you can see the `employees` schema was restored, as well as the table `book2.artist`; however, the `before_restore` schema still exists. Further analysis showed the following error on a restored table that appears to exist:

```
mysql> SELECT * FROM book2.artist LIMIT 10;
ERROR 1146 (42S02): Table 'book2.artist' doesn't exist
```

Investigation of the MySQL error log shows numerous errors to confirm that the restoration failed to complete successfully.

```
120408  0:38:50  InnoDB: Error: table 'employees'.'salaries' does not exist
in the InnoDB internal
InnoDB: data dictionary though MySQL is trying to drop it.
InnoDB: Have you copied the .frm file of the table to the
InnoDB: MySQL database directory from another database?
InnoDB: You can look for further help from
InnoDB: http://dev.mysql.com/doc/refman/5.1/en/innodb-troubleshooting.html
120408  0:38:50  InnoDB: Error: table 'employees'.'titles' does not exist
in the InnoDB internal
InnoDB: data dictionary though MySQL is trying to drop it.
InnoDB: Have you copied the .frm file of the table to the
InnoDB: MySQL database directory from another database?
InnoDB: You can look for further help from
InnoDB: http://dev.mysql.com/doc/refman/5.1/en/innodb-troubleshooting.html
120408  0:46:20 [ERROR] Cannot find or open table book2/artist from
the internal data dictionary of InnoDB though the .frm file for the
table exists. Maybe you have deleted and recreated InnoDB data
files but have forgotten to delete the corresponding .frm files
of InnoDB tables, or you have moved .frm files to another database?
or, the table contains indexes that this version of the engine
doesn't support.
See http://dev.mysql.com/doc/refman/5.1/en/innodb-troubleshooting.html
how you can resolve the problem.
```

This highlights two practices that are required:

1. Determine the necessary prerequisites for the restore process.

2. Always check the MySQL error log.

Handling InnoDB Specific Situations

The most commonly used storage engine in MySQL is InnoDB. One of the strengths of InnoDB is the ability to support transactions and the ability to perform automatic crash recovery. What happens when this does not work as designed? This section includes several InnoDB examples:

1. When automatic recovery fails

2. Internal data dictionary corruption

3. InnoDB data recovery

Automatic Recovery

The InnoDB storage engine will automatically perform a crash recovery when necessary, generally when the MySQL instance is not shut down safely. In this example, crash recovery was occurring every time MySQL was started.

```
$ cat /var/log/mysql/error.log
110426 14:05:53 [Note] /usr/sbin/mysqld: Normal shutdown
110426 14:05:56  InnoDB: Starting shutdown...

InnoDB: Log scan progressed past the checkpoint lsn 6 2726373466
110426 14:05:59  InnoDB: Database was not shut down normally!
InnoDB: Starting crash recovery.
InnoDB: Doing recovery: scanned up to log sequence number 6 2731616256
nnoDB: Doing recovery: scanned up to log sequence number 6 2750470428
110426 14:06:01  InnoDB: Starting an apply batch of log records to the
database...
InnoDB: Progress in percents: 0 1 2 3 4 5 6 7 8 9 10 11 12 13 14 15 16 17 18 ...
InnoDB: Apply batch completed
110426 14:07:56  InnoDB: Started; log sequence number 6 2750470428
110426 14:07:56 [Note] /usr/sbin/mysqld: ready for connections.
```

While MySQL was cleanly shut down, an automatic crash recovery was being performed. This would take several minutes before the system was available for general use. It is unclear exactly why this problem was occurring. The client reported the situation was the result of an unexpected MySQL instance failure on an Amazon Web Services (AWS) instance running on Elastic Block Storage (EBS).

InnoDB provides for a forced recovery mode, which enables six varying levels of disabling various crash recovery features. In a failed InnoDB crash recovery, you can use each of these modes, starting with 1, to attempt to retrieve as much data as possible. In this example, this configuration option was set to 1.

```
#my.cnf
[mysqld]
innodb_force_recovery=1

$ service mysql restart
110426 15:25:42 [Note] Event Scheduler: Purging the queue. 0 events
110426 15:25:42  InnoDB: Starting shutdown...
```

```
110426 15:25:45  InnoDB: Shutdown completed; log sequence number 6 2767325763
110426 15:25:45 [Note] /usr/sbin/mysqld: Shutdown complete

110426 15:27:02  InnoDB: Started; log sequence number 6 2767325763
InnoDB: !!! innodb_force_recovery is set to 1 !!!
110426 15:27:02 [Note] Event Scheduler: Loaded 0 events
110426 15:27:02 [Note] /usr/sbin/mysqld: ready for connections.
Version: '5.1.41-3ubuntu12.6'  socket: '/var/run/mysqld/mysqld.sock'
port: 3306  (Ubuntu)
```

At this time, the database has successfully started without performing a crash recovery. In any non-zero mode InnoDB will self-protect the data and prevent any modification with INSERT, UPDATE, or DELETE statements. In this example, a clean shutdown, the removal of the `innodb_force_recovery` option, and the restarting of MySQL addressed the issue.

InnoDB Data Dictionary Inconsistency

Every table in MySQL has a related table definition file that is located in the schema sub-directory within the data directory of the instance. This is known as an .frm file.In addition, InnoDB holds meta-data within the InnoDB common tablespace (e.g., the ibdata1 file) about the table definitions.

At times these may appear inconsistent or be inconsistent and report errors similar to:

```
120206 21:10:27  InnoDB: Error: table `test`.`person` does not exist in the
InnoDB internal
InnoDB: data dictionary though MySQL is trying to drop it.
InnoDB: Have you copied the .frm file of the table to the
InnoDB: MySQL database directory from another database?
InnoDB: You can look for further help from
InnoDB: http://dev.mysql.com/doc/refman/5.1/en/innodb-troubleshooting.html
```

and

```
110222 23:46:48 [ERROR] Cannot find or open table demo/tbl from
the internal data dictionary of InnoDB though the .frm file for the
table exists. Maybe you have deleted and recreated InnoDB data
files but have forgotten to delete the corresponding .frm files
of InnoDB tables, or you have moved .frm files to another database?
or, the table contains indexes that this version of the engine
doesn't support.
See http://dev.mysql.com/doc/refman/5.1/en/innodb-troubleshooting.html
how you can resolve the problem.
```

These situations occur where the InnoDB tablespace has been rebuilt and the underlying table definitions were in place. Alternatively insufficient file permissions with the MySQL data directory can cause an underlying inconsistency.

Automatic Recovery Crashes the Database Server

The InnoDB storage engine is designed to perform automatic crash recovery. This is possible because the InnoDB transaction logs (redo logs) record all successful transactions that may not have been applied to the underlying InnoDB data. The doublewrite buffer also holds committed data that may not be applied to the same underlying InnoDB data.

When the MySQL instance is started, InnoDB will detect a difference in the Log Sequence Number (LSN) between the InnoDB transaction logs and the InnoDB data. This is an indication that the MySQL instance was not shut down correctly. In this case InnoDB will automatically detect then rectify the situation to produce a consistent view. In the following example this then caused the MySQL server to crash:

```
...
InnoDB: The log sequence number in ibdata files does not match
InnoDB: the log sequence number in the ib_logfiles!
120125 16:39:48  InnoDB: Database was not shut down normally!
InnoDB: Starting crash recovery.
InnoDB: Reading tablespace information from the .ibd files...
InnoDB: Restoring possible half-written data pages from the doublewrite
InnoDB: buffer...
120125 16:39:48  InnoDB: Assertion failure in thread 2691024672 in file
fsp0fsp.c line 2101
InnoDB: Failing assertion: inode
InnoDB: We intentionally generate a memory trap.
InnoDB: Submit a detailed bug report to http://bugs.mysql.com.
InnoDB: If you get repeated assertion failures or crashes, even
InnoDB: immediately after the mysqld startup, there may be
InnoDB: corruption in the InnoDB tablespace. Please refer to
InnoDB: http://dev.mysql.com/doc/refman/5.5/en/forcing-innodb-recovery.html
InnoDB: about forcing recovery.
120125 16:39:48 - mysqld got signal 6 ;
This could be because you hit a bug. It is also possible that this binary
or one of the libraries it was linked against is corrupt, improperly built,
or misconfigured. This error can also be caused by malfunctioning hardware.
We will try our best to scrape up some info that will hopefully help diagnose
the problem, but since we have already crashed, something is definitely wrong
and this may fail.

...
```

Other MySQL Situations

The following examples complete some different situations using MySQL:

- Replication inconsistency
- Third party product recovery limitations

Replication Inconsistency

The following error message was discovered on a MySQL replication server:

```
mysql> SHOW SLAVE STATUS\G
*************************** 1. row ***************************
...
            Relay_Log_File: relay-log.007112
             Relay_Log_Pos: 664060
     Relay_Master_Log_File: mysql-bin.002334
...
        Exec_Master_Log_Pos: 59622948
...
          Slave_IO_Running: Yes
         Slave_SQL_Running: No
...
                Last_Errno: 1062
Last_Error: Error 'Duplicate entry '857867' for key 'id' on query.
Default database: 'db'. Query: 'INSERT INTO urls(url)
 VALUES('effectivemysql.com')'
              Skip_Counter: 0
...
             Last_IO_Errno: 0
             Last_IO_Error:
            Last_SQL_Errno: 1062
            Last_SQL_Error: Error 'Duplicate entry '857867' ...
```

A review of the data on the slave host shows the data for the SQL statement was already applied.

```
mysql> select * from urls where id=857867;
+--------+-------------------+
| id     | url               |
+--------+-------------------+
| 857867 | effectivemysql.com|
+--------+-------------------+
```

A number of checks were performed to look at the master database and binary logs to confirm this statement only occurred once.

A review of the slave host error log showed that MySQL has recently performed a crash recovery.

```
111214 17:19:20 [Note] Plugin 'FEDERATED' is disabled.
InnoDB: Log scan progressed past the checkpoint lsn 42 957070720
111214 17:19:20  InnoDB: Database was not shut down normally!
...
111214 17:19:54  InnoDB: Started; log sequence number 42 997980331
111214 17:19:54 [Note] Slave SQL thread initialized, starting replication
in log 'mysql-bin.002334' at position 58959139, relay log
'/var/lib/mysql/relay-log.007110' position: 58959284
111214 17:19:54 [Note] Event Scheduler: Loaded 0 events
111214 17:19:54 [Note] /usr/sbin/mysqld: ready for connections.
Version: '5.1.41-3ubuntu12.6'  socket: '/var/run/mysqld/mysqld.sock'
port: 3306  (Ubuntu)
111214 17:19:54 [Note] Slave I/O thread: connected to master 'repl@',replication
started in log 'mysql-bin.002334' at position 58959139
111214 17:19:55 [ERROR] Slave SQL: Error 'Duplicate entry '857867' for key ...
Query: 'INSERT INTO urls(url) VALUES('effectivemysql.com')', Error_code: 1062
111214 17:19:55 [Warning] Slave: Duplicate entry '857867' for key 'id'
Error_code: 1062
111214 17:19:55 [ERROR] Error running query, slave SQL thread aborted.
Fix the problem, and restart the slave SQL thread with "SLAVE
START". We stopped at log 'mysql-bin.002334' position 59622948
```

A review of the slave relay log, which details completed SQL statements, showed that this SQL command had actually been executed, yet MySQL replication appeared not to record this. A review of the underlying information file, defined by the `relay-log-info-file` configuration option, indicated an inconsistency with the error log of the actual master binary log executed log position. The error log indicates that MySQL replication started at the position of 58959139, while the relay log information file shows a different position. This inconsistency was the actual SQL statement that was being reported as the last failure.

```
# more relay-bin.info
/var/lib/mysql/relay-log.007112
664060
mysql-bin.002334

59622948
9
1
```

As a result, by skipping the SQL statement, the replication slave could be started and continued without incident.

By default the `sync_relay_log_info` configuration option has a value of 0, which implies the filesystem should flush this file to disk from time to time. In this situation, a database crash caused this file to become inconsistent. More information on this option can be found at http://dev.mysql.com/doc/refman/5.5/en/replication-options-slave.html#sysvar_sync_relay_log_info.

RDS Recovery Failure

Amazon Web Services (AWS) provides a Remote Database Service (RDS) for MySQL. This is popular when an organization does not have any skills to manage MySQL. This complete packaged solution has several limitations. There is no physical access to the database server. While there are API interfaces to change MySQL configuration settings and look at MySQL error and slow logs, it is not possible to look at the system resources being used, or look at the MySQL binary logs, for example.

An issue arose with a client when a database restore through an RDS snapshot failed. Amazon support informed the client there was some BLOB or TEXT field with bad characters and this prevented mysqlbinlog from performing a successful restoration. They were directed to the following bug: http://bugs.mysql.com/bug.php?id=33048.

The client was looking for a means of tracking down the potential offending records so a database restoration could be performed. First there was no way to confirm this was the actual failure of the restoration, as this third party managed service did not provide access to detailed logs. The listed bug, if this was indeed the true problem, provided two workaround solutions; the first was to analyze the mysqlbinlog output, and then correct if necessary before applying. The second option was to replay the binary log via the replication stream rather than converting to ASCII and then using the mysql client. Both of these options were not possible because the third party did not provide sufficient access. The binary logs, for example, are not accessible.

At this time, the client has no recovery capability. The backup process failed during recovery, and the service provider was both unwilling to help further or provide access to necessary MySQL information to perform more in-depth analysis.

Common Downtime Causes

What are the most common causes of downtime with MySQL systems? Leading service provider Percona published in the IOUG SELECT magazine, Q1 2011, an article titled "Causes of Downtime in Production MySQL Servers," which provides a very detailed picture of actual support situations.

One third of all reported downtime was not the result of MySQL in any way. Issues with the storage system were defined as the top factor, with the operating system and networking also attributing to downtime. A SAN or RAID storage system is not a backup solution. The following article by leading PostgreSQL expert Josh Berkus is a great reinforcement of why. In this disaster example, there was not even a physical failure—a vendor-provided firmware update led to eventual total data corruption. More information can be found at http://it.toolbox.com/blogs/database-soup/a-san-is-not-a-highavailability-solution-47644. The Sidekick data disaster as detailed earlier was reported as a SAN upgrade mistake.

CAUTION   A RAID system is only as good as the monitoring used to detect a degraded RAID configuration and the time taken to correct the problem. When a service provider, system administrator, or other resource states your data is protected by RAID, ask for proof the RAID system is not degraded. This question is always asked when reviewing a client backup and recovery strategy, and the results observed have been two clients unaware they had degraded production systems.

The whitepaper also shows a breakdown of replication related problems where data drift results in almost 50% of replication issues. The majority of data loss and corruption issues were the result of human factors. An important factor in the management of any system is the result of a failure due to other human factors. The lack of appropriate configuration management, unprepared and untested upgrading, or the lack of performing software upgrades all attribute to controllable situations. An important statement in the prevention of situations that can use a disaster situation clearly highlights a common problem found.

NOTE   Quoting from the "Causes of Downtime in Production MySQL Servers" whitepaper: "In most cases, emergencies analyzed could have been prevented best by a systematic, organization-wide effort to find and remove latent problems [before they occur]. Many of the activities involved in this effort could appear to be unproductive, and might be unrewarding for people to do."

A full copy of the whitepaper is available for download from the Percona website at http://www.percona.com/about-us/mysql-white-paper/causes-of-downtime-in-production-mysql-servers.

External Help

In some cases, a disaster is correctable. As shown in this chapter, understanding and describing the precise circumstances and seeking input from multiple reputable and experienced resources can be key to avoiding a disaster and career limiting situation. Organizations that provide dedicated MySQL services, that are active in the MySQL community ecosystem, and that are known by this author are included here:

- MySQL technical support services, part of Oracle support services, provides global 24/7 technical support. Details at http://www.mysql .com/support/.

- SkySQL provides world-wide support and services for the MariaDB and MySQL databases. Details at http://www.skysql.com/.

- FromDual provides independent and neutral MySQL, Percona Server, and MariaDB consulting and services. Details at http://fromdual.com/.

- The Pythian Group "love your data" provides remote database services for Oracle, MySQL, and SQL Server. Details at http://www .pythian.com/.

- Blue Gecko provides remote DBA services, database hosting services, and emergency DBA support. Details at http://www.bluegecko.net/.

- Percona provides consulting, support, training, development, and software in MySQL and InnoDB performance. Details at http://www .percona.com/.

- Open Query provides support, training, products, and remote maintenance for MySQL and MariaDB. Details at http://openquery .com/.

- PalominoDB provides remote DBA and system administration services in MySQL, MariaDB, and other open source products. Details at http://palominodb.com/.

- Effective MySQL provides practical education, training, and mentoring resources for MySQL DBAs, developers, and architects. Details at http://effectivemysql.com/.

- Continuent provides continuous data availability and database replication solutions, and provides support managing and running MySQL replication with industry leading experts. Details at http://www.continuent.com/.

Other organizations may state they provide MySQL services. While this list is not exclusive of all possible service providers, these companies are known within the MySQL ecosystem. As with any service you should always independently compare and evaluate for your needs.

Conclusion

World Backup Day is designated as the 31st of March. The tag line is "Don't be an April Fool. Back up your data. Check your restores." More information can be found at http://www.worldbackupday.com/. However, every day is your last day if you do not have a backup and recovery process in place. Disaster recovery (DR) can range from a mildly annoying occurrence to a once in a lifetime tsunami type event. This chapter and this book do not provide all the answers for all situations with a MySQL disaster. This book does provide extensive knowledge and presents all the common options and tools available, with supporting information of situations you should be aware of, plan for, and know how to address when necessary.

Copies of all referenced articles are available on the Effective MySQL website at http://effectivemysql.com/book/backup-recovery/.

8

Optimizing Backup and Recovery

Once you know there is a valid backup and restore process for your environment, how can you improve and refine this process? Depending on your locking strategy, diskspace availability, or business data recovery service level agreement (SLA), there are various techniques you can use to optimize and streamline your process. There are also architectural considerations for further optimizations.

171

In this chapter we will discuss:

- Use and benefits of compression
- Levering streaming
- Parallelism with mydumper
- Full and incremental backups
- Architectural considerations

Example Backup Environment

Chapter 2 discussed the primary backup options available for a MySQL instance. This chapter has specific demonstrations for `mysqldump`, MySQL Enterprise Backup (MEB), and XtraBackup products described as well as mydumper.

All tests were performed on an Amazon Web Services (AWS) Elastic Compute Cloud (EC2) large instance with a dedicated Elastic Block Storage (EBS) partition for the MySQL data and the MySQL backup location. An EC2 `m1.large` instance is defined with the following characteristics from http://aws.amazon.com/ec2/instance-types/:

- 7.5GB memory
- 4 EC2 Compute Units (2 virtual cores with 2 EC2 Compute Units each)
- 850GB instance storage
- 64-bit platform
- I/O Performance: High
- API name: m1.large

The following articles will provide all the steps necessary to start using AWS without any prior knowledge in order to repeat any examples in this chapter:

- http://effectivemysql.com/article/setting-up-amazon-web-services/
- http://effectivemysql.com/article/using-amazon-web-services/

Refer to the GitHub repository of code for this book to reproduce the full environment and commands used in the following examples. Details can be found at http://effectivemysql.com/book/backup-recovery/.

The small database environment used is approximately 5GB.

```
SELECT    SUM(data_length+index_length)/1024/1024 AS total_mb,
          SUM(data_length)/1024/1024 AS data_mb,
          SUM(index_length)/1024/1024 AS index_mb,
          COUNT(DISTINCT table_schema) AS schema_cnt,
          COUNT(*) AS tables,
          CURDATE() AS today,
          VERSION()
FROM      information_schema.tables\G

*************************** 1. row ***************************
  total_mb: 5344.63
   data_mb: 4545.49
  index_mb: 799.13
schema_cnt: 7
    tables: 103
     today: 2012-04-03
 VERSION(): 5.1.61-0ubuntu0.11.10.1-log
```

For the purposes of testing and providing shorter commands, the MySQL privileges have been recorded in a user MySQL configuration file. This does not represent the optimal MySQL user account or approach for securing MySQL backups. An appropriate and secure approach should be used for production systems.

```
$ cat $HOME/.my.cnf
[client]
user=root
password=passwd
```

All times shown are for a single execution of the respective command and are provided as an example representation. Appropriate error checking is not shown in the following examples. This should be applied accordingly in a production setting. Accurate benchmarking should involve several iterations of the same test and should include monitoring additional system resources, including CPU, disk, and network throughput to determine a more specific measurement.

Using Compression

One of the most common improvements to any backup strategy is the use of compression. The time savings for transferring backups offsite or to external media, including tape, can be an important benefit. Compression can also be used to reduce disk I/O during the backup or recovery approach. This feature has one significant limitation—that is, the time taken to compress or uncompress files may impact individual steps in the backup or recovery strategy.

mysqldump

When using `mysqldump`, compression can simply be included as an additional step or in the command line via a piped command. For example:

```
$ time mysqldump [options] > dump1.sql
$ ls -lh dump1.sql
$ time gzip dump1.sql
$ ls -lh dump1.sql.gz
```

or

```
$ time mysqldump [options] | gzip > dump2.sql.gz
$ ls -lh dump2.sql.gz
```

TIP   *While the `gzip` command is demonstrated here, other compression tools exist, including `bzip` and `7zip`. These tools can provide better compression ratios for certain types of data. Compressions tools also generally include different options between the fastest and best compression.*

Using the example MySQL database of approximately 5GB:

```
$ time mysqldump --all-databases > /mysql/backup/dump1.sql
real    1m31.631s
user    1m12.533s
sys     0m10.893s
$ ls -lh /mysql/backup/dump1.sql
-rw-rw-r-- 1 uid gid 2.9G 2012-04-03 03:04 /mysql/backup/dump1.sql
$ time gzip /mysql/backup/dump1.sql
real    4m28.237s
user    4m6.687s
sys     0m5.316s
$ ls -lh /mysql/backup/dump1.sql.gz
-rw-rw-r-- 1 uid gid 902M 2012-04-03 03:04 /mysql/backup/dump1.sql.gz
```

With compression combined as a single command the results are:

```
$ time mysqldump --all-databases | gzip > /mysql/backup/dump2.sql.gz
real    4m18.536s
user    5m4.371s
sys     0m7.792s
$ ls -lh dump2.sql.gz
-rw-rw-r-- 1 uid gid 902M 2012-04-03 03:15 /mysql/backup/dump2.sql.gz
```

When using a piped command the first benefit is that the output file is automatically compressed on the fly, without requiring any additional temporary disk space. This helps if your system has limited diskspace. The disadvantage is the additional time this command may take to execute. When combined with the `mysqldump` command using default settings, a lock of all tables can affect application access. In this example, the locking was increased from 91 seconds to 258 seconds. Locking is not a consideration for an InnoDB only database when the `--single-transaction` option is used.

Testing is necessary to confirm the benefits for your environment. It is easy to time the backup and compress commands separately and the time taken when combined. The combined time may not be a significant overhead in some situations. This will depend on disk throughput capacity and memory. In the preceding example, 359 seconds was reduced to 258 seconds when the statements were combined, producing a saving in time. In the following example of a different sized database on a different system, the time is about the same, 83 seconds compared with 81 seconds.

```
$ time mysqldump --all-databases > dump1.sql
real     0m36.801s
$ ls -lh dump1.sql
-rw-rw-r-- 1 uid gid 280M 2012-03-08 17:41 dump1.sql
$ time gzip dump1.sql
real     0m47.457s
$ ls -lh dump1.sql.gz
-rw-rw-r-- 1 uid gid 94M 2012-03-08 17:41 dump1.sql.gz
$ time mysqldump --all-databases | gzip > dump2.sql.gz
real     1m21.262s
$ ls -lh dump2.sql.gz
-rw-rw-r-- 1 uid gid 94M 2012-03-08 17:43 dump2.sql.gz
```

Compression with a filesystem snapshot is a process that occurs as a post-step, generally before copying the snapshot files. As the size of the backup grows, the negative impact on the production system and the recovery process becomes more obvious.

The compression on the database server can have an effect on the database I/O performance. Is the copy of an uncompressed backup that is five to ten times larger on a dedicated network interface less of an impact than the compression? This will be discussed in the following sections.

TIP   *The* `nice` *and* `ionice` *Linux commands can change the priority of work on a system and lower the system impact of certain commands.*

While you consider this, the greatest issue uncovered during consulting in a disaster recovery situation is either the time taken to uncompress the data before restoration, or insufficient disk space to uncompress a backup and restore accordingly. In the first situation, a client with a large centralized SAN for more than 30 databases had a 17 hour delay in the database restoration due to the time taken to uncompress data. In the second situation, your system may require at least two times the database size in diskspace, the uncompressed backup file, and the restored database.

Under normal circumstances the most common database recovery is that of the last physical backup. It would be optimal to always ensure an uncompressed copy of the system you wish to restore is on disk.

Compression Utilities

Using the mysqldump backup of 2.9GB the following testing was performed to compare the time and % compression savings of various available open source products.

Utility	Compression Time (sec)	Decompression Time (sec)	New Size(% Saving)
lzo (-3)	21	34	1.5GB (48%)
pigz (-1)	43	33	995MB (64%)
pigz (-3)	56	34	967MB (67%)
gzip (-1)	81	43	995MB (64%)
fastlz	92	128	1.3GB (55%)
pigz [-6]	**105**	**25**	**902MB (69%)**
gzip (-3)	106	43	967MB (67%)
compress	145	36	1.1GB (62%)
pigz (-9)	202	23	893MB (70%)
gzip [-6]	**232**	**78**	**902MB (69%)**
zip	234	50	902MB (69%)
gzip (-9)	405	43	893MB (70%)
bzip2	540	175	757MB (74%)
rzip	11 minutes	360	756MB (74%)
lzo (-9)	20 minutes	82	1.2GB (58%)
7z	33 minutes	122	669MB (77%)
lzip	47 minutes	132	669MB (77%)
lzma	58 minutes	180	639MB (78%)
xz	59 minutes	160	643MB (78%)

The percentage savings and compression time of results will vary depending on the type of data that is stored in the MySQL database.

NOTE   The `pigz` compression utility was the surprising winner in best compression time producing at least a size of `gzip`. This was a full 50% faster than `gzip`.

MySQL Enterprise Backup (MEB)

A backup with MEB can enable compression with the `--compress` option. With compression you are unable to apply the logs within a single backup command, i.e., `--compress` and the action `backup-and-apply-log` are incompatible. Compression is also incompatible with all incremental backup options including `--incremental` and `--incremental-with-redo-log-only`.

The following information is for a normal MEB backup:

```
$ sudo su - mysql
$ time /opt/meb/bin/mysqlbackup --user=root --password=passwd \
--backup-dir=/mysql/backup/meb/first backup-and-apply-log
real    3m30.879s
user    0m17.081s
sys     0m14.565s
$ du -sh /mysql/backup/meb/first
5.6G    /mysql/backup/meb/first
$ ls -lh /mysql/backup/meb/first/datadir/ibd*
-rw-rw-r-- 1 uid gid 5.4G 2012-04-03 03:25 /mysql/backup/meb/first/datadir/ibdata1
```

Only InnoDB tablespace files are compressed. These are given a `.ibz` extension accordingly for both the per tablespace `.ibd` data files and the common tablespace `ibdata` file. Large MyISAM data files are not compressed. For example:

```
$ time /opt/meb/bin/mysqlbackup --user=root --password=passwd --compress \
--backup-dir=/mysql/backup/meb/second-compressed backup
...
mysqlbackup: INFO: Unique generated backup id for this is 13334239375677869
 mysqlbackup: INFO: Uses posix_fadvise() for performance optimization.
 mysqlbackup: INFO: System tablespace file format is Antelope.
 mysqlbackup: INFO: Found checkpoint at lsn 6374642841.
 mysqlbackup: INFO: Starting log scan from lsn 6374642688.
120403  3:32:17 mysqlbackup: INFO: Copying log...
120403  3:32:17 mysqlbackup: INFO: Log copied, lsn 6374642841.
          We wait 1 second before starting copying the data files...
120403  3:32:18 mysqlbackup: INFO: Copying /var/lib/mysql/ibdata1
```

```
(Antelope file format).
mysqlbackup: Progress in MB: 200 400 600 800 ... 4800 5000 5200 5400
 mysqlbackup: INFO: Preparing to lock tables: Connected to mysqld server.
120403 03:36:59 mysqlbackup: INFO: Starting to lock all the tables....
120403 03:36:59 mysqlbackup: INFO: All tables are locked and flushed to disk
 mysqlbackup: INFO: Opening backup source directory '/var/lib/mysql/'
120403 03:36:59 mysqlbackup: INFO: Starting to backup all files in
subdirectories of '/var/lib/mysql/'
 mysqlbackup: INFO: Backing up the database directory 'employees'
 mysqlbackup: INFO: Backing up the database directory 'musicbrainz'
 mysqlbackup: INFO: Backing up the database directory 'mysql'
 mysqlbackup: INFO: Backing up the database directory 'sakila'
 mysqlbackup: INFO: Backing up the database directory 'world_innodb'
 mysqlbackup: INFO: Backing up the database directory 'world_myisam'
 mysqlbackup: INFO: Copying innodb data and logs during final stage ...
 mysqlbackup: INFO: A copied database page was modified at 6374642841.
         (This is the highest lsn found on page)
         Scanned log up to lsn 6374644872.
         Was able to parse the log up to lsn 6374644872.
         Maximum page number for a log record 229380
mysqlbackup: INFO: Compressed 5432 MB of data files to 1704 MB
(compression 68%).
...
real    4m42.160s
user    3m4.052s
sys     0m6.960s
$ du -sh /mysql/backup/meb/second-compressed/
1.7G    /mysql/backup/meb/second-compressed/
$ ls -lh /mysql/backup/meb/second-compressed/datadir/ibd*
-rw-rw-r-- 1 uid gid 1.7G 2012-04-03 03:36 /mysql/backup/meb/
second-compressed/datadir/ibdata1.ibz
$ ls -lh /mysql/backup/meb/second-compressed/datadir/world_myisam/
total 484K
-rw-rw-r-- 1 mysql mysql 8.6K 2012-04-03 03:36 City.frm
-rw-rw-r-- 1 mysql mysql 267K 2012-04-03 03:36 City.MYD
-rw-rw-r-- 1 mysql mysql  42K 2012-04-03 03:36 City.MYI
-rw-rw-r-- 1 mysql mysql 9.0K 2012-04-03 03:36 Country.frm
-rw-rw-r-- 1 mysql mysql 8.5K 2012-04-03 03:36 CountryLanguage.frm
-rw-rw-r-- 1 mysql mysql  38K 2012-04-03 03:36 CountryLanguage.MYD
-rw-rw-r-- 1 mysql mysql  18K 2012-04-03 03:36 CountryLanguage.MYI
-rw-rw-r-- 1 mysql mysql  61K 2012-04-03 03:36 Country.MYD
-rw-rw-r-- 1 mysql mysql 5.0K 2012-04-03 03:36 Country.MYI
-rw-rw-r-- 1 mysql mysql   65 2012-04-03 03:36 db.opt
```

By comparison the backup without the --compress option produced a 5.6GB backup in 210 seconds. This compressed backup of 1.7GB took 282 seconds to complete.

The --compress-level=N option enables further compression. A value of 1 is the default and fastest compression; 9 is the slowest compression. Subsequent tests with --compress-level=9 produced only slightly better compression; however, the time taken was six times longer.

XtraBackup

To enable compression with XtraBackup, you must first stream the data with the `--stream=tar` option and pipe accordingly to an applicable compression command. For example:

```
$ innobackupex--stream=tar ./ | gzip -> /path/to/backup.tar.gz
```

A normal XtraBackup produces the following results for the example database:

```
$ sudo su - mysql
$ time innobackupex --defaults-file=/etc/mysql/my.cnf --user=root \
--password=passwd --no-timestamp /mysql/backup/xtrabackup/first
real    2m41.339s
user    0m21.769s
sys     0m14.569s

$ du -sh /mysql/backup/xtrabackup/first/
5.4G    /mysql/backup/xtrabackup/first/
```

The following is produced for an XtraBackup with compression:

```
$ time innobackupex --defaults-file=/etc/mysql/my.cnf --user=root \
--password=passwd --stream=tar ./ | \
gzip - > /mysql/backup/xtrabackup/second.tar.gz
real    8m2.409s
user    7m9.551s
sys     0m9.025s

$ ls -lh /mysql/backup/xtrabackup/second.tar.gz
-rw-rw-r-- 1 uid gid 1.6G 2012-04-03 04:04 second.tar.gz
```

For comparison, without the streaming and compression the backup took 161 seconds and produced a backup directory 5.4GB in size compared with 482 seconds and a backup file of 1.6GB in size with compression.

When extracting the backup file, the following syntax is used:

```
$ tar xvfzi /mnt/backup/xtrabackup/second.tar.gz
```

CAUTION   *When uncompressing XtraBackup tar files, the* -i *option is required.*

Streaming Backups

A Linux pipe combined with an applicable command can be used to stream output across the network, avoiding the need to write any backup information on the database server.

Using SSH

Using standard SSH with keyed authentication you can automate the network transfer of a backup. In the following examples the SSH connection has been simplified to just using the alias backup:

```
$ cat $HOME/.ssh/config
Host backup
   IdentityFile /home/ubuntu/.ssh/admin.pem
   User ubuntu
   HostName ec2-XX-XX-XX-XX.compute-1.amazonaws.com
```

TIP   *You can remove the complexity for remote connections by defining the hostname, port, user, and key details in the SSH configuration file $HOME/.ssh/ config.*

For example:

```
$ time mysqldump --all-databases |  ssh backup "cat - > rdump1.sql"
real    2m20.774s
user    2m8.896s
sys     0m19.961s
$ ssh backup "ls -lh rdump1.sql"
-rw-rw-r-- 1 uid gid 2.9G 2012-04-03 04:13 rdump1.sql
```

This can be combined with compression as described previously. For example:

```
$ time mysqldump --all-databases | gzip | \
   ssh backup "cat - > rdump2.sql.gz"
real    4m32.434s
user    5m27.788s
sys     0m11.693s
$ ssh backup "ls -lh rdump2.sql.gz"
-rw-rw-r-- 1 uid gid 902M 2012-04-03 04:18 rdump2.sql.gz
```

It is also possible to offload the compression to the remote host by sending the data uncompressed and applying at the destination. For example:

```
$ time mysqldump --all-databases | ssh backup "cat - | \
   gzip > rdump3.sql.gz"
real    3m38.905s
user    1m57.011s
```

```
sys      0m12.265s
$ ssh backup "ls -lh rdump3.sql.gz"
-rw-rw-r-- 1 uid gid 902M 2012-04-03 04:23 rdump3.sql.gz
```

You can also throttle throughput in a pipe with the pv command. For example:

```
$ time mysqldump --all-databases |  pv -L5m -q | \
    ssh backup "cat - > backup.sql"
```

Using nc

Using netcat (nc) you can transfer a file via TCP/UDP directly on a given port. This generally requires defining the receiving communication on the destination server, and may require additional firewall access on a defined port. For example:

```
$ ssh backup "nc -l 9306 > /mysql/backup/nc/first.sql" &
$ time mysqldump --all-databases | nc backup 9306
real     2m21.778s
user     1m21.261s
sys      0m49.039s
ssh backup "ls -lh /mysql/backup/nc/first.sql"
-rw-rw-r-- 1 uid gid 2.9G 2012-04-08 00:07 /mysql/backup/nc/first.sql
```

This command is generally considered more lightweight than ssh and possibly a little faster. The size of this backup example does not represent what true savings may occur for larger files. The time saving can be attributed to less authentication and encryption requirements; however, this highlights a potential security impact for a plain text SQL dump. Adequate firewall security for an internal network is an important consideration. Compression can also be included with these piped commands at either the source or destination host.

MySQL Enterprise Backup (MEB)

To achieve streaming with MEB, the [backup-to-image] option can be used in conjunction with writing the output to standout and using an appropriate piped output. For example:

```
$ time /opt/meb/bin/mysqlbackup --backup-dir=/mysql/backup/meb/stream \
    --backup-image=- backup-to-image | \
    ssh backup "cat - > /mysql/backup/meb/stream.tar"
MySQL Enterprise Backup version 3.7.0 [2011/12/19]
Copyright (c) 2003, 2011, Oracle and/or its affiliates. All Rights Reserved.
...
```

```
Backup Image Path= -
 mysqlbackup: INFO: Unique generated backup id for this is 13339848429520965
mysqlbackup: Can't seek in file 'UNOPENED' (Errcode: 29)
 mysqlbackup: INFO: Uses posix_fadvise() for performance optimization.
 mysqlbackup: INFO: System tablespace file format is Antelope.
 mysqlbackup: INFO: Found checkpoint at lsn 5702886491.
 mysqlbackup: INFO: Starting log scan from lsn 5702886400.
120409 15:20:42 mysqlbackup: INFO: Copying log...
120409 15:20:42 mysqlbackup: INFO: Log copied,lsn 5702886491.
         We wait 1 second before starting copying the data files...
120409 15:20:43 mysqlbackup: INFO: Copying /var/lib/mysql/ibdata1
(Antelope file format).
120409 15:20:44 mysqlbackup: INFO: Copying /var/lib/mysql/sakila/rental.ibd
 (Antelope file format).
120409 15:20:44 mysqlbackup: INFO: Copying /var/lib/mysql/sakila/language.ibd
 (Antelope file format).
120409 15:20:44 mysqlbackup: INFO: Copying /var/lib/mysql/sakila/customer.ibd
 (Antelope file format).
...
 mysqlbackup: INFO: Backup image created successfully.:
         Image Path: '-'
-------------------------------------------------------------
  Parameters Summary
-------------------------------------------------------------
  Start LSN              : 5702886400
  End LSN                : 5702891809
-------------------------------------------------------------
mysqlbackup completed OK!
real    2m37.681s
user    1m54.003s
sys     0m14.689s
$ ssh backup 'ls -lh /mysql/backup/meb/stream.tar'
-rw-rw-r-- 1 uid gid 4.2G 2012-04-09 15:23 /mysql/backup/meb/stream.tar
```

While you are performing a remote backup, MEB does require a local
working directory and it does leave files on the backup server.

```
$ time /opt/meb/bin/mysqlbackup --backup-image=- backup-to-image \
ssh backup "cat - > /mysql/backup/meb/stream.tar"
MySQL Enterprise Backup version 3.7.0 [2011/12/19]
Copyright (c) 2003, 2011, Oracle and/or its affiliates. All Rights Reserved.

Error: Backup to image operation also requires --backup-dir option;
  The specified directory is used to create temporary
  generated files.
  Note: Incremental backup-to-image operation also uses
  --backup-dir option, not --incremental-backup-dir.

$ du -sh /mysql/backup/meb/stream
540K    /mysql/backup/meb/stream
$ ls -l /mysql/backup/meb/stream/
total 12
-rw-rw-r-- 1 mysql mysql  190 2012-04-09 15:20 backup-my.cnf
drwx------ 9 mysql mysql 4096 2012-04-09 15:23 datadir
drwx------ 2 mysql mysql 4096 2012-04-09 15:23 meta
```

With MEB version 3.7 the `backup-to-image` backup feature now includes checksum verification to ensure the backup data remains unchanged during any transfers to other systems. Each file within the backup image is tested against a checksum calculated using the CRC32 algorithm, either when files are extracted from the backup image, or using the new mysqlbackup option `validate` to test a backup image without extracting.

MEB also provides streaming options to high-capacity storage devices using the System Backup to Tape (SBT) interface. This enables MEB to integrate with Oracle Secure Backup (OSB) or other compatible media management software (MMS) products to manage the backup and restore process. More information about the various `--sbt` options can be found at http://dev.mysql.com/doc/mysql-enterprise-backup/3.7/en/meb-backup-tape.html.

XtraBackup

To enable streaming with XtraBackup, the `--stream=tar` option is required and combined with one of the preceding examples. For example:

```
$ innobackupex --stream=tar ./ | ssh user@backup "cat - > /path/to/backup.tar"
```

The `--incremental` option is not applicable if specified with the `--stream` option. The `--stream` option will always produce a full backup.

The execution time and resulting backup size are comparable to a standard XtraBackup command as shown previously.

```
$ time innobackupex --defaults-file=/etc/mysql/my.cnf \
    --user=root --password=passwd --stream=tar ./ \
    > /mysql/backup/xtrabackup/third.tar
real    2m32.682s
user    0m21.009s
sys     0m8.833s
$ ls -lh /mysql/backup/xtrabackup/third.tar
-rw-rw-r-- 1 uid gid 5.4G 2012-04-03 04:09 third.tar
```

XtraBackup also provides a push of a backup to a remote host with the `--remote-host` option.

```
$ time innobackupex --defaults-file=/etc/mysql/my.cnf \
    --user=root --password=passwd \
    --no-timestamp --remote-host=backup \
    /mysql/backup/xtrabackup/remote
InnoDB Backup Utility v1.5.1-xtrabackup; Copyright 2003, 2009 Innobase Oy
and Percona Inc 2009-2012.  All Rights Reserved.

120409 14:50:47  innobackupex: Starting ibbackup with command: xtrabackup_51
--defaults-file="/etc/mysql/my.cnf" --backup --suspend-at-end --target-dir=/tmp
```

```
--log-stream
xtrabackup_51 version 1.9.2 for MySQL server 5.1.59 unknown-linux-gnu (x86_64)
xtrabackup: Log only mode.
>> log scanned up to (1 1407919195)
120409 14:50:49  innobackupex: Continuing after ibbackup has suspended
innobackupex: Starting to backup InnoDB tables and indexes
innobackupex: to '/mysql/backup/xtrabackup/remote'
innobackupex: from original InnoDB data directory '/var/lib/mysql'
innobackupex: Backing up file '/var/lib/mysql/ibdata1'
ibdata1      100%  18MB   9.0MB/s   00:02
innobackupex: Backing up files '/var/lib/mysql/sakila/*.ibd' (15 files)
actor.ibd    100%  112KB 112.0KB/s   00:00
>> log scanned up to (1 1407919195)
address.ibd  100%  160KB 160.0KB/s   00:00
category.ibd 100%   96KB  96.0KB/s   00:00


...
country.frm  100% 8638     8.4KB/s   00:00
db.opt       100%   65     0.1KB/s   00:00
120409 14:59:28  innobackupex: Finished backing up .frm, .MRG, .MYD, .MYI,
.TRG, .TRN, .ARM, .ARZ, .CSV, .CSM and .opt files
innobackupex: Resuming ibbackup
xtrabackup: The latest check point (for incremental): '1:1407919195'
xtrabackup: Stopping log copying thread.
.>>log scanned up to (1 1407919195)
xtrabackup: Transaction log of lsn (1 1407919195) to (1 1407919195) was copied.
120409 14:59:30  innobackupex: All tables unlocked
120409 14:59:30  innobackupex: Connection to database server closed
xtrabackup_logfile 100% 2560     2.5KB/s   00:00
xtrabackup_checkpoints 100%  89     0.1KB/s   00:00
innobackupex: Backup created in directory '/mysql/backup/xtrabackup/remote'
innobackupex: MySQL binlog position: filename 'mysql-bin.000062',
position 106
120409 14:59:31  innobackupex: completed OK!

real    8m54.157s
user    7m29.480s
sys     0m22.377s
$ du -sh /mysql/backup/xtrabackup/remote
du: cannot access '/mysql/backup/xtrabackup/remote': No such file or directory
$ ssh backup 'du -sh /mysql/backup/xtrabackup/remote'
4.2G    /mysql/backup/xtrabackup/remote
```

For more information and other examples see http://www.percona.com/
doc/percona-xtrabackup/howtos/recipes_ibkx_stream.html.

Remote Backups

In the previous section it was possible to push a MySQL backup to an external
server. With all client/server backup options it is possible to pull a MySQL
backup from the database server. One of the benefits of this process is the

necessary access requirements. In a pull process the only permissions on the database server are the necessary MySQL permissions and firewall access to the MySQL port; no operating system user is necessary.

mysqldump

Using the `--host` option enables the `mysqldump` command to connect to a remote server.

The use of `--compress` can provide some assistance in client/server network communications of the data; however, this does not result in a compressed backup file.

```
$ time mysqldump -u<user> -p<password> --host db-server --compress \
  --all-databases > backup.sql
Using the
$ time mysqldump -h10.0.0.1 --all-databases > /mysql/backup/ldump1.sql
real    1m39.484s
user    1m3.252s
sys     0m24.906s
$ time mysqldump -h10.0.0.1 --all-databases --compress >\
     /mysql/backup/ldump1c.sql
real    4m45.219s
user    1m34.762s
sys     0m13.857s
$ ls -lh /mysql/backup/ldump*
-rw-rw-r-- 1 uid gid 2.9G 2012-04-03 04:59 ldump1c.sql
-rw-rw-r-- 1 uid gid 2.9G 2012-04-03 04:54 ldump1.sql
```

Surprisingly, the use of the `--compress` option results in a much slower backup.

MySQL Enterprise Backup (MEB)

MEB does not support connecting to a remote host.

NOTE   While MEB has a `--host` configuration option, this is used only for the validation of parsing this option when it exists in a [client] configuration section without producing an error message during execution.

XtraBackup

XtraBackup does not support connecting to a remote host.

Parallel Processing

Using the default `mysqldump` command has the limitation of being a single threaded process. This is particularly important during the restoration process of a large database. While `mysqldump` natively does not support parallel processing, the open source mydumper provides a suitable replacement.

mydumper

Mydumper (http://www.mydumper.org/) is a high-performance MySQL backup and restore toolset released under the GNU GPLv3 license. Domas Mituzas, Andrew Hutchings, and Mark Leith created the mydumper toolset for use in both MySQL and Drizzle. Mydumper was created as a tool that competes with the mysqldump client program. Although there are many installations currently using mysqldump, it can be slow considering that it is not multi-threaded.

Given that mydumper is multi-threaded it can create a MySQL backup much faster than the mysqldump tool distributed with MySQL. Mydumper also has the capability to retrieve the binary logs from a remote server. Copying the binary logs at the same time as the dump has the advantage of supporting a point in time backup.

The major advantages of mydumper are as follows:

- Multi-threaded, which makes dumping data much faster.

- Mydumper output is easy to manage and parse because there are separate files for tables and meta-data.

- All threads maintain a consistent snapshot that provides accurate master and slave positions.

- Mydumper supports Perl Regular Expressions (PCRE), which enable pattern matching for database names and table names to be included or excluded.

- The mydumper toolset also comes with the ability to restore data from a mydumper backup through the multi-threaded tool called myloader.

Installation

Mydumper must be compiled from source code. This will require a system that has a C++ compiler available. Additional dependencies include:

- CMake

- Glib2 with development packages

- PCRE with development packages

- MySQL client libraries and development packages

Refer to http://docs.mydumper.org/compiling.html for operating specific commands to install these dependencies.

The following commands were used for an Ubuntu environment:

```
$ sudo apt-get install -y make cmake g++
$ sudo apt-get install -y libglib2.0-dev libmysqlclient-dev zlib1g-dev \
libpcre3-dev
$ wget http://launchpad.net/mydumper/0.2/0.2.3/+download/mydumper-0.2.3.tar.gz
$ tar xvfz mydumper-0.2.3.tar.gz
$ cd mydumper-0.2.3/
$ cmake .
$ make
$ ./mydumper -help
$ sudo cp mydumper /usr/local/bin
```

NOTE *The current stable version is 0.2.3. The current development version is 0.5.1. This development version includes additional options for enabling daemon mode, defining an interval between snapshots, and an output log file option.*

Usage

On an operational MySQL system, mydumper can operate with no arguments and will attempt to connect to MySQL via the local socket file. For example:

```
$ mkdir /mysql/backup/mydumper
$ cd /mysql/backup/mydumper
$ time mydumper
real    1m55.070s
user    0m39.198s
sys     0m7.864s
$ echo $?
```

No output is produced to indicate success or failure, or to provide details of the export produced. By default a directory with a name of export-[date/time] will be produced.

```
$ ls -ld export-*
drwx------ 2 uid gid 12288 2012-04-07 19:24 export-20120407-192341
$ du -sh export-20120407-192341/
2.9G    export-20120407-192341/
```

During the backup you can monitor the multiple threads with the SHOW PROCESSLIST command. For example:

```
mysql> SHOW PROCESSLIST
|  97 |52 |                     | NULL
|  98 | 6 | Writing to net   | SELECT ... * FROM 'musicbrainz'.'track_name' |
|  99 |29 | Sending data     | SELECT ... * FROM 'musicbrainz'.'recording' |
| 100 | 7 | Writing to net   | SELECT ... * FROM 'musicbrainz'.'track'     |
| 101 |29 | Writing to net   | SELECT ... * FROM 'musicbrainz'.'release'   |
```

Running in verbose mode produces additional output; however, the full output directory is not included in the information provided:

```
$ ./mydumper -v 3
** Message: Connected to a MySQL server
** Message: Started dump at: 2012-04-07 19:31:42

** Message: Written master status
** Message: Thread 3 dumping data for 'mysql'.'backup_progress'
** Message: Thread 1 dumping data for 'mysql'.'backup_history'
** Message: Thread 1 dumping data for 'mysql'.'event'
** Message: Thread 3 dumping data for 'mysql'.'func'
** Message: Thread 3 dumping data for 'mysql'.'general_log'
...
** Message: Thread 3 dumping data for 'world_myisam'.'City'
** Message: Thread 1 dumping data for 'world_myisam'.'Country'
** Message: Thread 4 dumping data for 'world_myisam'.'CountryLanguage'
** Message: Thread 4 dumping data for 'employees'.'departments'
** Message: Thread 4 dumping data for 'employees'.'dept_emp'
** Message: Thread 2 dumping data for 'employees'.'dept_manager'
** Message: Thread 2 dumping data for 'employees'.'employees'
** Message: Thread 1 dumping data for 'employees'.'salaries'
** Message: Non-InnoDB dump complete, unlocking tables
** Message: Thread 3 dumping data for 'employees'.'titles'
** Message: Thread 4 dumping data for 'musicbrainz'.'artist'
** Message: Thread 3 dumping data for 'musicbrainz'.'artist_credit'
...
** Message: Thread 2 dumping data for 'musicbrainz'.'release_group'
** Message: Thread 3 shutting down
** Message: Thread 1 shutting down
** Message: Thread 4 shutting down
** Message: Thread 2 shutting down
** Message: Finished dump at: 2012-04-07 19:34:50
```

The output provides some additional insight into the operation. As shown by the message, non-InnoDB tables are backed first to improve locking during the entire dump process.

The following example uses the regular expression options to exclude any mysql and test schema objects.

```
$ ./mydumper --user root --regex '^(?!(mysql|test))'
```

Compression

By default all output files are uncompressed. By using the -c option, all files will be compressed, producing a much smaller database backup. All files in the directory are compressed with gzip.

```
$ time /home/ubuntu/mydumper-0.2.3/mydumper -c
real     3m7.203s
user     4m49.802s
sys      0m4.636s
$ du -sh export-20120407-*
2.9G     export-20120407-192341
903M     export-20120407-192605
```

More Information

Mydumper generates several files pertaining to meta-data, table data, table schemas, and binary logs.

The .metadata file stores the start and end times of the dump as well as the master binary log position. When a dump is executed a .metadata file is created in the output directory.

```
$ LAST_EXPORT='ls -dtr export-* | tail -1'
$ cat $LAST_EXPORT/.metadata
Started dump at: 2012-04-07 19:26:05
SHOW MASTER STATUS:
    Log: mysql-bin.000017
    Pos: 106

Finished dump at: 2012-04-07 19:29:12
```

Table data can be stored in two different ways, one file with all table data or many files with chunks of data for one table. If the --rows option is added to the command, then many files will be created for one table with a naming convention like database.table.chunk.sql. If the --rows option is not specified, one file per table will be create with a naming convention like database.table.sql.

```
$ ls -lh export-20120407-192341 | more
total 2.9G
...
-rw-rw-r-- 1 uid gid  207 2012-04-07 19:24 musicbrainz.gender-schema.sql
-rw-rw-r-- 1 uid gid  133 2012-04-07 19:23 musicbrainz.gender.sql
-rw-rw-r-- 1 uid gid  471 2012-04-07 19:24 musicbrainz.medium-schema.sql
-rw-rw-r-- 1 uid gid  74M 2012-04-07 19:23 musicbrainz.medium.sql
-rw-rw-r-- 1 uid gid  445 2012-04-07 19:24 musicbrainz.recording-schema.sql
-rw-rw-r-- 1 uid gid 910M 2012-04-07 19:25 musicbrainz.recording.sql
-rw-rw-r-- 1 uid gid  424 2012-04-07 19:24 musicbrainz.release_group-schema.sql
```

When using the compression option, all files are included:

```
$ ls -lh export-20120407-192605 | more
total 903M
...
-rw-rw-r-- 1 uid gid  190 2012-04-07 19:27 musicbrainz.gender-schema.sql.gz
-rw-rw-r-- 1 uid gid  139 2012-04-07 19:26 musicbrainz.gender.sql.gz
-rw-rw-r-- 1 uid gid  275 2012-04-07 19:27 musicbrainz.medium-schema.sql.gz
-rw-rw-r-- 1 uid gid  13M 2012-04-07 19:26 musicbrainz.medium.sql.gz
-rw-rw-r-- 1 uid gid  270 2012-04-07 19:27 musicbrainz.recording-schema.sql.gz
-rw-rw-r-- 1 uid gid 368M 2012-04-07 19:29 musicbrainz.recording.sql.gz
```

Table schemas are created by default and stored in individual files named databases.table-schema.sql. These files can be removed from the dump process with the --no-schemas option. There is no companion option to produce only the schema objects. You should use mysqldump for this functionality.

When the --binlogs option is used mydumper will store binary logs in a sub-directory inside the dump directory unless otherwise specified by the --binlog-outdir option. Binary logs will have the same filename as the MySQL server that supplies them. The meta-file will also reflect the current master position:

```
$  ls -lh export-20120407-230027/binlog_snapshot/
total 2.7G
-rw-r--r-- 1 uid gid  168 2012-04-07 23:01 mysql-bin.000001
-rw-r--r-- 1 uid gid  168 2012-04-07 23:01 mysql-bin.000002
...
-rw-r--r-- 1 uid gid  17K 2012-04-07 23:02 mysql-bin.000012
-rw-r--r-- 1 uid gid  13K 2012-04-07 23:02 mysql-bin.000013
-rw-r--r-- 1 uid gid  149 2012-04-07 23:02 mysql-bin.000014
-rw-r--r-- 1 uid gid  149 2012-04-07 23:02 mysql-bin.000015
-rw-r--r-- 1 uid gid  149 2012-04-07 23:02 mysql-bin.000016
-rw-r--r-- 1 uid gid 8.2K 2012-04-07 23:02 mysql-bin.000017

$ cat export-20120407-230027/metadata
Started dump at: 2012-04-07 23:00:27
SHOW MASTER STATUS:
    Log: mysql-bin.000017
    Pos: 8328

Finished dump at: 2012-04-07 23:02:56
```

XtraBackup

Parallel copying for a local backup with XtraBackup is possible when multiple InnoDB data files exist, either from using the innodb_file_per_table configuration option or when multiple data files in the `innodb_data_file_` `path` configuration option exist. Parallel processing is enabled by adding the `--parallel` option to the backup process. For example:

```
$ time innobackupex --defaults-file=/etc/mysql/my.cnf \
--user=root --password=passwd --no-timestamp --parallel 3 \
/mysql/backup/xtrabackup/parallel

InnoDB Backup Utility v1.5.1-xtrabackup; Copyright 2003, 2009 Innobase Oy
...
xtrabackup: Starting 3 threads for parallel data files transfer
[01] Copying ./ibdata1 to /mysql/backup/xtrabackup/parallel/ibdata1
[03] Copying ./sakila/rental.ibd to
 /mysql/backup/xtrabackup/parallel/./sakila/rental.ibd
[02] Copying ./sakila/language.ibd to
 /mysql/backup/xtrabackup/parallel/./sakila/language.ibd
[02]         ...done
[02] Copying ./sakila/customer.ibd to
/mysql/backup/xtrabackup/parallel/./sakila/customer.ibd
[02]         ...done
[01]         ...done
[03]         ...done
[02] Copying ./sakila/inventory.ibd to
/mysql/backup/xtrabackup/parallel/./sakila/inventory.ibd
[01] Copying ./sakila/film.ibd to
 /mysql/backup/xtrabackup/parallel/./sakila/film.ibd
[03] Copying ./sakila/city.ibd to
 /mysql/backup/xtrabackup/parallel/./sakila/city.ibd
[02]         ...done
[03]         ...done
[01]         ...done
[02] Copying ./sakila/category.ibd to
 /mysql/backup/xtrabackup/parallel/./sakila/category.ibd
[03] Copying ./sakila/country.ibd to
 /mysql/backup/xtrabackup/parallel/./sakila/country.ibd
[02]         ...done
[03]         ...done
[01] Copying ./sakila/film_category.ibd to
 /mysql/backup/xtrabackup/parallel/./sakila/film_category.ibd
[02] Copying ./sakila/store.ibd to
/mysql/backup/xtrabackup/parallel/./sakila/store.ibd
[03] Copying ./sakila/staff.ibd to
 /mysql/backup/xtrabackup/parallel/./sakila/staff.ibd
[02]         ...done
[03]         ...done
[01]         ...done
[01] Copying ./sakila/address.ibd to
 /mysql/backup/xtrabackup/parallel/./sakila/address.ibd
[02] Copying ./sakila/film_actor.ibd to
/mysql/backup/xtrabackup/parallel/./sakila/film_actor.ibd
[03] Copying ./sakila/actor.ibd to
/mysql/backup/xtrabackup/parallel/./sakila/actor.ibd
[03]         ...done
```

```
[01]         ...done
[03] Copying ./sakila/payment.ibd to
/mysql/backup/xtrabackup/parallel/./sakila/payment.ibd
[02]         ...done
...
120408 04:59:58 innobackupex: Finished backing up .frm, .MRG, .MYD, .MYI,
.TRG, .TRN, .ARM, .ARZ, .CSV, .CSM and .opt files

innobackupex: Resuming ibbackup

xtrabackup: The latest check point (for incremental): '1:1355186644'
xtrabackup: Stopping log copying thread.
.>>log scanned up to (1 1355186644)

xtrabackup: Transaction log of lsn (1 1355186644) to (1 1355186644) was copied.
120408 05:00:00 innobackupex: All tables unlocked
120408 05:00:00 innobackupex: Connection to database server closed

innobackupex: Backup created in directory '/mysql/backup/xtrabackup/parallel'
innobackupex: MySQL binlog position: filename 'mysql-bin.000060',
position 49717825
120408 05:00:00 innobackupex: completed OK!

real    1m54.351s
user    0m17.221s
sys     0m11.585s
```

Incremental Backups

In addition to performing a full backup of your MySQL database, several options exist to perform incremental backups. These can reduce the time to perform a backup and the size of backup files; however, a restore process will be more complex and may be more time consuming.

The choice for using a full backup versus an incremental backup can depend also on physical resources. The added steps during the restore process may introduce an additional chance of error under a crisis situation. The simplicity of a full server restore may also be more easily automated.

Depending on the volume and rate of change of data, an incremental backup may result in a smaller backup; however, it may take a similar amount of time to execute.

MySQL Enterprise Backup (MEB)

With the `--incremental` option and either the `--incremental-base` option or the `--start-lsn` of an appropriate backup, an incremental backup can be performed. For example:

```
$ time /opt/meb/bin/mysqlbackup --incremental \
--incremental-base=dir:/mysql/backup/meb/first \
--incremental-backup-dir=/mysql/backup/meb/first-inc backup
MySQL Enterprise Backup version 3.7.0 [2011/12/19]
Copyright (c) 2003, 2011, Oracle and/or its affiliates. All Rights Reserved.
...

mysqlbackup: INFO: Using start_lsn=6374639598, calculated from
backup_history table of MySQL server and backup_variables.txt file of
incremental-base backup.
 mysqlbackup: INFO: Found checkpoint at lsn 6529488284.
 mysqlbackup: INFO: Starting log scan from lsn 6529487872.
120407 20:19:19 mysqlbackup: INFO: Copying log...
120407 20:19:19 mysqlbackup: INFO: Log copied, lsn 6529488284.
         We wait 1 second before starting copying the data files...
120407 20:19:20 mysqlbackup: INFO: Copying /var/lib/mysql/ibdata1
(Antelope file format).
mysqlbackup: Progress in MB: 200 400 600 800 1000 ... 5000 5200 5400
 mysqlbackup: INFO: Preparing to lock tables: Connected to mysqld server.
120407 20:20:14 mysqlbackup: INFO: Starting to lock all the tables....
120407 20:20:15 mysqlbackup: INFO: All tables are locked and flushed to disk
 mysqlbackup: INFO: Opening backup source directory '/var/lib/mysql/'
120407 20:20:15 mysqlbackup: INFO: Starting to backup all files in
subdirectories of '/var/lib/mysql/'
 mysqlbackup: INFO: Backing up the database directory 'book2'
 mysqlbackup: INFO: Backing up the database directory 'employees'
 mysqlbackup: INFO: Backing up the database directory 'musicbrainz'
 mysqlbackup: INFO: Backing up the database directory 'mysql'
 mysqlbackup: INFO: Backing up the database directory 'sakila'
 mysqlbackup: INFO: Backing up the database directory 'world_innodb'
 mysqlbackup: INFO: Backing up the database directory 'world_myisam'
 mysqlbackup: INFO: Copying innodb data and logs during final stage ...
 mysqlbackup: INFO: A copied database page was modified at 6529488284.
         (This is the highest lsn found on page)
         Scanned log up to lsn 6529491094.
         Was able to parse the log up to lsn 6529491094.
         Maximum page number for a log record 262152
120407 20:20:15 mysqlbackup: INFO: All tables unlocked
 mysqlbackup: INFO: All MySQL tables were locked for 0.000 seconds
 mysqlbackup: INFO: Backup contains changes from lsn 6374639599
to lsn 6529491094
120407 20:20:15 mysqlbackup: INFO: Incremental backup completed!
 mysqlbackup: INFO: MySQL binlog position: filename mysql-bin.000017,
position 5555
 mysqlbackup: INFO: Backup created in directory
'/mysql/backup/meb/first-inc'

-------------------------------------------------------------
   Parameters Summary
-------------------------------------------------------------
   Start LSN                  : 6374639599
   End LSN                    : 6529491094
-------------------------------------------------------------
```

```
mysqlbackup completed OK!

real    0m56.133s
user    0m17.561s
sys     0m3.992s
```

The backup directory is significantly smaller than the previous full backup. The saving is in the ibdata1 tablespace file, which is not the full size.

```
$ du -sh /mysql/backup/meb/first*
5.6G    /mysql/backup/meb/first
92M     /mysql/backup/meb/first-inc
$ ls -lh /mysql/backup/meb/first-inc/datadir/
total 90M
drwx------ 2 uid gid 4.0K 2012-04-07 20:20 book2
drwx------ 2 uid gid 4.0K 2012-04-07 20:20 employees
-rw-rw-r-- 1 uid gid    0 2012-04-07 20:20 ibbackup_ibd_files
-rw-rw---- 1 uid gid 4.0K 2012-04-07 20:20 ibbackup_logfile
-rw-rw-r-- 1 uid gid  90M 2012-04-07 20:20 ibdata1
drwx------ 2 uid gid 4.0K 2012-04-07 20:20 musicbrainz
drwx------ 2 uid gid 4.0K 2012-04-07 20:20 mysql
drwx------ 2 uid gid 4.0K 2012-04-07 20:20 sakila
drwx------ 2 uid gid 4.0K 2012-04-07 20:20 world_innodb
drwx------ 2 uid gid 4.0K 2012-04-07 20:20 world_myisam
```

The --incremental option is for InnoDB tables, or for infrequent updates of non-InnoDB tables. If a non-InnoDB table has been modified, the entire file is included in the backup. The --incremental option is incompatible with the --compress option and also with the backup-and-apply-log command.

Producing a Full Restore

In order to utilize an incremental backup, this has to be applied to the full backup with the apply-incremental-backup command. For example:

```
$ time /opt/meb/bin/mysqlbackup \
    --backup-dir=/mysql/backup/meb/first \
    --incremental-backup-dir=/mysql/backup/meb/first-inc \
    apply-incremental-backup
MySQL Enterprise Backup version 3.7.0 [2011/12/19]
Copyright (c) 2003, 2011, Oracle and/or its affiliates. All Rights Reserved.

120407 21:29:40 mysqlbackup: INFO: Copying all non-InnoDB files in
subdirectories of
 mysqlbackup: INFO: '/mysql/backup/meb/first-inc/datadir'
 mysqlbackup: INFO: to the corresponding subdirectories in
 mysqlbackup: INFO: '/mysql/backup/meb/first/datadir'
 mysqlbackup: INFO: Copying file '/mysql/backup/meb/first-
inc/datadir/book2/album.frm'
 ...
```

```
mysqlbackup: INFO: Copying file '/mysql/backup/meb/first-inc/datadir/world_
myisam/CountryLanguage.frm'
mysqlbackup: INFO: Copying file '/mysql/backup/meb/first-
inc/datadir/world_myisam/db.opt'
mysqlbackup: INFO: Checking for deleted databases and non-InnoDB files
120407 21:29:40 mysqlbackup: INFO: Finished copying all non-InnoDB files
mysqlbackup: INFO: incremental backup to the full backup.
mysqlbackup: INFO: Uses posix_fadvise() for performance optimization.
mysqlbackup: INFO: ibbackup: Progress in MB:
120407 21:29:43 mysqlbackup: INFO:  ibbackup_logfile's creation parameters:
        start lsn 6529487872, end lsn 6529491094,
        start checkpoint 6529488284.
InnoDB: Doing recovery: scanned up to log sequence number 6529491094
InnoDB: Starting an apply batch of log records to the database...
InnoDB: Progress in percents: 0 1 2 3 4 5 6 .. 94 95 96 97 98 99
Setting log file size to 0 134217728
InnoDB: Progress in MB: 100
Setting log file size to 0 134217728
InnoDB: Progress in MB: 100
120407 21:29:50 mysqlbackup: INFO: We were able to parse ibbackup_logfile
up to lsn 6529491094.
ibbackup: Last MySQL binlog file position 0 5555, file name ./mysql-bin.000017
120407 21:29:50 mysqlbackup: INFO: The first data file is '/mysql/backup/meb/
first/datadir/ibdata1'
and the new created log files are at '/mysql/backup/meb/first/datadir/'
 mysqlbackup: INFO: System tablespace file format is Antelope.
120407 21:29:50 mysqlbackup: INFO: Incremental backup applied successfully!
mysqlbackup completed OK!

real    0m10.685s
user    0m0.020s
sys     0m0.908s
```

For more information visit the MEB Reference Manual at http://dev
.mysql.com/doc/mysql-enterprise-backup/3.7/en/mysqlbackup
.incremental.html and the blog post at https://blogs.oracle.com/MySQL/
entry/mysql_enterprise_backup_taking_incremental.

MEB also provides an alternative means of producing an incremental
backup with the `--incremental-with-redo-log-only` option. This
option uses the InnoDB transactional log files and requires that all information is still contained within these circular files. See more details from the
MEB Reference Manual at http://dev.mysql.com/doc/mysql-enterprise-
backup/3.7/en/backup-incremental-options.html and the blog post at
https://blogs.oracle.com/MySQL/entry/mysql_enterprise_backup_
redo_log.

XtraBackup

XtraBackup supports the ability to perform an incremental backup with the
`--incremental` and `--incremental-basedir` options. A previous full
backup is required to perform an incremental backup. For example:

```
$ time innobackupex --defaults-file=/etc/mysql/my.cnf \
--user=root --password=passwd --no-timestamp \
/mysql/backup/xtrabackup/first
...
xtrabackup: Transaction log of lsn (1 2234524172) to (1 2234524172) was copied.
120408 02:34:13  innobackupex: All tables unlocked
120408 02:34:13  innobackupex: Connection to database server closed
innobackupex: Backup created in directory '/mysql/backup/xtrabackup/first'
innobackupex: MySQL binlog position: filename 'mysql-bin.000001',
position 37522
120408 02:34:13  innobackupex: completed OK!

real    2m30.667s
user    0m21.933s
sys     0m14.713s
```

An incremental backup can now be created:

```
$ time innobackupex --user=root --password=passwd \
--defaults-file=/etc/mysql/my.cnf \
--incremental-basedir=/mysql/backup/xtrabackup/first \
--incremental --no-timestamp /mysql/backup/xtrabackup/first-inc
...
[01] Copying ./ibdata1 to /mysql/backup/xtrabackup/first-inc/ibdata1.delta
...
innobackupex: Backup created in directory '/mysql/backup/xtrabackup/first-inc'
innobackupex: MySQL binlog position: filename 'mysql-bin.000001',
position 41912727
120408 03:04:27  innobackupex: completed OK!

real    1m22.469s
user    0m20.345s
sys     0m1.592s
```

The output will show a delta of the InnoDB common tablespace files was
generated:

```
$ ls -lh /mysql/backup/xtrabackup/first-inc
...
-rw-rw---- 1 uid gid 58M 2012-04-08 03:04 ibdata1.delta
...
```

Two additional steps are required to apply the incremental backup to the
full backup to enable the successful restore of this backup:

```
$ time innobackupex --user=root --password=passwd \
  --defaults-file=/etc/mysql/my.cnf --apply-log --redo-only \
  /mysql/backup/xtrabackup/first
...
xtrabackup: cd to /mysql/backup/xtrabackup/first
xtrabackup: This target seems to be already prepared.
xtrabackup: notice: xtrabackup_logfile was already used to '--prepare'.
xtrabackup: Temporary instance for recovery is set as followings.
xtrabackup:   innodb_data_home_dir = ./
xtrabackup:   innodb_data_file_path = ibdata1:5000M:autoextend
xtrabackup:   innodb_log_group_home_dir = ./
xtrabackup:   innodb_log_files_in_group = 2
xtrabackup:   innodb_log_file_size = 134217728
xtrabackup: Starting InnoDB instance for recovery.
xtrabackup: Using 104857600 bytes for buffer pool
(set by --use-memory parameter)
InnoDB: The InnoDB memory heap is disabled
120408  3:55:51  InnoDB: Initializing buffer pool, size = 100.0M
120408  3:55:51  InnoDB: Completed initialization of buffer pool
InnoDB: Last MySQL binlog file position 0 5555, file name ./mysql-bin.000017
120408  3:55:51  InnoDB: Starting shutdown...
120408  3:55:52  InnoDB: Shutdown completed; log sequence number 1 2234524684
120408 03:55:52  innobackupex: completed OK!

real    0m0.736s
user    0m0.128s
sys     0m0.084s

$ time innobackupex --user=root --password=passwd \
  --defaults-file=/etc/mysql/my.cnf --apply-log \
  /mysql/backup/xtrabackup/first \
--incremental-dir=/mysql/backup/xtrabackup/first-inc
InnoDB Backup Utility v1.5.1-xtrabackup; Copyright 2003, 2009 Innobase Oy
and Percona Inc 2009-2012.  All Rights Reserved.
xtrabackup_51 version 1.9.2 for MySQL server 5.1.59 unknown-linux-gnu (x86_64)
incremental backup from 1:2234524172 is enabled.
xtrabackup: cd to /mysql/backup/xtrabackup/first
xtrabackup: This target seems to be already prepared.
xtrabackup: xtrabackup_logfile detected: size=2359296, start_lsn=(1 2325677247)
xtrabackup: page size for /mysql/backup/xtrabackup/first-inc/ibdata1.delta
is 16384 bytes
Applying /mysql/backup/xtrabackup/first-inc/ibdata1.delta ...
xtrabackup: Temporary instance for recovery is set as followings.
xtrabackup:   innodb_data_home_dir = ./
xtrabackup:   innodb_data_file_path = ibdata1:5000M:autoextend
xtrabackup:   innodb_log_group_home_dir = /mysql/backup/xtrabackup/first-inc
xtrabackup:   innodb_log_files_in_group = 1
xtrabackup:   innodb_log_file_size = 2359296
xtrabackup: Starting InnoDB instance for recovery.
xtrabackup: Using 104857600 bytes for buffer pool (set by --use-memory
parameter)
InnoDB: The InnoDB memory heap is disabled
```

```
120408  4:00:49  InnoDB: Initializing buffer pool, size = 100.0M
120408  4:00:49  InnoDB: Completed initialization of buffer pool
InnoDB: The log sequence number in ibdata files does not match
InnoDB: the log sequence number in the ib_logfiles!
120408  4:00:49  InnoDB: Database was not shut down normally!
InnoDB: Starting crash recovery.
InnoDB: Reading tablespace information from the .ibd files...
InnoDB: Last MySQL binlog file position 0 41912727, file name ./mysql-bin.000001
120408  4:00:51  InnoDB: Started; log sequence number 1 2325677247
InnoDB: Last MySQL binlog file position 0 41912727, file name ./mysql-bin.000001
120408  4:00:51  InnoDB: Starting shutdown...
120408  4:00:54  InnoDB: Shutdown completed; log sequence number 1 2325677247
innobackupex: Starting to copy non-InnoDB files in
 '/mysql/backup/xtrabackup/first-inc'
innobackupex: to the full backup directory '/mysql/backup/xtrabackup/first'
innobackupex: Copying file '/mysql/backup/xtrabackup/first/
xtrabackup_binlog_info'
innobackupex: Copying file '/mysql/backup/xtrabackup/first/ibdata1'
...
innobackupex: Copying file '/mysql/backup/xtrabackup/first/artist.frm'
innobackupex: Copying file '/mysql/backup/xtrabackup/first/album.frm'
120408 04:03:44  innobackupex: completed OK!

real    2m56.405s
user    0m0.300s
sys     0m13.709s
```

The end result is a complete backup in the original full backup directory that contains all information from the incremental backup.

Partial Backups

Generally for a backup and recovery strategy, partial backups are not practical due to absence of some data. A relational database also defines consistency with database constraints, including foreign keys, which may not be included in a partial backup. These options, however, may be of benefit in a partial data recovery process for a corrupt or dropped table, or for convenience in testing.

A partial backup may be practical in an ETL process when only a subset of data is necessary and additional data can be regenerated without a backup. This can be an optimization that saves backup space and time.

mysqldump

The mysqldump command allows for the specification of various database schemas or tables with the --databases and --tables options.

MySQL Enterprise Backup (MEB)

MEB supports the ability to perform partial backups. These options include `--only-innodb`, `--only-innodb-with-frm`, `--only-known-file-types`, `--databases`, `--databases-list-path`, and `--include`. For more information see http://dev.mysql.com/doc/mysql-enterprise-backup/3.7/en/backup-partial-options.html.

XtraBackup

XtraBackup provides an export of an individual InnoDB and XtraDB table with the `--export` option; however, an import is only possible with Percona Server using XtraDB.

More information can be found at http://www.percona.com/doc/percona-xtrabackup/innobackupex/importing_exporting_tables_ibk.html.

MySQL Backup Security

Throughout these examples the topic of appropriate MySQL security has not been discussed. This is an important consideration for any complete backup and recovery strategy. A recent poll at the 2012 annual MySQL conference highlighted that very few organizations use SSL for accessing MySQL data.

MySQL provides SSL support for client connections, for example a remote backup, and for MySQL replication. In Chapter 3 of *Effective MySQL: Advanced Replication Techniques*, SSL usage is described in detail. The following sections can be found in the MySQL Reference Manual.

- Client connections – http://dev.mysql.com/doc/refman/5.5/en/secure-connections.html

- Replication – http://dev.mysql.com/doc/refman/5.5/en/replication-solutions-ssl.html

With the wider adoption of MySQL in the Cloud as discussed in Chapter 9, the use of SSL for client communications and MySQL replication will become an important requirement. It is possible to encrypt files created on a production server before network transfer with generally available utilities including `openssl` and `gpg`.

Using transparent encryption techniques can provide a level of adequate security on the filesystem and can be integrated into the existing MySQL backup and recovery options with little impact. The ezNcrypt product from Gazzang (http://www.gazzang.com/) is one offering that provides examples for implementation with MySQL. This blog post by Mike Frank provides an introduction: http://mikefrank.wordpress.com/tag/mysql-mysqldump-ezncrypt-gazzang-linux-backup-xtrabackup-transparent-encryption/.

Encryption with ezNcrypt

The following steps demonstrate how to set up a `mysqldump` encrypted backup with ezNcrypt. You can request a free trial evaluation of the software from http://blog.gazzang.com/request-a-free-trial-of-ezncrypt/. Following installation and configuration, the first step is to verify the ezNcrypt process is running:

```
$ sudo ezncrypt-service status
  ezncrypt | Checking system dependencies
** ezncrypt system is UP and running **
      log | File: /var/log/ezncrypt/ezncrypt-service.log
```

If the process is not running you would find the following error message:

```
$ sudo ezncrypt-service status
  ezncrypt | Checking system dependencies
** ezncrypt system is NOT running **
      log | File: /var/log/ezncrypt/ezncrypt-service.log
$ sudo ezncrypt-service start
  ezncrypt | Checking system dependencies
  ezncrypt | checking encryption directories
   keymgr | Retrieving key from KSS
          |  > Encryption password retrieved from KSS
  ezncrypt | starting service
          |  > using "aes_256" cipher algorithm
          | done!
   access | Loading access control list
          | done!
  ezncrypt | Thank you for using ezncrypt.
      log | File: /var/log/ezncrypt/ezncrypt-service.log
```

Under the covers you will find the following attached devices, and no actual processes.

```
$ df -h
Filesystem ...
...
/var/lib/ezncrypt/storage/encrypted_private
/var/lib/ezncrypt/ezncrypted
$ ps -ef | grep ezn
uid  4947  3327  0 23:15 pts/3     00:00:00 grep ezn
$ ps -ef | grep cry
```

```
root           30     2   0 21:41 ?          00:00:00 [ecryptfs-kthrea]
root           31     2   0 21:41 ?          00:00:00 [crypto]
uid  4951   3327   0 23:15 pts/3     00:00:00 grep cry
```

The first step is to create a backup directory and encrypt all contents that are placed in the directory. ezNcrypt uses the concept of an @category for reference with an encrypted file or directory.

```
$ mkdir /mysql/backup/ezncrypt
$ sudo ezncrypt --encrypt @backup /mysql/backup/encrypted
   ezncrypt | Checking system dependencies
            | Verifying ezncrypt license
            | getting information about location
            |   > path: /var/lib/ezncrypt/ezncrypted/backup
   ezncrypt | Checking encryption status
            | done!
     keymgr | Retrieving key from KSS
            |   > Encryption password retrieved from KSS
            | generating keys
            | done!
     backup | backing up data
            | This can take a while. Please be patient
            |   > backing up /mysql/backup/encrypted
            |   > File: /opt/ezncrypt/backup/2012-04-27/encrypted.tar.gz
            | done!
   ezncrypt | encrypting files
            |   > checking disk space
            |   > encrypting /mysql/backup/encrypted
            | done!
   ezncrypt | congratulations. you have encrypted your Files!!
        log | File: /var/log/ezncrypt/ezncrypt.log
```

The underlying regular directory is now replaced:

```
$ ls -l /mysql/backup
total 0
lrwxrwxrwx 1 root root 59 2012-04-27 00:03 encrypted ->
/var/lib/ezncrypt/ezncrypted/backup//mysql/backup/encrypted
```

Any attempts to write to this directory will fail, even with the Linux super user:

```
$ mysqldump --all-databases > /mysql/backup/encrypted/edump1.sql
-bash: /mysql/backup/encrypted/edump1.sql: Permission denied
$ sudo mysqldump --all-databases > /mysql/backup/encrypted/edump1.sql
-bash: /mysql/backup/encrypted/edump1.sql: Permission denied
```

mysqldump

In order to read and write from an encrypted directory you need to grant access controls to a given program, for example `mysqldump`:

```
$ sudo ezncrypt-access-control -a "ALLOW @backup * /usr/bin/mysqldump"
passphrase:
salt:
Rule added
```

You verify the defined access control rules with:

```
$ sudo ezncrypt-access-control -L
passphrase:
salt:
# -   Type      Category      Path      Process
1     ALLOW     @backup       *         /usr/bin/mysqldump
```

However, writing with `mysqldump` still causes an error because it is the shell redirection that is performing the writing, as seen in the system error log:

```
$ mysqldump --all-databases > /mysql/backup/encrypted/edump1.sql
-bash: /mysql/backup/encrypted/edump1.sql: Permission denied

$ dmesg | tail
[4138848.618559] ezncryptfs: DENIED type="acl" exec="/bin/bash"
 script="/dev/pts/4" comm="bash" path="/var/lib/ezncrypt/ezncrypted/backup"
 pid=7448 uid=1000
```

You can use the `--result-file` option with `mysqldump` to enable the process to create the file directly. For example:

```
$ time mysqldump --all-databases \
  --result-file=/mysql/backup/encrypted/edump2.sql
real    1m34.714s
user    0m59.388s
sys     0m9.589s
$ sudo ezncrypt-run "ls -l /mysql/backup/encrypted/"
passphrase:
salt:
total 3.0G
-rw-rw-r-- 1 uid gid 2.9G 2012-04-27 02:43 edump2.sql
```

In this single test, the transparent encryption added only a very nominal overhead. You can easily extract the file from the encrypted directory; however, that would defeat the purpose of using encryption. The following syntax is shown just to confirm the validity of the encrypted file:

```
$ sudo /usr/sbin/ezncrypt-run "cp /mysql/backup/encrypted/edump2.sql ."
passphrase:
salt:
$ ls -al edump*
total 3916
-rw-r--r-- 1 uid gid 2.9G 2012-04-27 02:55 edump2.sql
$ grep "^CREATE.*DATABASE" edump2.sql
```

```
CREATE DATABASE /*!32312 IF NOT EXISTS*/ `book2` /*!40100 DEFAULT CHARACTER SET
latin1 */;
CREATE DATABASE /*!32312 IF NOT EXISTS*/ `employees` ...
CREATE DATABASE /*!32312 IF NOT EXISTS*/ `musicbrainz` ...
CREATE DATABASE /*!32312 IF NOT EXISTS*/ `mysql` ...
CREATE DATABASE /*!32312 IF NOT EXISTS*/ `sakila` ...
CREATE DATABASE /*!32312 IF NOT EXISTS*/ `world_innodb` ...
CREATE DATABASE /*!32312 IF NOT EXISTS*/ `world_myisam` ...
```

When using correctly configured directories and access controls, the use is truly transparent to the backup process.

Restoring an encrypted file is a little more involved. The best approach is to create a script to perform the work, then encrypt this script. When executed, this script will have the permissions necessary to read and apply the encrypted file.

TIP   *Using transparent encryption it is possible to encrypt the MySQL user and password securely in a plain text configuration file and used with appropriate MySQL client commands.*

Architectural Considerations

Given the various options for backup, it is possible to optimize a recovery strategy to minimize downtime. A failover to a standby system is generally the best approach for critical operations.

The archiving of data from an OLTP system to a secondary MySQL instance can be a great benefit for ensuring smaller backups and a more efficient restore process. If your application stores logging, history, or archive information in individual tables or large amounts of reproducible transient data or read-only data, considering the separation of this information into different instances can also serve to reduce the dependency on a primary system. This is an approach for designing your application to support sharding and partitioning.

A simple example is a new system for analyzing stock information. With a large amount of historical information (over 30 years and approximately 500GB), the application was designed for data recorded in two individual tables: a historical table of data before the system went live and a second table for data following the go live date. The application was written to query one or both tables appropriately based on date parameters. By recommending the client split the MySQL instance into two separate instances, placing all histori-cal data on one instance, the only application modification was an additional database connection management.

The backup strategy was also optimized now for two different sets of data. The first set was a static copy of historical data, no daily backup was needed, and no binary logging was necessary. This requirement actually enabled an additional benefit of parallelism and enabling the MySQL query cache. The second set of current data, which was much smaller, could be managed with a different backup and recovery process to meet SLA requirements. This ar-chitectural change enabled a different strategy for read scalability and negat-ing the requirement of replication for historical information. The system was also able to support a partial failure of any historical information by report-ing this information as unavailable.

TIP   *A well designed and configured MySQL replication topology can be the first step for a minimal recovery time. MySQL replication is not a complete backup solution but can support optimizing many common failure scenarios. The* Effective MySQL: Advanced Replication Techniques *book will focus on the various options that are available with MySQL.*

Conclusion

With any RDBMS system, time and new features will always result in more data being recorded. While an appropriate MySQL backup and recovery strategy may meet business expectations today, this may not be so in six months' time. The decision of which backup strategy to use can also be affected by optimization factors. The addition of more hardware such as an additional network card or an additional low cost hard drive can change the decision process for optimizing backup and recovery.

The SQL statements and web links listed in this chapter can be down-loaded from http://effectivemysql.com/book/backup-recovery/.

9

MySQL in the Cloud

"Everything fails all the time."
Dr Werner Vogels, CTO of Amazon (http:/allthingsdistributed.com/)

The emergence of the cloud in recent years has seen a number of MySQL specific and MySQL like database solutions. These offerings are in addition to running a stock MySQL implementation in a virtualized environment. Amazon, HP, and Google currently provide MySQL cloud deployments that are based on using the core MySQL server. There are solutions including ScaleDB that use new MySQL storage engines to provide many cloud scalable features. Xeround and Clustrix are custom solutions that use the MySQL protocol for communication and ease of application integration; however, they have an entirely different

205

underlying product solution. In this chapter we will be discussing the options that most closely represent a standard MySQL environment:

- Amazon Relational Database Service (RDS)
- Google Cloud SQL
- HP Cloud Database as a Service (DBaaS)

Amazon Relational Database Service (RDS)

AWS RDS is the most mature cloud based MySQL product. RDS provides a managed MySQL service offering for versions 5.1 and 5.5, including several point releases. This includes a web based console and command line APIs for creating and maintaining RDS instances. RDS supports two HA options, a master and read replicas topology via MySQL asynchronous replication and a Multi Availability Zone (AZ) deployment that provides a proprietary synchronous replication solution. The Multi AZ instance supports failover capability via internal management of the RDS instances; however, the second Multi AZ instance is not accessible for read load like a normal replication topology.

Some of the benefits of the managed RDS service include:

- Ability to enable automatic minor updates of MySQL software (using `--auto-minor-version-upgrade=true` option)
- Ability to upgrade or downgrade the size of the RDS instance without additional work (using `rds-modify-db-instance --db-instance-class=<newsize>` command)

The RDS implementation of MySQL has some restrictions including:

- No direct access to the MySQL configuration file (i.e. `my.cnf`). Access to change parameters is via the `rds-modify-db-parameter-group` command.
- Lack of SUPER privilege for any user.
- No access to read binary logs.
- No access to the MySQL error log.

See the blog post http://effectivemysql.com/article/setting-up-aws-rds/ for the necessary steps to set up and create a new RDS instance.

Example Database Creation

Using the example database from Chapter 8, the following data was added to RDS by restoring a `mysqldump` backup.

```
+--------------------+---------------+---------------+---------------+
| table_schema       | total_mb      | data_mb       | index_mb      |
+--------------------+---------------+---------------+---------------+
| musicbrainz        | 5152.71875000 | 4412.64062500 | 740.07812500  |
| employees          |  196.43750000 |  141.25000000 |  55.18750000  |
| mysql              |    5.40359974 |    3.03738880 |   2.36621094  |
| world_innodb       |    0.76562500 |    0.57812500 |   0.18750000  |
| sakila             |    0.46972656 |    0.29687500 |   0.17285156  |
| world_myisam       |    0.42019653 |    0.35671997 |   0.06347656  |
| information_schema |    0.00878906 |    0.00000000 |   0.00878906  |
| performance_schema |    0.00000000 |    0.00000000 |   0.00000000  |
+--------------------+---------------+---------------+---------------+
```

MySQL Versions

These current versions are presently available with RDS.

```
$ rds-describe-db-engine-versions -e mysql
VERSION  mysql  5.1.45  mysql5.1  MySQL Community Edition  Mysql 5.1.45
VERSION  mysql  5.1.49  mysql5.1  MySQL Community Edition  MySQL 5.1.49-R1
with innodb plugin
VERSION  mysql  5.1.50  mysql5.1  MySQL Community Edition  MySQL 5.1.50-R3
VERSION  mysql  5.1.57  mysql5.1  MySQL Community Edition  MySQL 5.1.57-R1
VERSION  mysql  5.1.61  mysql5.1  MySQL Community Edition  MySQL 5.1.61-R1
VERSION  mysql  5.5.12  mysql5.5  MySQL Community Edition  MySQL 5.5.12-R1
VERSION  mysql  5.5.20  mysql5.5  MySQL Community Edition  MySQL 5.5.20-R1
VERSION  mysql  5.5.8   mysql5.5  MySQL Community Edition  MySQL 5.5.8.R1 GA
```

Backup Options

RDS enables the use of standard client tools to connect to MySQL. The `mysql` and `mysqldump` commands can be used when connecting to a remote host. MySQL Enterprise Backup and XtraBackup cannot be used with RDS.

mysqldump

As described in Chapter 2 and Chapter 8, the standard options for using `mysqldump` are possible providing you connect to the appropriate remote host. For example:

```
$ cat ~/.my.cnf
[client]
user=dba
```

```
password=passwd
host=book2.XXX.us-east-1.rds.amazonaws.com

$ time mysqldump --all-databases > /mysql/backup/rds1.sql
mysqldump: Got error: 1142: SELECT,LOCK TABL command denied to user
'dba'@'ip-10-194-163-1.ec2.internal' for table 'cond_instances'
when using LOCK TABLES
real    1m22.818s
user    0m49.579s
sys     0m17.545s
$ ls -lh /mysql/backup/rds1.sql
-rw-rw-r-- 1 uid gid 2.9G 2012-04-18 17:22 /mysql/backup/rds1.sql
```

As you can see, an error occurred. This is due to a change in mysqldump between MySQL 5.1 and MySQL 5.5. In this example the MySQL server running the client command mysqldump is an older version than the RDS database server version.

CAUTION   *When using mysqldump to connect to a remote database host for backups, the mysqldump version must be at least the same version as the remote MySQL database.*

Using a correct version produces:

```
$ time mysqldump --all-databases > /mysql/backup/rds1.sql
real    1m18.115s
user    0m48.591s
sys     0m18.149s

$ ls -lh /mysql/backup/rds1.sql
-rw-rw-r-- 1 uid gid 2.9G 2012-04-18 17:27 /mysql/backup/rds1.sql
```

This execution time includes the network overhead between an EC2 instance and an RDS instance. This is comparable with a standard EC2 instance running a local MySQL instance.

A more advanced option for excluding the mysql meta-schema (which will become relevant in the restore section) can be achieved by:

```
$ time mysqldump --databases 'mysql --skip-column-names \
  -e "SELECT GROUP_CONCAT(schema_name SEPARATOR ' ') FROM \
information_schema.schemata WHERE schema_name NOT IN \
('mysql','performance_schema','information_schema');"' > /mysql/backup/rds2.sql
real    1m16.358s
user    0m49.943s
sys     0m18.897s
```

The SQL statement in this solution has a limitation on the length of the string output from the GROUP_CONCAT function. For MySQL instances with a large number of database schemas this query will fail. This length restriction can be increased with the `group_concat_max_len` configuration variable. Giuseppe Maxia provides an improvement with two more possible options; the first, however, is limited to the maximum length of an OS command. See http://datacharmer.blogspot.com/2012/04/few-hacks-to-simulate-mysqldump-ignore.html for more details. Within a day of posting a related blog post about this syntax, Mark Leith provided a code patch to the `mysqldump` command that implements an actual `--ignore-database` option. The beauty of the MySQL community and open source software is seen in these immediate responses. See more information at http://www.markleith.co.uk/?p=768 and MySQL bug #3228 at http://bugs.mysql.com/bug.php?id=3228.

TIP *There is currently no `--ignore-database` option with `mysqldump`. The previously mentioned command provides one of several suitable alternatives.*

Database Snapshot

RDS provides a native snapshot option to produce a consistent backup of MySQL data. This occurs while the database is online. It is unclear how locking occurs with MyISAM tables to ensure database consistency. Using the RDS CLI tools, you can produce a snapshot with:

```
$ rds-create-db-snapshot -i book2 -s backup-1
DBSNAPSHOT  backup-1  book2  2012-04-18T15:09:08.420Z  mysql  20  creating
   dba  5.5.20  general-public-license  manual
```

NOTE *Unlike most other commands that can be timed, this is an asynchronous process. You must poll the results via the `rds-describe-db-snapshots` command to determine when the backup is completed. There is no estimated percentage completion like an AWS EBS filesystem snapshot. There is no execution time or size information available following the backup.*

You can monitor the state of the snapshot creation with the following command:

```
$ while [ : ];do date;rds-describe-db-snapshots -s backup-1;sleep 15;done
Wed Apr 18 20:13:24 UTC 2012
DBSNAPSHOT  backup-1  book2  2012-04-18T19:31:51.919Z
   mysql  20  creating  dba  5.5.20  general-public-license  manual
   ...
```

```
Wed Apr 18 20:33:17 UTC 2012
DBSNAPSHOT  backup-1  2012-04-18T20:13:30.178Z  book2  2012-04-18T19:31:51.919Z
  mysql  20  available  dba  5.5.20  general-public-license  manual
```

Or interactively with the command:

```
$ watch -n 15 --differences "rds-describe-db-snapshots"
```

This snapshot took approximately 20 minutes to complete for a 20GB RDS instance.

An RDS snapshot can also be scheduled with the RDS management tools using the rds-modify-db-instance command with the --preferred-backup-window and --backup-retention-period configuration options.

MySQL Binary Logs

RDS does not provide access to the binary logs. This means it is not possible to perform data analysis or auditing via the binary log. RDS does provide a capability to restore to a given point in time via the rds-restore-db-instance-to-point-in-time command within the last five minutes.

```
$ date
Wed Apr 18 20:42:03 UTC 2012
$ rds-describe-db-instances book2 --headers --show-long | head -2 | cut -d, -f22
Latest Restorable Time
2012-04-18T20:40:00Z
```

This information is not available with the standard rds-describe-db-instances command. The --show-long option is required.

You can use the MySQL status variables to determine that RDS uses binary logs and flushes these to disk every five minutes, and this infers a redundancy of binary logs at a filesystem level.

Recovery Options

The following steps describe how to restore an RDS backup.

SQL Dump

You can use the mysql command line tool to restore a mysqldump backup.

```
$ time mysql -udba -ppasswd -hbook2.XXX.us-east-1.rds.amazonaws.com \
  < /mysql/backup/dump1.sql > dump1.out 2>&1
real    25m2.568s
user    1m17.869s
sys     0m4.764s
```

A verification of the data shows:

```
mysql> source allschemas.sql
+---------------------+----------------+----------------+---------------+
| table_schema        | total_mb       | data_mb        | index_mb      |
+---------------------+----------------+----------------+---------------+
| musicbrainz         | 3681.85937500  | 2970.82812500  | 711.03125000  |
| employees           |  196.43750000  |  141.25000000  |  55.18750000  |
| book2               |   83.76562500  |   57.17187500  |  26.59375000  |
| mysql               |    5.38966751  |    3.02736282  |   2.36230469  |
| information_schema  |    0.00878906  |    0.00000000  |   0.00878906  |
| performance_schema  |    0.00000000  |    0.00000000  |   0.00000000  |
+---------------------+----------------+----------------+---------------+
```

CAUTION   *Do not be fooled by a significant and appropriate restore time and a database that appears to contain a large amount of data (e.g., 3.6GB for the* musicbrainz *schema).*

However, you should always check for any errors and perform a more in-depth validation to ensure your database has been completely restored. The average time to perform a restore, the total database size, and additional checks and balances are necessary in a production system. A review of the output file shows:

```
$ cat dump1.out
ERROR 1044 (42000) at line 3827: Access denied for user 'dba'@'%'
to database 'mysql'
```

This error condition is due to the RDS implementation restricting user permissions. This type of error is unavoidable for a full `mysqldump` of all schemas. A normal restoration on a more traditional MySQL database system can overcome this with applicable user privileges. In order to address this limitation with RDS, you need to use the `-f` option during the restore; however, this introduces other problems. This type of situation is not limited to RDS instances with the lack of non-adjustable user privileges, which some may state as an appropriate security feature.

```
$ time mysql -f  < /mysql/backup/dump1.sql > dump1.out 2>&1
real    23m57.580s
user    1m17.405s
sys     0m4.732s
$ echo $?
0
$ more dump3.out
ERROR 1044 (42000) at line 3827: Access denied for user 'dba'@'%' to database
ERROR 1044 (42000) at line 3835: Access denied for user 'dba'@'%' to database
ERROR 1044 (42000) at line 3838: Access denied for user 'dba'@'%' to database
```

```
ERROR 1146 (42S02) at line 3871: Table 'mysql.backup_history' doesn't exist
ERROR 1044 (42000) at line 3872: Access denied for user 'dba'@'%' to database
ERROR 1146 (42S02) at line 3873: Table 'mysql.backup_history' doesn't exist
...
mysql> source allschemas.sql
+--------------------+----------------+----------------+----------------+
| table_schema       | total_mb       | data_mb        | index_mb       |
+--------------------+----------------+----------------+----------------+
| musicbrainz        | 3681.85937500  | 2970.82812500  | 711.03125000   |
| employees          |  196.43750000  |  141.25000000  |  55.18750000   |
| book2              |   83.76562500  |   57.17187500  |  26.59375000   |
| sakila             |    6.56817627  |    4.09844971  |   2.46972656   |
| mysql              |    5.38966751  |    3.02736282  |   2.36230469   |
| world_innodb       |    0.76562500  |    0.57812500  |   0.18750000   |
| world_myisam       |    0.42019653  |    0.35671997  |   0.06347656   |
| information_schema |    0.00878906  |    0.00000000  |   0.00878906   |
| performance_schema |    0.00000000  |    0.00000000  |   0.00000000   |
+--------------------+----------------+----------------+----------------+
```

With no actual error state and numerous error messages it is difficult to verify a successful restore. In addition, several errors occur when importing the MySQL `sakila` database due to stored procedures. These errors can be reproduced with:

```
$ mysql < sakila-schema.sql
ERROR 1419 (HY000) at line 183: You do not have the SUPER privilege and binary
  logging is enabled (you *might* want to use the less safe
  log_bin_trust_function_creators variable)
$ mysql < sakila-data.sql
ERROR 1419 (HY000) at line 73: You do not have the SUPER privilege and binary
  logging is enabled (you *might* want to use the less safe
  log_bin_trust_function_creators variable)
```

An import of the second `mysqldump` file excluding the `mysql` meta-schema produced:

```
$ time mysql < /mysql/backup/rds2.sql > rds2.out 2>&1
real    24m21.368s
user    1m18.557s
sys     0m4.644s
echo $?
0
$ cat rds2.out
```

As described in Chapter 5, the modification of various configuration variables can improve the performance of a restore, for example, `innodb_flush_log_at_trx_commit`. You can also disable MySQL binary logging by setting the `backup-retention-period` value to 0. This, however, requires a MySQL restart to disable, and then to re-enable when completed.

RDS Snapshot

To perform a restoration for a given snapshot that can be identified by the `rds-describe-db-snapshots` command, use the following syntax. This will create a new RDS instance.

```
$ rds-restore-db-instance-from-db-snapshot book2s -s backup-1
...
Wed Apr 18 20:48:03 UTC 2012
DBINSTANCE  book2s  db.m1.large  mysql  20  dba  creating  us-east-1b  1  n
  5.5.20  general-public-license
        SECGROUP  default  active
        PARAMGRP  default.mysql5.5  in-sync
...
Wed Apr 18 20:53:00 UTC 2012
DBINSTANCE  book2s  2012-04-18T20:51:25.083Z  db.m1.large  mysql  20  dba
  available  book2s.cqmcgpjfkies.us-east-1.rds.amazonaws.com  3306  us-east-1b
  1  n
  5.5.20  general-public-license
        SECGROUP  default  active
        PARAMGRP  default.mysql5.5  in-sync
```

This restoration took approximately five minutes.

A restoration from a given snapshot cannot use the binary logs to perform a point in time recovery. In order to use this, you must use the `rds-restore-db-instance-to-point-in-time` command.

Point in Time Recovery

For the purposes of verifying a point in time recovery, two new schemas were created at the given time interval of the schema name in the following example:

```
mysql> CREATE SCHEMA 20120418_204605;
...
mysql> SHOW SCHEMAS;
+--------------------+
| Database           |
+--------------------+
| information_schema |
| 20120418_203846    |
| 20120418_204605    |
...
+--------------------+
11 rows in set (0.00 sec)
```

A point in time recovery was specified before the creation of the second schema with the `--restore-time` option. This value does not have to correspond with a specific five minute interval value. This can be anytime after an available snapshot and before or equal to the last restorable time.

```
$ rds-restore-db-instance-to-point-in-time \
    --target-db-instance-identifier book2n \
    --source-db-instance-identifier book2 \
    --restore-time 2012-04-18T20:41:25Z
...
Wed Apr 18 21:02:26 UTC 2012
DBINSTANCE  book2n  db.m1.large  mysql  20  dba  creating  1  n  5.5.20
general-public-license
        SECGROUP  default  active
        PARAMGRP  running-mysql55  in-sync
..
Wed Apr 18 21:13:16 UTC 2012
DBINSTANCE  book2n  2012-04-18T21:07:04.160Z  db.m1.large  mysql  20  dba
    available  book2n.cqmcgpjfkies.us-east-1.rds.amazonaws.com  3306  us-east-1b
    1  n
    5.5.20  general-public-license
        SECGROUP  default  active
        PARAMGRP  running-mysql55  in-sync
```

This restore took approximately 11 minutes.

A verification of the restored schemas shows the second schema does not exist as expected. In a production system a more detailed verification is necessary. This example is only used to highlight the syntax for the commands.

```
mysql> SHOW SCHEMAS;
+--------------------+
| Database           |
+--------------------+
| information_schema |
| 20120418_203846    |
...
+--------------------+
11 rows in set (0.00 sec)
```

NOTE   *Be sure to remove RDS instances no longer used with the* `rds-delete-db-instance`.

More information about RDS can be found at http://aws.amazon.com/rds/.

Google Cloud SQL

Google provides a MySQL version 5.5 cloud offering with a few additional features and a few unsupported features. At publication of this book, this is available in a limited beta program. It is recommended that InnoDB is used for tables; however, it is possible to use MyISAM.

This offering automatically replicates data synchronously to multiple geographic regions to provide high data availability. There is currently no asynchronous option via traditional replication. With this synchronous functionality, Cloud SQL provides automatic failover with no data loss. Software upgrades and database management are automatically managed by the service.

Google Cloud SQL is tightly integrated with Google App Engine (GAE) using Java and Python. A web based SQL interface and custom CLI interface are available for access to run SQL statements. Any product that can communicate with a JDBC connection can connect to Google Cloud SQL.

See the blog post http://effectiveMySQL.com/article/setting-up-google-cloud-sql/ for the necessary steps to set up and create a new Google Cloud SQL instance.

Example Database Creation

Using the example database in Chapter 8, an uncompressed or compressed (via `gzip`) `mysqldump` file can be used to populate a Cloud SQL environment. In order to import any data you must first store the file on Google Cloud Storage. For example:

```
$ gsutil mb gs://effectivemysql
Creating gs://effectivemysql/...
$ time gsutil cp dump1.sql gs://effectivemysql
Copying file:///mysql/backup/dump1.sql...
    [Setting Content-Type=application/x-sql]
Uploading: 659.0 MB/2.92 GB
real    7m39.020s
user    0m50.079s
sys     0m10.441s

$ gsutil ls -l gs://effectivemysql
3106569645  2012-04-17T03:40:54  gs://effectivemysql/dump1.sql
TOTAL: 1 objects, 3106569645 bytes (2.89 GB)
$ ls -al dump1.sql
-rw-rw-r-- 1 uid gid 3106569645 2012-04-08 02:58 dump1.sql
```

The only verification option is file size.

You can then use the Google APIs web console to import the given file. There is no CLI interface to initiate this process or determine the total execution time.

The web interface provides a log of the process after completion.

```
Apr 18, 2012 1:23 PM  Started importing gs://effectivemysql/rds2.sql
Apr 18, 2012 3:45 PM  Imported gs://effectivemysql/rds2.sql
```

The import process took two hours and 22 minutes.

If there is a problem, the log will report an error but will not provide any additional information. For example:

```
Failed to import gs://effectivemysql/dump1.sql: An unknown problem
occurred (ERROR_RDBMS)
```

CAUTION   *You should not import the* mysql *meta-schema, as this can cause problems including permissions for the root MySQL user and meta-table structure issues. Refer to the RDS section for a* mysqldump *option to exclude this schema.*

The first step of the verification process can be confirmed with the Google provided SQL CLI tool:

```
+-------------------+---------------+---------------+---------------+
| table_schema      | total_mb      | data_mb       | index_mb      |
+-------------------+---------------+---------------+---------------+
| musicbrainz       | 3681.85937500 | 2970.82812500 |  711.03125000 |
| employees         |  196.43750000 |  141.25000000 |   55.18750000 |
| test              |   81.10937500 |   66.59375000 |   14.51562500 |
| world_innodb      |    0.76562500 |    0.57812500 |    0.18750000 |
| sakila            |    0.46972656 |    0.29687500 |    0.17285156 |
| world_myisam      |    0.42019653 |    0.35671997 |    0.06347656 |
| mysql             |    0.04379368 |    0.00180149 |    0.04199219 |
| information_schema |   0.00878906 |    0.00000000 |    0.00878906 |
+-------------------+---------------+---------------+---------------+
```

Backup Options

Only one option exists to perform an independent backup from Google Cloud SQL.

mysqldump

A mysqldump export is possible. This can only be initiated from the Google APIs web console. You are not able to specify per-schema or per-table information or any other additional options at this time. The output file, compressed or uncompressed, is available in Google Cloud Storage when completed. The web console provides a log of the process start and completion.

```
Apr 18, 2012 5:23 PM Started backing up to gs://effectivemysql/cloud1.sql.gz
Apr 18, 2012 6:05 PM Backed up to gs://effectivemysql/cloud1.sql.gz
```

This backup took 42 minutes.

You can verify and obtain the backup file for offsite management with:

```
$ time gsutil cp gs://effectivemysql/cloud1* .
Copying gs://effectivemysql/cloud1.sql.gz...
Copying gs://effectivemysql/cloud1.sql.gz.log.1334795000328424...
real    1m33.916s
user    0m25.618s
sys     0m11.369s
$ ls -lh cloud1.sql.gz
-rw-rw-r-- 1 uid gid 929M 2012-04-19 01:39 cloud1.sql.gz
$ gunzip cloud1.sql.gz
$ ls -lh cloud1.sql
-rw-rw-r-- 1 uid gid 3.0G 2012-04-19 01:39 cloud1.sql
```

A scheduled backup feature is also available for regular daily backups.

Restore Options

As described in the example database creation, the restore of a mysqldump file generated by the export or scheduled process is possible. Google Cloud SQL does not currently provide a point in time recovery capability. Due to the synchronous nature of this product, high availability and failover features are provided by default, reducing the need for a database restore. More selective disaster recoverability options or data analysis of SQL statements in the binary log is not currently possible.

For obtaining a copy of data at a given time, the recommendation is to use the export functionality. It is then possible to import this for verification and use if necessary.

At the time of this book's publication, Google Cloud SQL was in limited beta. More information can be found at https://developers.google.com/cloud-sql/.

HP Cloud Database as a Service (DBaaS)

The HP Public Cloud (http://hpcloud.com) provides a number of services based on the popular Open Stack cloud software (http://openstack.org/). These services include compute, storage, content delivery network (CDN), identity management, and a managed MySQL relational database offering. This MySQL offering is a DBaaS based on the Red Dwarf project from Open Stack (http://wiki.openstack.org/DatabaseAsAService).

Access to creating, deleting, and restarting instances, and creating and using snapshots is via a RESTful HTTP API providing JSON formatted response. The standard MySQL client tools, including mysql and mysqldump, can be used for access to the MySQL database.

The HP DBaaS offering is fully integrated with the Openstack Keystone Identity Service. To access the DBaaS API, you first need to obtain a token to be used for the X-Auth-Token HTTP header. In addition the X-Auth-Project-Id (generally your e-mail, or tenant name) is required for all requests. The credentials required to obtain an auth-token and the project-id can be found from the HP Management Console.

As of this writing, the HP Cloud DBaaS (currently in private beta) offers the following features. These are subject to change in the future:

- Create and terminate database instances
- Reset password
- Create and delete snapshots
- Create instance from an existing snapshot

MySQL Versions

DBaaS currently uses Percona Server version 5.5, available from http://www.percona.com/software/percona-server/. This is a fork of MySQL version 5.5 providing XtraDB (a modified version of InnoDB), better instrumentation, performance improvements, and a shorter deployment life cycle for new features.

Example Database Creation

A request has to be made to the Identity Service to obtain the auth token to use for DBaaS access. For example:

```
$ curl -i https://[IdentityServiceHost]/v2.0/tokens -X POST \
-H "Content-Type: application/json" -d \
'{"auth": {"tenantName": "tenant@domain.com",
"passwordCredentials": {"username": "user@domain.com", "password": "changeit"}}}'

{"access": {
 "token": {
   "expires": "2012-04-05T04:28:29.405Z",
   "id": "HPAuth_4f7c6456e4b01a25ab011e74",
```

```
    "tenant": {
      "id": "123456789",
      "name": "tenant@domain.com"
    }
  },
  "user": {
.....
}
```

Using the `id` value you can create a new instance with:

```
$ curl -i https://[DBaaSHost]/v1.0/12345/instances -X POST \
  -H "Content-Type: application/json" -H "X-Auth-Token: \
HPAuth_4f7c6456e4b01a25ab011e74" -H "X-Auth-Project-Id: tenant@domain.com" \
-d '{"instance": {"name": "My_Instance", "flavorRef": "medium", \
"port": "3306", "dbtype": { "name": "mysql", "version": "5.5" }}}'
{
  "instance":
    {
      "status": "BUILD",
      "updated": null,
      "name": "My_Instance",
      "links": [
        {
          "href": "http://127.0.0.1/v1.0/12345/instances/1fff96e1-1504-4dcc-
9b30-8ae784ee0788",
          "rel": "self"
        }
      ],
      "created": "2012-03-07T19:04:02Z",
      "hostname": "15.100.100.100",
      "id": "1fff96e1-1504-4dcc-9b30-8ae784ee0788"
    }
}
```

Backup Options

DBaaS provides for backup options via `mysqldump` or by a database snapshot.

mysqldump

Refer to the `mysqldump` syntax in Chapters 2 and 8 and the syntax in the RDS section for example usage.

Database Snapshot

DBaaS provides several API calls to manage database snapshots. A database snapshot can be performed on a running MySQL instance with the following command:

```
$ curl -i https://[DBaaSHost]/v1.0/12345/snapshots -X POST -H \
"Content-Type: application/json" -H "X-Auth-Token: \
HPAuth_4f7c6456e4b01a25ab011e74" -H "X-Auth-Project-Id: tenant@domain.com" \
-d '{"snapshot": {"name": "My_Instance_Snapshot", \
"instanceId": "1fff96e1-1504-4dcc-9b30-8ae784ee0788"}}'
```

Snapshots are automatically replicated to multiple Availability Zones for higher availability.

Recovery Options

mysqldump

Refer to the syntax in Chapter 5 and the RDS section for example usage.

Database Snapshot

A DBaaS instance can be created from a pre-existing snapshot. The request is identical to creating a new instance, with the additional `snapshotId` parameter. For example:

```
$ curl -i https://[DBaaSHost]/v1.0/12345/instances -X POST -H \
"Content-Type: application/json" -H "X-Auth-Token: \
HPAuth_4f7c6456e4b01a25ab011e74" -H "X-Auth-Project-Id: tenant@domain.com" \
-d '{"instance": {"name": "Backup", "snapshotId": "id_of_snapshot", \
flavorRef": "medium", "port": "3306", "dbtype": { "name": "mysql", \
"version": "5.5" }}}'
```

Point in Time Recovery

No information was available at this time regarding point in time capabilities.

At the time of this publication DBaaS was in closed beta and access for more detailed testing was not possible. More information can be found at http://www.hpcloud.com/products/RDB.

Cloud Impact on Backup and Recovery

The use of the cloud does not mean that disasters will no longer occur. This is a myth. The cloud has made the case to ensure appropriate DR operations are more prevalent. As the control and management of data systems become the responsibility of service providers, it is more important that your business understands the risks of entrusting this responsibility to a third party.

The cloud has enabled a new way of testing and verifying your processes. The availability of systems on demand provides the ability to easily test and verify your system at production scale, for a very small cost. The ability to also test with additional size and load is possible immediately without any hardware provisioning requirements (except a credit card). That same ability enables options to fully test backup and restore procedures with full production volume without any hindrances.

Organizations are also using the cloud for storing backup files externally, read scalability via replication, and ancillary services including analytics, reporting, and data warehousing. The use of the cloud is becoming an ideal hybrid implementation that scales on demand with no upfront hardware costs. The use of the cloud does introduce additional security concerns regarding the access to your business data and appropriate encryption techniques become more important. Backup options that have been discussed in this book generally store and transfer data in clear text. Chapter 8 discusses some more information on MySQL backup security. Amazon, the current leading cloud provider, recognizes security as the top priority and is constantly improving the level of fine grained access via techniques including security groups, virtual private network (VPN) access, and AWS direct connect.

In some organizations, cloud deployments have now streamlined the disaster preparedness to an art form, giving backup and recovery the top priority in business needs. For example, using a quote from Netflix: "The Chaos Monkey's (and simian army's) job is to randomly kill instances and services within our architecture. If we aren't constantly testing our ability to succeed despite failure, then it isn't likely to work when it matters most—in the event of an unexpected outage." This is a brilliant concept for being prepared.

See http://techblog.netflix.com/2010/12/5-lessons-weve-learned-using-aws.html and http://techblog.netflix.com/2011/07/netflix-simian-army.html for more background information.

Ironically, the best advice for creating an effective MySQL backup and recovery strategy is a quote now possible because of these cloud based technology capabilities.

"The best way to avoid failure is to fail constantly."

John Ciancutti, Netflix

Conclusion

Cloud based services are becoming more easily available to consumers. While the Amazon RDS service has been available for some time, the HP and Google offerings are recent editions not yet generally available when this book was published. More cloud based MySQL products will definitely become available in the future. Each option has its relative merits of providing a managed service; however, you must evaluate the strengths and interoperability needs with any existing production environment to determine the best approach to maintaining your business continuity effectively.

The commands, SQL statements, and web links listed in this chapter can be downloaded from http://effectivemysql.com/book/backup-recovery/.

Index

GET YOUR FREE SUBSCRIPTION
TO *ORACLE MAGAZINE*

Oracle Magazine is essential gear for today's information technology professionals. Stay informed and increase your productivity with every issue of *Oracle Magazine*. Inside each free bimonthly issue you'll get:

- Up-to-date information on Oracle Database, Oracle Application Server, Web development, enterprise grid computing, database technology, and business trends
- Third-party news and announcements
- Technical articles on Oracle and partner products, technologies, and operating environments
- Development and administration tips
- Real-world customer stories

If there are other Oracle users at your location who would like to receive their own subscription to *Oracle Magazine*, please photocopy this form and pass it along.

Three easy ways to subscribe:

① **Web**
Visit our Web site at **oracle.com/oraclemagazine**
You'll find a subscription form there, plus much more

② **Fax**
Complete the questionnaire on the back of this card and fax the questionnaire side only to **+1.847.763.9638**

③ **Mail**
Complete the questionnaire on the back of this card and mail it to **P.O. Box 1263, Skokie, IL 60076-8263**

ORACLE®

Want your own FREE subscription?

To receive a free subscription to *Oracle Magazine*, you must fill out the entire card, sign it, and date it (incomplete cards cannot be processed or acknowledged). You can also fax your application to **+1.847.763.9638. Or subscribe at our Web site at oracle.com/oraclemagazine**

O **Yes, please send me a FREE subscription** *Oracle Magazine*.   O No.

O From time to time, Oracle Publishing allows our partners exclusive access to our e-mail addresses for special promotions and announcements. To be included in this program, please check this circle. If you do not wish to be included, you will only receive notices about your subscription via e-mail.

O Oracle Publishing allows sharing of our postal mailing list with selected third parties. If you prefer your mailing address not to be included in this program, please check this circle.

If at any time you would like to be removed from either mailing list, please contact Customer Service at +1.847.763.9635 or send an e-mail to oracle@halldata.com. If you opt in to the sharing of information, Oracle may also provide you with e-mail related to Oracle products, services, and events. If you want to completely unsubscribe from any e-mail communication from Oracle, please send an e-mail to: unsubscribe@oracle-mail.com with the following in the subject line: REMOVE [your e-mail address]. For complete information on Oracle Publishing's privacy practices, please visit oracle.com/html/privacy/html

X
_____
signature (required)   date

name   title

company   e-mail address

street/p.o. box

city/state/zip or postal code   telephone

country   fax

Would you like to receive your free subscription in digital format instead of print if it becomes available? O Yes O No

YOU MUST ANSWER ALL 10 QUESTIONS BELOW.

(1) WHAT IS THE PRIMARY BUSINESS ACTIVITY OF YOUR FIRM AT THIS LOCATION? (check one only)

- ☐ 01 Aerospace and Defense Manufacturing
- ☐ 02 Application Service Provider
- ☐ 03 Automotive Manufacturing
- ☐ 04 Chemicals
- ☐ 05 Media and Entertainment
- ☐ 06 Construction/Engineering
- ☐ 07 Consumer Sector/Consumer Packaged Goods
- ☐ 08 Education
- ☐ 09 Financial Services/Insurance
- ☐ 10 Health Care
- ☐ 11 High Technology Manufacturing, OEM
- ☐ 12 Industrial Manufacturing
- ☐ 13 Independent Software Vendor
- ☐ 14 Life Sciences (biotech, pharmaceuticals)
- ☐ 15 Natural Resources
- ☐ 16 Oil and Gas
- ☐ 17 Professional Services
- ☐ 18 Public Sector (government)
- ☐ 19 Research
- ☐ 20 Retail/Wholesale/Distribution
- ☐ 21 Systems Integrator, VAR/VAD
- ☐ 22 Telecommunications
- ☐ 23 Travel and Transportation
- ☐ 24 Utilities (electric, gas, sanitation, water)
- ☐ 98 Other Business and Services _____

(2) WHICH OF THE FOLLOWING BEST DESCRIBES YOUR PRIMARY JOB FUNCTION? (check one only)

CORPORATE MANAGEMENT/STAFF
- ☐ 01 Executive Management (President, Chair, CEO, CFO, Owner, Partner, Principal)
- ☐ 02 Finance/Administrative Management (VP/Director/ Manager/Controller, Purchasing, Administration)
- ☐ 03 Sales/Marketing Management (VP/Director/Manager)
- ☐ 04 Computer Systems/Operations Management (CIO/VP/Director/Manager MIS/IS/IT, Ops)

IS/IT STAFF
- ☐ 05 Application Development/Programming Management
- ☐ 06 Application Development/Programming Staff
- ☐ 07 Consulting
- ☐ 08 DBA/Systems Administrator
- ☐ 09 Education/Training
- ☐ 10 Technical Support Director/Manager
- ☐ 11 Other Technical Management/Staff
- ☐ 98 Other

(3) WHAT IS YOUR CURRENT PRIMARY OPERATING PLATFORM (check all that apply)

- ☐ 01 Digital Equipment Corp UNIX/VAX/VMS
- ☐ 02 HP UNIX
- ☐ 03 IBM AIX
- ☐ 04 IBM UNIX
- ☐ 05 Linux (Red Hat)
- ☐ 06 Linux (SUSE)
- ☐ 07 Linux (Oracle Enterprise)
- ☐ 08 Linux (other)
- ☐ 09 Macintosh
- ☐ 10 MVS
- ☐ 11 Netware
- ☐ 12 Network Computing
- ☐ 13 SCO UNIX
- ☐ 14 Sun Solaris/SunOS
- ☐ 15 Windows
- ☐ 16 Other UNIX
- ☐ 98 Other
- ☐ 99 None of the Above

(4) DO YOU EVALUATE, SPECIFY, RECOMMEND, OR AUTHORIZE THE PURCHASE OF ANY OF THE FOLLOWING? (check all that apply)

- ☐ 01 Hardware
- ☐ 02 Business Applications (ERP, CRM, etc.)
- ☐ 03 Application Development Tools
- ☐ 04 Database Products
- ☐ 05 Internet or Intranet Products
- ☐ 06 Other Software
- ☐ 07 Middleware Products
- ☐ 99 None of the Above

(5) IN YOUR JOB, DO YOU USE OR PLAN TO PURCHASE ANY OF THE FOLLOWING PRODUCTS? (check all that apply)

SOFTWARE
- ☐ 01 CAD/CAE/CAM
- ☐ 02 Collaboration Software
- ☐ 03 Communications
- ☐ 04 Database Management
- ☐ 05 File Management
- ☐ 06 Finance
- ☐ 07 Java
- ☐ 08 Multimedia Authoring
- ☐ 09 Networking
- ☐ 10 Programming
- ☐ 11 Project Management
- ☐ 12 Scientific and Engineering
- ☐ 13 Systems Management
- ☐ 14 Workflow

HARDWARE
- ☐ 15 Macintosh
- ☐ 16 Mainframe
- ☐ 17 Massively Parallel Processing

- ☐ 18 Minicomputer
- ☐ 19 Intel x86(32)
- ☐ 20 Intel x86(64)
- ☐ 21 Network Computer
- ☐ 22 Symmetric Multiprocessing
- ☐ 23 Workstation Services

SERVICES
- ☐ 24 Consulting
- ☐ 25 Education/Training
- ☐ 26 Maintenance
- ☐ 27 Online Database
- ☐ 28 Support
- ☐ 29 Technology-Based Training
- ☐ 30 Other
- ☐ 99 None of the Above

(6) WHAT IS YOUR COMPANY'S SIZE? (check one only)

- ☐ 01 More than 25,000 Employees
- ☐ 02 10,001 to 25,000 Employees
- ☐ 03 5,001 to 10,000 Employees
- ☐ 04 1,001 to 5,000 Employees
- ☐ 05 101 to 1,000 Employees
- ☐ 06 Fewer than 100 Employees

(7) DURING THE NEXT 12 MONTHS, HOW MUCH DO YOU ANTICIPATE YOUR ORGANIZATION WILL SPEND ON COMPUTER HARDWARE, SOFTWARE, PERIPHERALS, AND SERVICES FOR YOUR LOCATION? (check one only)

- ☐ 01 Less than $10,000
- ☐ 02 $10,000 to $49,999
- ☐ 03 $50,000 to $99,999
- ☐ 04 $100,000 to $499,999
- ☐ 05 $500,000 to $999,999
- ☐ 06 $1,000,000 and Over

(8) WHAT IS YOUR COMPANY'S YEARLY SALES REVENUE? (check one only)

- ☐ 01 $500, 000, 000 and above
- ☐ 02 $100, 000, 000 to $500, 000, 000
- ☐ 03 $50, 000, 000 to $100, 000, 000
- ☐ 04 $5, 000, 000 to $50, 000, 000
- ☐ 05 $1, 000, 000 to $5, 000, 000

(9) WHAT LANGUAGES AND FRAMEWORKS DO YOU USE? (check all that apply)

- ☐ 01 Ajax
- ☐ 02 C
- ☐ 03 C++
- ☐ 04 C#
- ☐ 13 Python
- ☐ 14 Ruby/Rails
- ☐ 15 Spring
- ☐ 16 Struts
- ☐ 05 Hibernate
- ☐ 06 J++/J#
- ☐ 07 Java
- ☐ 08 JSP
- ☐ 09 .NET
- ☐ 10 Perl
- ☐ 11 PHP
- ☐ 12 PL/SQL
- ☐ 17 SQL
- ☐ 18 Visual Basic
- ☐ 98 Other

(10) WHAT ORACLE PRODUCTS ARE IN USE AT YOUR SITE? (check all that apply)

ORACLE DATABASE
- ☐ 01 Oracle Database 11g
- ☐ 02 Oracle Database 10g
- ☐ 03 Oracle9i Database
- ☐ 04 Oracle Embedded Database (Oracle Lite, Times Ten, Berkeley DB)
- ☐ 05 Other Oracle Database Release

ORACLE FUSION MIDDLEWARE
- ☐ 06 Oracle Application Server
- ☐ 07 Oracle Portal
- ☐ 08 Oracle Enterprise Manager
- ☐ 09 Oracle BPEL Process Manager
- ☐ 10 Oracle Identity Management
- ☐ 11 Oracle SOA Suite
- ☐ 12 Oracle Data Hubs

ORACLE DEVELOPMENT TOOLS
- ☐ 13 Oracle JDeveloper
- ☐ 14 Oracle Forms
- ☐ 15 Oracle Reports
- ☐ 16 Oracle Designer
- ☐ 17 Oracle Discoverer
- ☐ 18 Oracle BI Beans
- ☐ 19 Oracle Warehouse Builder
- ☐ 20 Oracle WebCenter
- ☐ 21 Oracle Application Express

ORACLE APPLICATIONS
- ☐ 22 Oracle E-Business Suite
- ☐ 23 PeopleSoft Enterprise
- ☐ 24 JD Edwards EnterpriseOne
- ☐ 25 JD Edwards World
- ☐ 26 Oracle Fusion
- ☐ 27 Hyperion
- ☐ 28 Siebel CRM

ORACLE SERVICES
- ☐ 28 Oracle E-Business Suite On Demand
- ☐ 29 Oracle Technology On Demand
- ☐ 30 Siebel CRM On Demand
- ☐ 31 Oracle Consulting
- ☐ 32 Oracle Education
- ☐ 33 Oracle Support
- ☐ 98 Other
- ☐ 99 None of the Above